Python Apps
on
Visual Studio Code

Develop apps and utilize the true potential of
Visual Studio Code

Swapnil Saurav

www.bpbonline.com

First Edition 2024

ISBN: 978-93-55519-504

LIMITS OF LIABILITY AND DISCLAIMER OF WARRANTY

Distributors:

BPB PUBLICATIONS
20, Ansari Road, Darya Ganj
New Delhi-110002
Ph: 23254990 / 23254991

DECCAN AGENCIES
4-3-329, Bank Street,
Hyderabad-500195
Ph: 24756967 / 24756400

MICRO MEDIA
Shop No. 5, Mahendra Chambers,
150 DN Rd. Next to Capital Cinema,
V.T. (C.S.T.) Station, MUMBAI-400 001
Ph: 22078296 / 22078297

To View Complete
BPB Publications Catalogue
Scan the QR Code:

Published by Manish Jain for BPB Publications, 20 Ansari Road, Darya Ganj, New Delhi-110002 and Printed by him at Manipal Technologies, Manipal

Dedicated to

My beloved wife:

Rupali

&

My son **Ojass**

About the Author

Swapnil Saurav is a highly accomplished and versatile professional with over 20 years of experience in various industries, including CPG and Retail. Passionate about understanding customer challenges and driving business growth in competitive markets. Skilled in process consulting, market analysis, sales and marketing support, product development, customer service, and project management. Known for being a perceptive troubleshooter with a unique ability to solve large-scale problems using data analytics skills. Career progression includes roles in product development, value delivery in sales cycle, and IT operations. Strong educational background includes an MBA from S. P. Jain Institute of Management & Research and a Master of Science in Software Systems from BITS, Pilani.

Swapnil is a results-oriented leader with a track record of driving organizational success. He has a proven ability to effectively manage large teams and motivate employees to achieve their full potential. He excels at creating a positive and collaborative work environment, fostering a culture of continuous improvement and innovation.

Acknowledgement

First and foremost, I would like to express my deepest gratitude to my family and friends for their unwavering support and encouragement throughout this book's writing, especially my wife Rupali, my son Ojass and my sister Smriti, I could not have achieved this milestone without your unending support..

I would like to extend my heartfelt appreciation to my publishers, who believed in the potential of this manuscript and gave me the opportunity to share my thoughts with the world. Their unwavering support, insightful feedback, and meticulous editing have been instrumental in shaping this book into its final form. I am truly grateful for their expertise and professionalism.

To my friends and colleagues, thank you for your invaluable contributions and inspiration. Your insightful conversations, wise advice, and constructive criticism have played a vital role in shaping my ideas and improving the quality of this book.

I would also like to extend my appreciation to the team of reviewers who provided their valuable feedback, thank you for your time and dedication in crafting constructive suggestions.

Lastly, I would like to thank the readers for their interest in this book. Your support and enthusiasm continue to fuel my passion for writing, and for that, I am truly grateful. I hope that the words within these pages resonate with you, inspire you, and bring about positive change in your technical career.

This book would not have been possible without the support and contributions of these incredible individuals. I am deeply grateful to each and every one of you for your role in the creation of this work. May this book serve as a testament to our collective belief in the power of knowledge, dedication, and unity.

Preface

Welcome to the world of **Python Apps on Visual Studio Code**! In this book, we aim to provide you with a comprehensive guide on building Python applications using the Visual Studio Code editor. Python has gained immense popularity in recent years due to its simplicity, versatility, and an ever-growing community of developers. As a result, there has been a surge in demand for tools and editors that cater specifically to Python development.

Visual Studio Code, commonly known as VS Code, has emerged as one of the most preferred code editors for Python developers. Its lightweight nature, extensive customization options, and powerful features make it an ideal choice for anyone looking to write Python applications. Whether you are a beginner or an experienced Python developer, this book presents a step-by-step approach to using Visual Studio Code for Python development. We will cover essential concepts, techniques, and best practices that will empower you to build robust Python applications efficiently.

In this book, readers take their basic programming skills to more productive and delivering outstanding results and fully functioning applications using a rich tool, VS Code. This book helps lazy programmers skip the long learning hours and start being efficient and effective as a smart python developer.

In this book, the author covers practical teaching, how to use Python in developing desktop GUI applications, websites and web applications. You will explore VS Code and its capabilities. You will also get to know all the popular and high performing extensions available in VS Code. Furthermore, you will learn to work around various python high-performing libraries such as Flask, NumPy, Pandas, and others. You will come across how to code data structures and implement algorithms, how to configure web servers, how to add authentication to apps and various tools to improve the capabilities of your python apps.

Throughout this book, we have strived to provide practical examples, code snippets, and tips to help you grasp the concepts and apply them to your own projects. We believe that by the end of this book, you will not only have a solid understanding of Python development on Visual Studio Code but also be equipped with the necessary skills to build sophisticated Python applications.

We hope you find this book to be a valuable resource in your quest to become a proficient Python developer.

Happy coding!

Chapter 1: Introduction to VS Code - This chapter covers the basics of using Visual Studio Code, a popular and versatile code editor. Its features and functionalities, such as creating and managing projects, writing code, debugging, and integrating with other tools and extensions are covered. We also learn various tips and tricks to enhance productivity and efficiency while using Visual Studio Code for coding and development tasks.

Chapter 2: Setting up the Environment - covers the nuts and bolts of the VS Code environment and builds the first Python program. This chapter covers the installation of Python and VS Code, setting up the Python environment using Python extension, installing default extensions along with it, and learning about editing settings.

Chapter 3: Top Extensions in VS Code for Python - This chapter covers the top 10 popular extensions used by developers across the world and the powerful features of these extensions. Also, you will learn how to configure these Python extensions and the Python-specific settings, which can be edited in VS Code. This chapter also covers the installation of packages in Python. Python, and focuses focuses on how to create functions, modules, and packages for application development.

Chapter 4: Developing Visualizing Python App in VS Code - In this chapter, we will cover the Python concepts such as Numpy, Scipy, Pandas, and Matplotlib and work on data analysis. This chapter also introduces basic statistical concepts and focuses on how to plot using Matplotlib. The chapter then explains the practice of data analytics by analyzing sample datasets. This chapter also provides clear explanations and examples to help the reader understand these concepts and apply them in practice. Towards the end of the chapter, the authors guide the reader on how to use GitHub with VS Code.

Chapter 5: Developing Desktop Application using Database - In this chapter, the author discusses how Python applications can be used to create and manage databases for various purposes. Python's comprehensive object-oriented library and its ability to interface with popular database systems make it an ideal choice for the rapid development of database applications. This chapter emphasizes the importance of learning to use Python for database applications, an efficient tool for data analysis and processing. In the last part of the chapter, the author covers debugging in VS Code. Debugging helps identify potential performance issues and allows for code optimization.

Chapter 6: Advanced Algorithm Design - This chapter focusses on learning and using different algorithms. The following algorithms are covered in this chapter: Divide and conquer, Backtracking Binary tree, Heaps, Hash table, and Graph algorithm. This chapter discusses the concept of Big O notation, which is a way of measuring the complexity of an algorithm.

Chapter 7: Building Multithreading Application - This chapter provides an overview of the concept of threads and how they can be utilized to optimize the execution of multiple tasks simultaneously. This chapter discusses the threading module in Python and its various components, such as threads, locks, and semaphores. It explains how to create and manage threads, as well as how to implement synchronization mechanisms to prevent data corruption and race conditions. The chapter also explores different threading techniques, including thread pooling and communication between threads.

Chapter 8: Building an Interactive Dashboard using Jupyter Notebook - This chapter introduces the process of developing a dashboard using Jupyter Notebooks on Visual Studio Code. This chapter explains how to set up the necessary environment and dependencies, including installing the Jupyter extension. The chapter also provides step-by-step instructions on creating a new Jupyter Notebook file within VS Code and importing libraries such as Pandas and Matplotlib for data manipulation and visualization. This chapter concludes with an example of creating a simple dashboard by analyzing and displaying data from a CSV file.

Chapter 9: Editing and Debugging Jupyter Notebook - This chapter provides a comprehensive guide for effectively editing and debugging Jupyter Notebooks using VS Code. By reading this chapter, you will understand various features and functionalities that VS Code offers for editing Jupyter Notebooks, such as cell manipulation, code execution, and markdown formatting. This chapter also covers debugging techniques, including setting breakpoints, inspecting variables, and using the built-in debugger in VS Code.

Chapter 10: Mastering Tkinter GUI Capabilities using VS Code - This chapter provides a comprehensive overview of Tkinter's GUI capabilities and demonstrates how to utilize them effectively using Visual Studio Code. The chapter begins with an introduction to the Tkinter library and its features and then dives into the process of building a graphical user interface using Tkinter in Visual Studio Code. The topics covered includes creating windows and frames, adding buttons and labels, using various widgets and layout managers, and handling events.

Chapter 11: Developing Flask-based Web Applications - In this chapter, we learned how to build web applications using the Flask framework provided by Python. The chapter covers a wide range of topics, from setting up a development environment and creating a basic Flask application to implementing authentication and authorization, handling forms, and database interactions. This chapter also provides clear explanations, step-by-step instructions, and practical examples, making it an invaluable resource for both beginner and experienced developers looking to build their own Flask-based web applications.

Chapter 12: Working with Containers in Azure - This chapter details the necessary steps for working with containers in Azure from Visual Studio Code using Python. By using the right tools and a bit of knowledge, developers can easily containerize their code in Azure. This chapter also covers deploying the Flask App developed in *Chapter 11* on Azure.

Code Bundle and Coloured Images

Please follow the link to download the
Code Bundle and the *Coloured Images* of the book:

https://rebrand.ly/98a8d0

The code bundle for the book is also hosted on GitHub at
https://github.com/bpbpublications/Python-Apps-on-Visual-Studio-Code.
In case there's an update to the code, it will be updated on the existing GitHub repository.
We have code bundles from our rich catalogue of books and videos available at
https://github.com/bpbpublications. Check them out!

Errata

We take immense pride in our work at BPB Publications and follow best practices to ensure the accuracy of our content to provide with an indulging reading experience to our subscribers. Our readers are our mirrors, and we use their inputs to reflect and improve upon human errors, if any, that may have occurred during the publishing processes involved. To let us maintain the quality and help us reach out to any readers who might be having difficulties due to any unforeseen errors, please write to us at :

errata@bpbonline.com

Your support, suggestions and feedbacks are highly appreciated by the BPB Publications' Family.

Did you know that BPB offers eBook versions of every book published, with PDF and ePub files available? You can upgrade to the eBook version at www.bpbonline.com and as a print book customer, you are entitled to a discount on the eBook copy. Get in touch with us at :

business@bpbonline.com for more details.

At **www.bpbonline.com**, you can also read a collection of free technical articles, sign up for a range of free newsletters, and receive exclusive discounts and offers on BPB books and eBooks.

Piracy

If you are interested in becoming an author

If there is a topic that you have expertise in, and you are interested in either writing or contributing to a book, please visit **www.bpbonline.com**. We have worked with thousands of developers and tech professionals, just like you, to help them share their insights with the global tech community. You can make a general application, apply for a specific hot topic that we are recruiting an author for, or submit your own idea.

Reviews

Please leave a review. Once you have read and used this book, why not leave a review on the site that you purchased it from? Potential readers can then see and use your unbiased opinion to make purchase decisions. We at BPB can understand what you think about our products, and our authors can see your feedback on their book. Thank you!

For more information about BPB, please visit **www.bpbonline.com**.

Join our book's Discord space

Join the book's Discord Workspace for Latest updates, Offers, Tech happenings around the world, New Release and Sessions with the Authors:

https://discord.bpbonline.com

Table of Contents

CHAPTER 1
Introduction to VS Code

People don't buy what you do, they buy why you do it.
— Simon Sinek

Introduction

Welcome to the first chapter of this book, *Python Apps on Visual Studio Code*. You would have guessed correctly by now that we will build lots of Python applications in this book. But why Visual Studio Code or VS Code? The first step to learning any programming language is to pick a code editor and learn the tips and tricks to get the most out of your code editor. You will come across many code editors to program in Python from, but the most popular, and my favourite, is VS Code. Do not confuse VS Code with Visual Studio. VS Code is a free, open-source platform, and you will learn more about this editor in this chapter.

Over a decade ago, *Simon Sinek* in his TedTalk, had said, *People don't buy what you do, they buy why you do it*. It is stuck in my mind till today. So, the first thing we will talk about is why we should use VS Code for Python. Next, we will discuss what VS Code is and how to use it.

Visual Studio Code is an open-source code editor that is free to use and fully supports development in Python programming language. It has useful features, such as real-time collaboration with other programmers around the world. This chapter is meant to introduce VS Code to help you understand its development process and its different components.

This chapter is for readers who have not yet heard about VS Code and wonder why they should even consider it for their development work. This chapter will provide information about VS Code; we will discuss why it is probably the most popular code editor, look at its features, and discuss the different components of VS Code. We will look at the architecture of VS Code to understand why it is a perfect tool for software development needs and how a developer can quickly perform a code-build-debug cycle and leave more complex workflows to fuller featured IDEs, such as Pycharm or Visual Studio IDE.

Structure

We will be looking at the following topics in this chapter:

- Why use VS Code?
- What is VS Code?
    o VS Code: Context View
    o VS Code: Development View
    o VS Code: Functional View
    o Performance and Scalability
- VS Code vs Visual Studio

Now, let us dive deep into each of these topics.

Why use VS Code?

Visual Studio Code, or VS Code, is the best code editor by far for multiple reasons. As per the official documentation, VS Code provides *the delightfully frictionless edit-build-debug cycle means less time fiddling with your environment, and more time executing on your ideas.* In terms of the number of users, VS Code has the largest user base (December 2021, source: JetBrains/Python Software Foundation). *JetBrains,* along with Python Software Foundation, conducted a Python developer survey in which respondents were asked one question, 'What is the main editor you use for your current Python development?' More than 23,000 Python developers answered the survey. Around 35% answered VS Code, making it number one, ahead of PyCharm. One interesting finding was that the web developers preferred PyCharm and VS Code almost equally (about 39%), but data scientists preferred VS Code as their main editor. The result is represented in *Figure 1.1:*

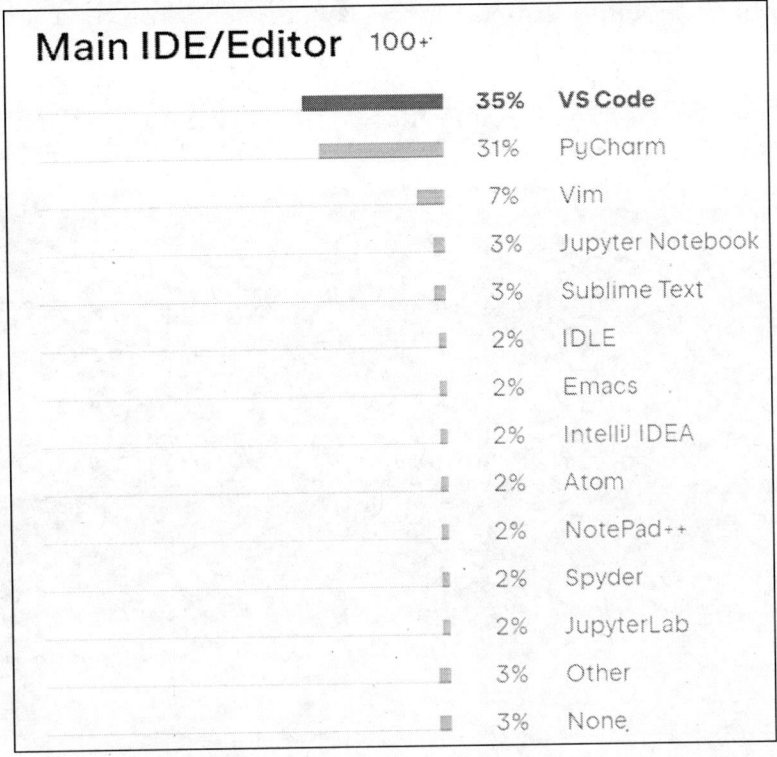

Figure 1.1: Main IDE/Editor (source: JetBrains/Python Software Foundation)

According to a report published by Visual Studio Magazine (*visualstudiomagazine.com*, July 2022), the Python extension for Visual Studio Code has seen over 60 million installs, which is, by far, the highest number of installs. Jupyter has (40.8 million), Pylance (33.5 million), and Jupyter Keymap (23.4 million), with these extensions (also related to Python), taking the second, third, and fifth positions, respectively. But, this did not happen overnight. *Visual Studio Code, along with GitHub, Codespaces, and Azure Machine Learning, have been investing substantially into tools and platforms to make the lives of Python data scientists easier* (source: EuroPython show 2021). The amazing thing is that we will cover all these in the later chapters of this book, so rest assured that you will learn the best tools available today.

Let us look at some of its features and why it has become programmers' favourite code editor:

- It is a free open-source (under the MIT License) cross-platform application.

- It is easy to use.

- It is a lightweight, fast but powerful source code editor.

- It can be integrated with scripting tools and perform common tasks like developing everyday workflows.

- It comes with built-in support for tools like IntelliSense code completion, code refactoring, parameter hints, multi-cursor editing, and rich semantic code understanding, which takes programming to the next level. For example, if the user forgets to declare a certain variable before being used in the program, intelli-sense will declare that variable. A sample screenshot is shown in the *Figure 1.2*:

```
6   #we have divided the dataset into X (independent variables) and y(dependent variables)
7   X = dataset.iloc[:,:4].values
8   y = dataset.iloc[:,4].values
9   plt.scatter(dataset['R&D Spend'],dataset['Profit'])
10  plt.
        ⬡ show
        ⬡ acorr
        ⬡ angle_spectrum
        ⬡ annotate
        [◉] ArrayLike
        ⬡ arrow
        ⬡ autoscale
        ⬡ autumn
        ⚏ Axes
        ⬡ axes
        ⬡ axhline
        ⬡ axhspan
```

Figure 1.2: *Auto completion in VS Code using Intelli-Sense*

- It has an integrated interactive debugger, which helps step through the code, inspect values of variables, and view call stacks. It can also execute commands in the console. *Figure 1.3* shows the various options of integrated interactive debugger marked on the image:

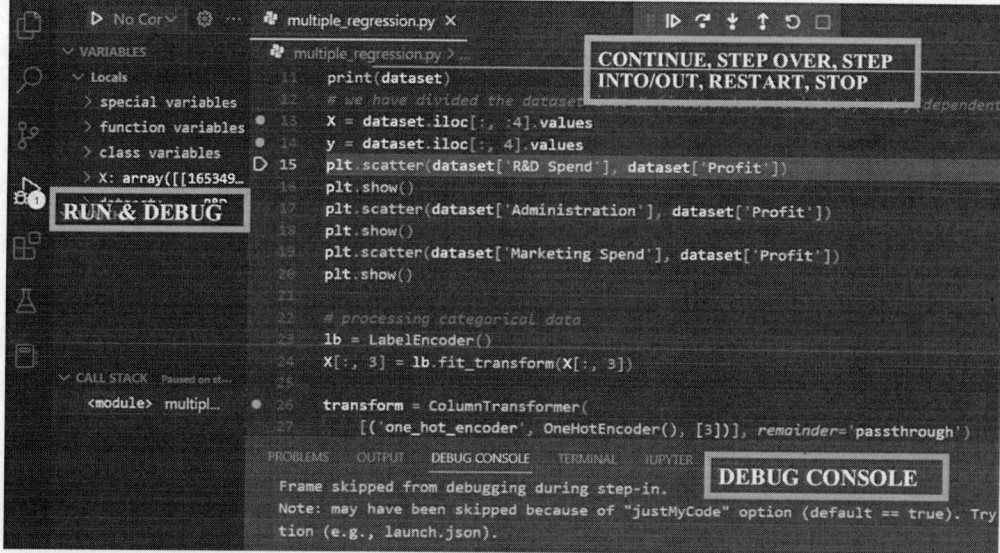

Figure 1.3: *Debugging in VS Code*

- It runs on a desktop and is available for Windows, macOS, and Linux. Earlier, editors used to support one of the operating systems, Windows, Linux, or Mac. But VS Code is cross-platform, so it can easily work on all three platforms.

- It is fully customizable to fit any developer's preferences and project requirements.

- It has great support from the community and tons of extensions. So, if a programmer cannot find support for a given programming language, they can easily download the extension and continue working.

- It has built-in support for web programming languages like JavaScript, TypeScript, and Node.js. It also has an ecosystem of extensions for multiple other languages and runtimes, such as C++, C#, Java, Python, PHP, Go, and .NET. These are just a few of more than 30 languages that are supported. This has another advantage here; VS Code can easily detect if there is any fault in the cross-language reference.

- It can be configured to anybody's liking through its various settings: language, user, and workspace. Several scopes for settings are provided by VS Code, which enables us to modify almost every part of Code's editor, user interface, and functional behavior.

- It provides comprehensive facilities to computer programmers to be instantly productive with features like syntax highlighting, bracket-matching, auto-indentation, box-selection, snippets, and many more.

- It has support for Git, which means the programmers can work with source control without leaving the editor, even for viewing pending changes differences.

- It supports multiple projects. It is possible to work with projects containing multiple files / folders that can be opened simultaneously. These projects or folders can even be unrelated to each other.

- It provides an ides inbuilt terminal / console, so the user need not switch between VS Code and command prompt or terminal.

- It is liked by front-end and back-end developers because of the multiple language support. Along with this, common zoom-in, zoom-out, brightness, and theme selection features are also available.

- It is updated monthly with new features and bug fixes.

What is VS Code?

Now, let us understand why VS Code is probably a better choice among all the code editors available right now. First, it is free to use and has very useful features that fully featured IDEs generally have. It enables a programmer to write code, debug, and autocomplete or correct the code. It is difficult for a code editor to have such features, but since VS Code has Intelli-sense integrated with itself, it makes this possible. In this section, we will learn what the VS Code editor is and how VS Code can integrate such powerful features. *Figure 1.4* shows a sample program running on VS Code editor:

Figure 1.4: VS Code running a multiple regression code on Windows 10

VS Code is developed with the Electron Framework and made open-source by Microsoft to create a lightweight alternative to Microsoft's Visual Studio, a complex, fully featured **Integrated Development Environment (IDE)**. There are differences between an IDE and Code Editor. IDEs are robust and self-contained software aimed at making programming easier. All the tools of an IDE are integrated. On the other hand, a code editor is a text editor, which has robust built-in features. IDEs also have code editors built into themselves where the developers write their code. The source-code of VS Code is under the MIT License and is maintained at the VS Code repository at GitHub (*github.com/microsoft/vscode*). Though VS Code ships under a standard Microsoft product license, it's free to use. The commercial license is attached because it has a small percentage of Microsoft-specific customizations. As it is open-source, developers can contribute to improving VS Code by adding issues or making pull requests from the GitHub location. Electron's open-source framework, maintained by GitHub, is designed to develop desktop-based applications using web technologies like HTML, Javascript, and CSS.

VS Code: Context view

In this section, we will look at the context diagram of VS Code. A **System Context Diagram (SCD)** is a block or engineering diagram that defines the boundary of the system and its environment and represents all the external entities that interact with the system. This provides a high-level understanding of the system. The objective of creating and understanding a system context diagram is to understand and focus on external components and events considered in developing the entire system. *Figure 1.5* shows the context view diagram; we identify different entities and see how they connect to Visual Studio Code:

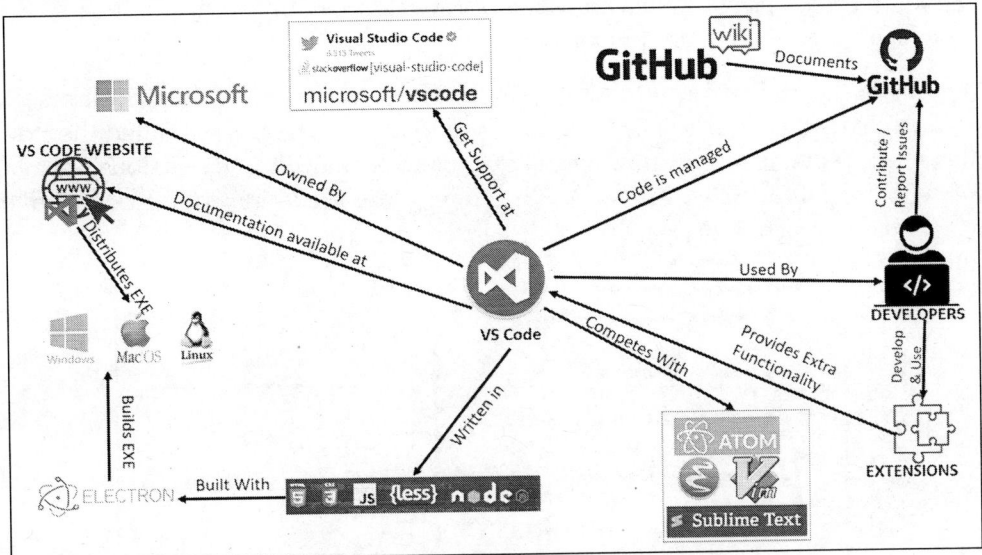

Figure 1.5: Context Diagram for Visual Studio Code

The preceding *Figure 1.5* shows multiple stakeholders and external processes that are involved with the development, maintenance, and use of VS Code. The VS Code project is built using the Electron framework. This framework uses programming languages like HTML, Javascript, CSS, and TypeScript, and it builds the installers for different operating systems. The VS Code website (**https://code.visualstudio.com**) then distributes the installers for each of the three operating systems. VS Code website also provides documentation (Docs), updates on new releases (Updates), VS Code Community Discussion (Blog), documentation related to APIs (API), and a list of extensions available (Extensions). The use of extensions can also help personalize the VS Code editor, for example, choosing your own font type and size for the editor.

GitHub provides a cloud-based Git repository that provides software development and version control services. VS Code's code and issues/bugs are managed and tracked by developers at GitHub, where they are solved through contributions made by the community. The wiki contains information such as project structure, how one can contribute to the code, and links to various resources.

Next in the context diagram are the main stakeholders. Microsoft developed the VS Code. Developers contribute to adding new features or fixing bugs identified by the community. Atom, Vim, Emacs, and Sublime Text are some of the editors identified as the competitors, as these are also lightweight text editors used to develop applications. We do not consider IDEs like Visual Studio, Pycharm, or IntelliJ as competitors, as these are more complex than code editors.

VS Code: Development view

The development or implementation view illustrates a software system from a programmer's perspective and is about software management. In this section, we will look at the architecture and software development process, how the code is structured, and how design and testing are performed.

VS Code has a layered and modular core (folder location at *github: src/vs*). These can be extended while using extensions. Extensions run in a separate process called the extension host and are implemented by utilizing the extension API. Built-in extensions are available in the extensions folder. Six core layers work together to make VS Code a powerful editor. These layers are shown in *Figure 1.6*:

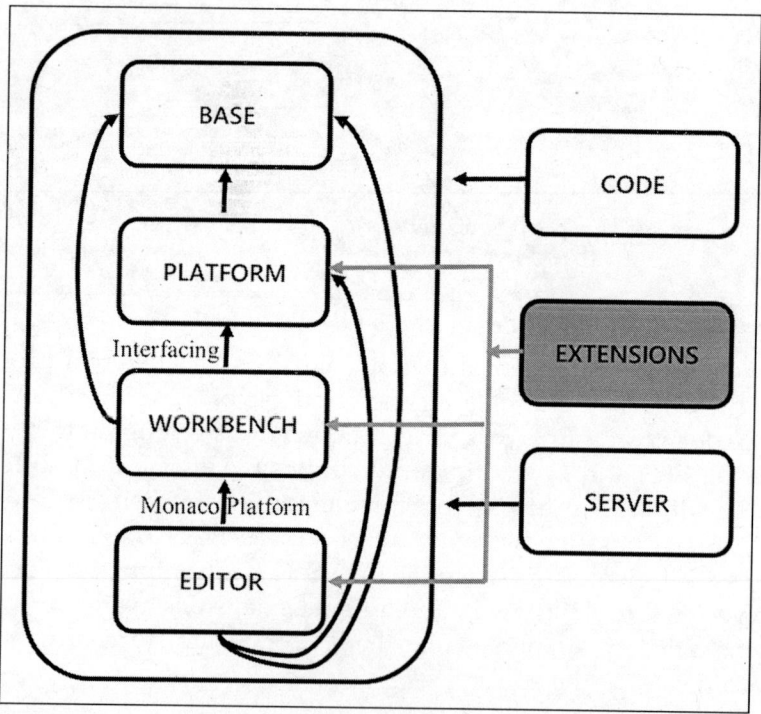

Figure 1.6: VS Code Module Diagram

Let us now understand the purpose of these layers:

- **Base**: This folder has user interface building blocks and general utilities, which any other layer can use. This common environment approach provides, among others, the structure to handle errors, process events, and do other web-related things. In the common environment, the code ranges widely, from simple functions to reduce code duplication, such as returning a hash value for an object, to complex code that handles asynchronous processes. It also has other functionalities, such as:

o Reading the configuration files,

o Handling the checksum for encryption,

o Character encoding and decoding,

o Operating system functionalities for directory and file manipulation, and

o Network handling to interact with the web.

- **Platform**: This layer defines service injection support and the base services for VS Code that are shared across layers, and it excludes editor or workbench-specific code or services. Most of the services around which the VS Code project is organized are defined in the platform layer. The platform layer builds upon the base layer, creates instances, and registers services for almost everything. Extensions are all instantiated and registered through the platform layer. The workbench layer is built upon the platform layer, which initializes much more details, like CSS, that are not handled by the platform.

- **Editor**: By now, we know that VS Code has a high-productivity code editor, which gives the power of an IDE and the efficiency of a text editor. Now, let us look at how this is possible at all! The power behind VS Code editor is Monaco editor. Monaco started as a project at Microsoft's Switzerland lab, which was part of a plan to build online development tools. It was built using TypeScript and launched in 2013. The first job of Monaco editor was as Azure's website editing tool, and it was also used as the editor for Office 365's extension development site. The editor layer handles everything from syntax highlighting for different languages to user input, like copying, pasting, and selecting text. Services defined in the editor layer can be used by the controllers to fetch certain data. One of these services is TextMate, which interprets grammar files for text highlighting. The final part of the editor layer is contributions. Contributions extend functionalities like hiding and unhiding (blocking) comments, code indentation, and the usage of links.

- **Workbench**: It contains the Monaco editor and code notebooks. It also provides the framework for panels like the Explorer, Status Bar, or Menu Bar. It leverages the Electron framework to implement the VS Code desktop application and browser APIs for VS Code for the web. The actual GUI of the workbench is implemented using the electron-browser environment. When the main component fires up the workbench, the shell component is called first. The shell component has five components that constitute the actual workbench:

  o **crashReporter**: It handles the workbench in case of a crash.

  o **nodeCachedDataManager**: It saves the settings of the workbench.

  o **command**: It handles the different keybindings that can be used in the workbench.

- o   **extensionHost**: It handles the different extensions installed in the workbench.

- o   **actions**: It handles all sorts of actions that can be done in the workbench, such as zooming in/out, switching from the window, and opening a new window.

- **Code**: It puts Electron main file, shared process, and the CLI together and forms the entry point to the desktop app.

- **Server**: This forms the entry point to the server app for remote development.

Extensions use the extension API and run in a separate process called the extension host. Inside each layer, VS Code is organized by the target runtime environment to ensure that only the runtime-specific APIs are used. The VS Code project has the following target environments:

- **common**: Source code that needs only basic JavaScript APIs and runs in all the other target environments

- **browser**: Source code that requires the browser APIs

- **node**: Source code that requires Nodejs APIs

- **electron-browser**: Source code that requires the Electron renderer-process APIs

- **electron-main**: Source code that requires the Electron main-process APIs

There are advantages to such a layered approach. It becomes easy to inject a service into VS Code.

Standardization

VS Code has a large, vibrant community of developers that helps find and resolve software bugs. Without following a standard process for coding and testing, it would become a mess to manage the code base. In this section, we will briefly see how a contributor can suggest new features, submit bug details, build extensions, comment on new ideas, or submit pull requests.

But before you can proceed as a contributor, you need to understand the standard very well. VS Code has a wiki where developers can find information about the code base and instructions on how to work with the source code. A detailed explanation of how you can contribute and coding guidelines are listed on the wiki. It defines how code should be written to keep every file readable and maintainable.

Visual Studio Code uses tools, called linters, to enforce the coding guidelines. These tools have configuration files and are set up in the Git root of VS Code. By installing these linters as extensions in Visual Studio Code, developers get notified by visualized errors and other kind-of messages in the editor.

Visual Studio Code is tested by using the JavaScript testing framework Mocha. A smoke test is performed before each release. This smoke test is carried out to ensure that all major functionalities work as intended. VS Code uses Travis CI and Appveyor for continuous integration on GitHub. Travis CI is used for testing Linux and Mac OS builds. whereas AppVeyor runs the build test on Windows.

Technical Debt

Technical debt, also known as design debt or code debt in the software engineering world, is a concept that shows and reflects the extra development work that is a result of software developers choosing limited or easy development work to address an issue instead of using a better approach that would take longer time and possibly delay the release. Technical debt can also arise from implementing poor programming syntaxes, leading to poor code readability and difficulty in maintaining code later. The term 'technical debt' was coined by software developer Ward Cunningham, one of the 17 Agile Manifesto authors who created the first wiki. He first used the technical debt metaphor to explain the non-technical stakeholders at WyCash why they should invest in resources for code refactoring to improve the existing code and add new features.

VS Code has multiple extensions available for the users to catch poor code, and manage and reduce technical debt. These extensions can be installed on demand. Some extensions that help in achieving better and efficient code are Stepsize, TODO Highlight, SonarLint, and Code Runner. A linter (or simple Lint) derives its name from a Unix utility originally written to manage C language source code, and it is a static code analysis tool. Linters highlight programming errors, bugs, coding standard errors, and possible construct errors. In the linters, the rules for naming conventions, type casting, and code styles are written to ensure that the contributors do not increase technical debt. If a developer pushing the code to VS Code GitHub, does not install linters, then they get notified by the pre-commit checks for the same. If these pre-commit checks fail, some technical debt must be fixed before being able to commit and push the desired contribution.

VS Code: Functional view

The functional view of VS Code defines the architectural elements that add to the functionalities. It talks about what VS Code can and can't do. In this section, we will look at the key functionalities and the external interfaces.

Functionalities

The functionalities are listed in the following table:

Functionality	Description
Editor	The main component displays code, syntax highlighting, and capability to edit

Functionality	Description
Search	Displays the capability to search and replace a piece of text
Explorer	Displays the folder structure of an opened folder and shows the contained files
Debugging	Allows you to add breakpoints, watch variables, and step into/out of the block
Marketplace	Shows paid and free extensions available
Implement Extensions	Lets you choose and install the right extension for your work
Git	Maintains version control

Table 1.1: List of core functions of Visual Studio Code

External Interfaces

There are several external interfaces to which VS Code connects. Listed here are just a few of them:

Functionality	Description
window	Shows the current window of the editor to the user and keeps track of all the open editors
extensions	Install and activate extensions by their ID so that extensions can use other extensions
CommentRule	Line and block (multi-line) comments for different languages
TextDocument	Represents a test file and holds all the information like file path, content, and so on
TextEditor	Text editor attached to a document helps in editing the content

Table 1.2: List of external interfaces

Performance and Scalability

The source code for any software can get much larger and more complex. Code editors' performance and scalability have become very important considerations for the development team. Performance is an indication of the responsiveness of a system to execute any action within a given time interval, while scalability is the ability of a system either to handle increases in load without impact on performance or for to increase the available resources. Let us look at a few factors considered while choosing VS Code over other editors.

Desired quality

The desired quality of Visual Studio Code is to be a lightweight code editor while supporting multiple programming languages. Language support will include debugging, implementation, and displaying results regardless of the type of application.

Applicability

It is recommended to use a processor of 1.6GHz or faster and at least 1 GB of RAM. Though the performance of Visual Studio Code itself is tested and known, there are elements like extensions, whose performance is unknown. This is so because the extensions available on the marketplace are developed by third-party developers and they do not necessarily test on various platforms and different conditions.

Concerns

One of the biggest concerns for Visual Studio Code is the response time. It is important that users do not have to wait long to open files, since this reduces the time they can spend on productive tasks like software development. This response time can be combined with the peak load behavior when large files are opened. This causes third-party behavior concerns since the whole file needs to be loaded at once. To reduce these concerns, Visual Studio Code tries to tackle the predictability concern by providing stable releases every month.

Tactics

Tactics in Visual Studio Code refer to a set of strategies or techniques that can be used to improve productivity and efficiency while working with the code editor. Visual Studio Code tries to optimize processing is by spending an entire week after a release to test and optimize the implementation. Some parts of the code may be rushed to ship with the release. Since Visual Studio Code depends on certain frameworks such as IntelliSense, which can make large files difficult to handle. In such cases, prioritization of code becomes important. Modules are divided into different layers, base and common, to minimize the use of shared resources. Visual Studio Code uses asynchronous processing in the form of a worker. Workers can be used to run desired processes in the background, which do not affect the performance of the current page of Visual Studio Code. Tactics, along with various extensions and customization options available in Visual Studio Code, can significantly enhance your coding experience and productivity.

VS Code vs Visual Studio

Visual Studio Code and Visual Studio are Microsoft-made products with similar-sounding names, but that is where the similarity ends. They have different features and uses. We have already seen that Visual Studio is a full-fledged **Integrated Development Environment (IDE)** with many features that are loved by millions of developers worldwide. But VS

Code is proving to be a tough competitor to Visual Studio. Let us get into the details to understand when to use VS Code and when to use Visual Studio.

Visual Studio helps develop desktop applications, web applications, web services, and mobile applications with the help of Microsoft's software development platform, that is, Windows API, Windows Presentation Foundation, Windows Forms, Microsoft Silverlight, and Windows Store. They help produce and manage the code. VS Code is used to write, edit, and debug the code in a single editor, without requiring any web support. Everything that is required is built-in.

To develop programs using Visual Studio, developers do not need to install any special software. VS Code is very powerful, but you need to know the right tools to be installed before you realize their benefits.

Looking at the license cost, VS Code wins hands down. VS Code is free, while Visual Code can cost you around $45 per month. You can refer to the Visual Studio website for detailed pricing.

Visual Studio is available for Windows and macOS but not for Linux platforms, whereas VS Code is available for all three platforms.

Let us look at a few situations where Visual Studio can be used:

- Since Visual Studio is functionally feature-rich, developers do not need to install extensions or plugins. So, when you do not want to keep looking for the right plugin, this is your choice of IDE.

- Visual Studio provides the right collaboration platform where the entire team can come together and debug the code; collaboration is super smooth.

- For heavy-duty code analysis, Visual Studio has no match. It has incredible options for debugging and performance profiling.

- Game development, **Augmented Reality (AR) / Virtual Reality (VR)** industries prefer Visual Studio because they can work effortlessly to build cross-platform applications. UNITY, a multi-platform environment, is integrated with Visual Studio.

Now, let us look at a few situations where Visual Studio Code should be preferred:

- VS Code is a lightweight application that doesn't require a lot of computing power or hard disk space.

- VS Code works faster as compared to Visual Studio.

- The code generated by VS Code is incredibly flexible and can be moved to another platform easily.

- Visual Studio Code is the number #1 choice for web development.

Conclusion

New technologies are emerging every day, and new frameworks are developed to use these technologies efficiently and effectively for our work. With the focus of software developers in today's times, and more so with cloud computing booming, the shift has focused on developing applications faster and more securely. It is a sure thing to learn this new framework thoroughly to make the best of it; this is where VS Code scores over other code editors.

This chapter introduced readers to the open-source project Visual Studio code and helped them understand its architecture. We discussed why VS Code is programmers' favorite choice of tool for developing different types of applications. We looked at the different layers of VS Code, which makes it powerful and, at the same time, retains its lightweight nature. We also looked at VS Code from different perspectives like context view, development view, performance and scalability, and technical debt.

Another thing we can say for sure is that as new frameworks are developed in the future, these will be made available to VS Code using extensions. This would bring into play a great variety of code effectiveness and help programmers, testers, and data administrators–experienced and newbies–to write better and more effective code faster. The community drives visual Studio Code development, prioritization of features comes from issue tracking, and a feature is implemented and optimized by the internal development team every week.

In the next chapter, we will see how to install VS Code and Python extension and set up the path so that we are ready to code our applications.

Join our book's Discord space

Join the book's Discord Workspace for Latest updates, Offers, Tech happenings around the world, New Release and Sessions with the Authors:

https://discord.bpbonline.com

CHAPTER 2
Setting up the Environment

I will prepare and someday my chance will come.
— Abraham Lincoln

Introduction

The first chapter aimed to introduce you to the VS Code, and this chapter is about getting started. You must be excited to do the first program in Python on VS Code. That will also help us understand different concepts well. This chapter will use simple programming concepts to revise basic Python programs and VS Code features like task running, editing the default settings, getting to know keyboard shortcuts, and running a Python program. The first thing we must do is set up a working development environment. We will start with Python installation and VS Code installation, and then we will set up the Python environment. The second part of the chapter is about understanding the *what* and *how* of the global and virtual environment. You must be excited to build and debug our first Python program. Let us get started!

Structure

In this chapter, we will discuss the following topics:

- Setting up a working development environment
- Installing Python extension

- Project Work: Design a Simple Battleship Game
- Setting up and configuring the editor
- Keyboard arguments

Objectives

The objective of this chapter is to introduce simple programming concepts to revise basic Python programs, but before that, we need to familiarize ourselves with the VS Code features. You will look at tasks like debugging, task running, and version control, to name a few. We will demonstrate the concepts with the help of programs.

Setting up a working development environment

This section focuses on downloading and installing the VS Code, setting up the VS Code environment, setting up the Python environment, and writing our first program.

Setting up a Python environment

First, the Python interpreter needs to be installed. We must connect to python.org and select the correct installer based on your operating system. Python is also available in the Microsoft Store on Windows devices. If you are on Linux, you might have Python3. You can verify if Python is already installed on your computer by typing **python3 --version** in a terminal. If it gives an error, it means you need to install it.

Follow these steps to install the software:

1. Open your favorite browser, type download Python, and click on the first link that appears on your search result – it should take you to *python.org*. Alternatively, you can directly enter the following address in the browser: **https://www.python. org/downloads/**.

2. Python interpreter is available for all the major platforms, including **Windows, MacOS, Linux/UNIX**. Refer to the following figure:

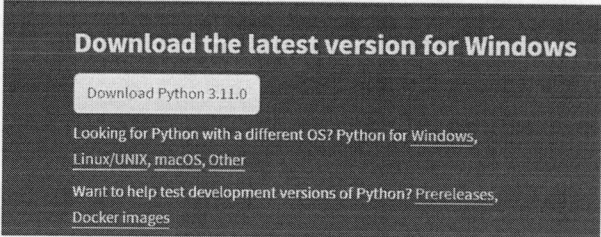

Figure 2.1: *Screenshot from Python download web page*

Installing on Windows

- You can directly click on **Download Python 3.11.0** or navigate to the **Python Releases for Windows** section and click the download link to get the latest Python 3 release. As of today, the latest version is Python 3.11.0. Select the Python installer executable for 32-bit or 64-bit and click on download. When the download is finished, move to the next step.

- Run the downloaded installer file by double-clicking on it. A dialog box similar to the one shown in *Figure 2.2* will appear:

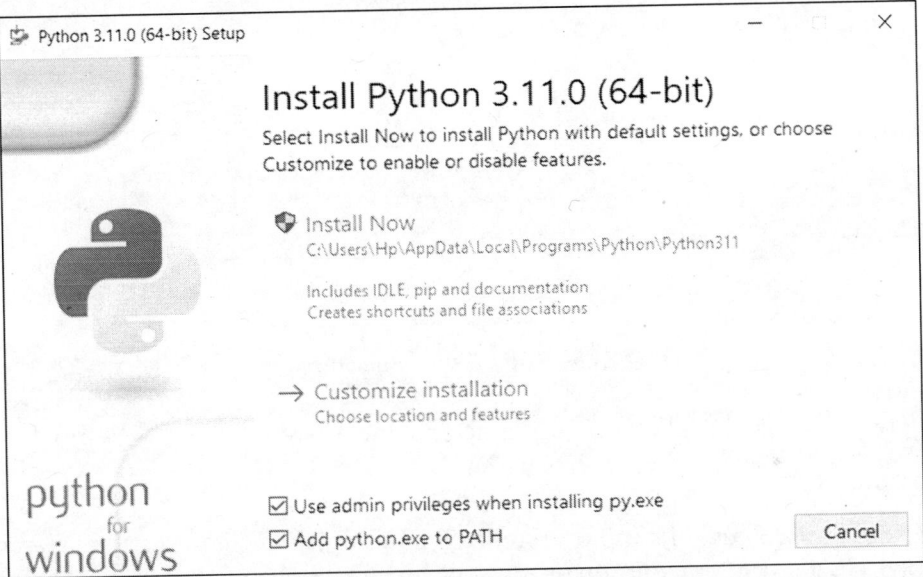

Figure 2.2: Python interpreter installer

There are a few things one needs to know before clicking on **Install Now** to move ahead:

- **Install Now** shows where Python will be installed and run from.

- The **Customize installation** option customizes the location and additional installation features. We can also manage this later using the **pip** command.

- The **Install launcher for all users (recommended)** box is checked by default on the dialog box. It can be unchecked to restrict other users from launching Python.

- Add **Python.exe to PATH** (unchecked by default). Python allows the installation of multiple versions on a single machine, and different projects can connect to different versions of Python. This is possible by creating multiple virtual environments. We also create a global environment by adding **Python.exe to PATH** (under environment variables). If you are installing for the first time, then checking this option is recommended.

Make the customization based on your needs and then click **Install Now**. Wait for the installation to complete. Refer to the following figure:

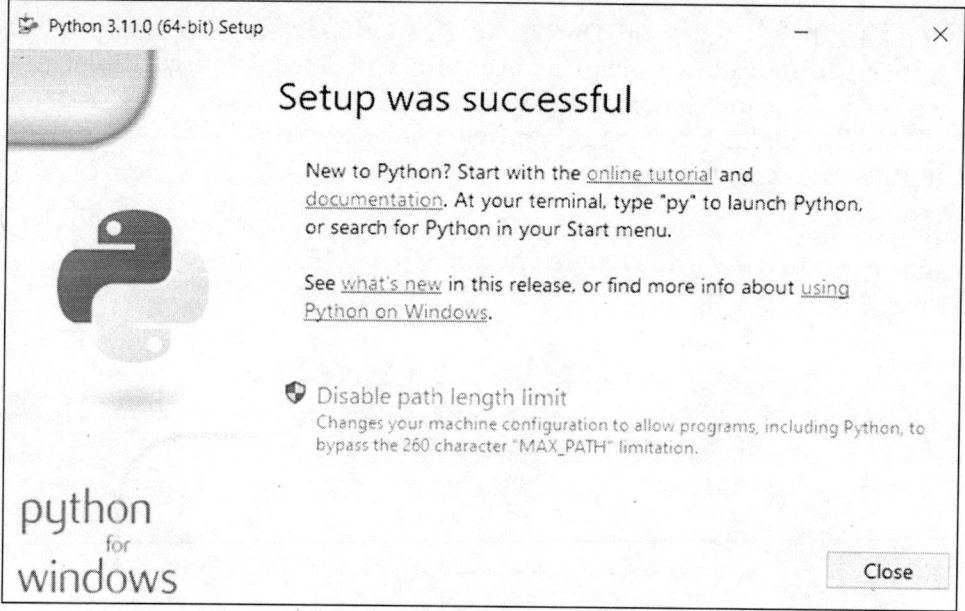

Figure 2.3: Successful installation

Now you have Python installed on your machine. We are ready to code Python!

Installing on macOS

- Older macOS versions (up until macOS Catalina) came with Python 2 (an old and phased-out version). Python needs to be installed on new Mac machines. Installing Python from **www.python.org** (the official website) is the most reliable method.

- You can navigate to the **Python Releases for macOS** section and click the download link for the latest Python 3 release. As of today, the latest version is Python 3.11.0. Click on download. When the download is finished, move to the next step.

- Run the macOS installer by double-clicking the file that was downloaded. You must click the **Continue** button a few times before agreeing to the software license agreement presented on the screen. Accept the agreement, and a window will pop up with details like install destination and how much space it will take, among other options. You can continue with the default location and click **Install** to proceed. The installer will finish copying files; you know this when you see the **Close** option. Click on **Close** to close the installer window. Congratulations! Python 3 is now installed on your macOS computer.

- You can refer to the online tutorial to install Python interpreters on Linux/UNIX machines.

Setting up VS Code Environment

Let us shift our focus to installing and setting up VS Code environments. First, we will see how to download the VS Code and install it. Let us go step by step:

1. Open your favorite browser and type download visual studio code. The first link you will see is **https://code.visualstudio.com/download**.

2. Go to the link and choose the installer based on the operating system, as discussed in *Chapter 1, Introduction to VS Code*. VS Code is available for **Windows**, **Linux**, and **Mac**. Click on download based on the OS and the machine type. Refer to the following figure:

Figure 2.4: Screenshot from https://code.visualstudio.com/download

3. After the download is complete, install it like any other application. It is lightweight; the file size is less than 100 MB for **Windows** and **Linux** machines, and the Mac file could be about 200 MB. It is lightning fast to install. Refer to the following figure:

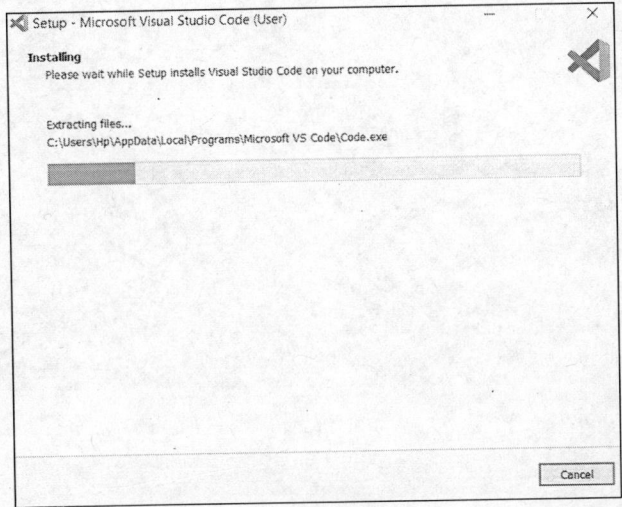

Figure 2.5: Installing on Windows 10

4. VS Code is now installed on your computer. Now you are ready to program.

5. If you are planning to program in HTML, then you are ready to go, but we need to install a Python extension to develop Python applications.

Installing Python extension

We will install the Python extension, which is a must to run Python programs from VS Code. The Python extension is helpful; it is what converts the lightweight VS Code editor into a powerful editor. It not only supports the Python language (for all actively supported versions of the language: >=3.7) but also includes features like IntelliSense (Pylance), linting, debugging, code navigation, code formatting, refactoring, variable explorer, and test explorer. We discussed these features in *Chapter 1, Introduction to Visual Studio Code*, so if you missed it and are wondering what they means, you can revisit the previous chapter.

You can run a Python file from VS Code by taking the Python interpreter's help and ignoring the VS Code's capabilities. Open your VS Code editor and select **New File** from the **File** menu. Type the following code in the editor:

```
print("Hello from VS Code")
```

Now, save this file to your desktop as **myfile1.py**. Python files have the **.py** extension, so save it in this format.

Next, click on the **Terminal** menu in VS Code, and you will see the **Terminal** window open at the bottom of your screen, similar to what you see in *Figure 2.6*:

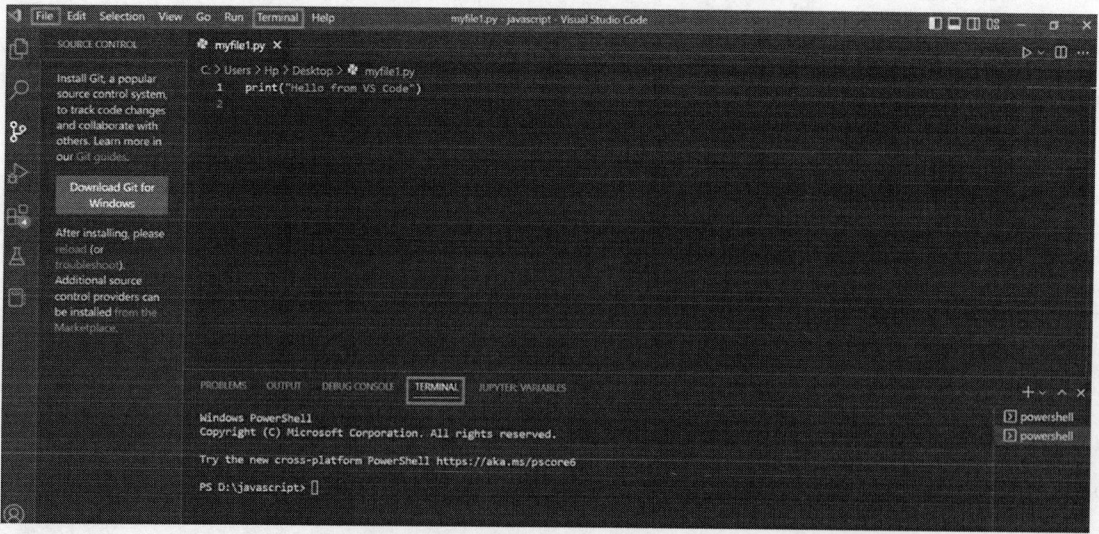

Figure 2.6: *VS Code screen with Python code and Terminal open*

In the terminal window, browse to desktop since our program is saved there. Then, type the following:

```
py myfile1.py
```

You will see the following output printed on the screen:

```
Hello from VS Code
```

This is shown in *Figure 2.7*:

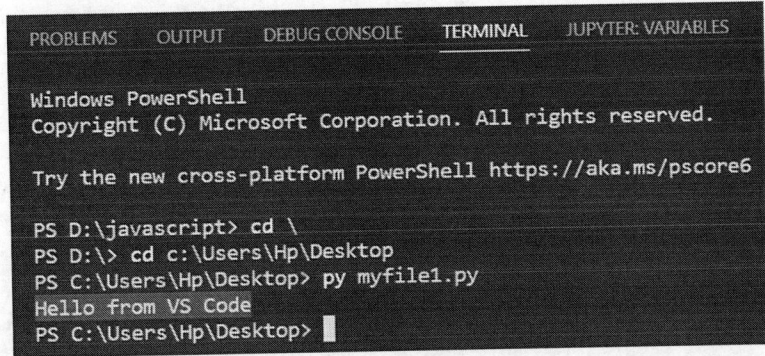

Figure 2.7: *Screenshot of Terminal running Python program*

In this example, we used the VS Code as a simple editor to write code and execute it on **Terminal** by calling the Python interpreter. This can be achieved using Notepad editor as well. In the next few sections, we will see how to install the Python extension on VS Code and use its features to enhance our code efficiency.

Go to the extension tab (on the left side of the screen) and search for the **Python** extension. The first result, as shown in *Figure 2.8*, is what we need to install. Click on the **Install** option that would be displayed next to the extension. As soon as you do that, the Python extension gets installed.

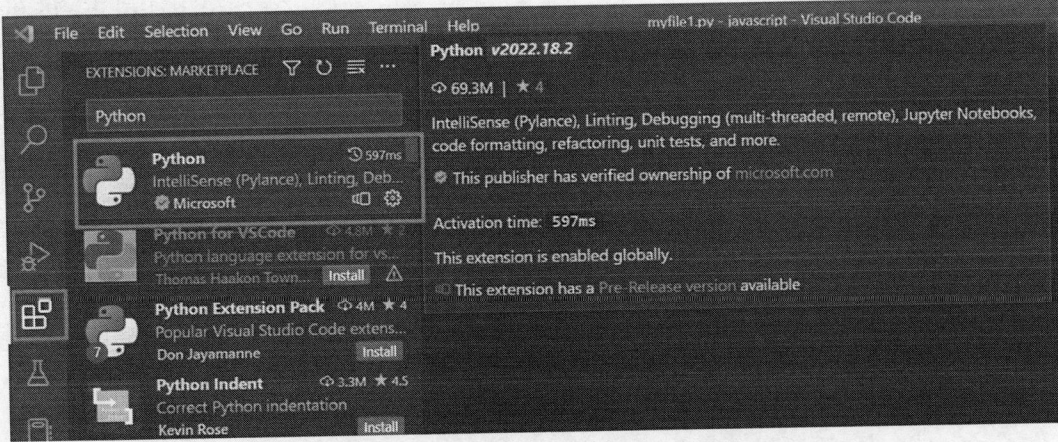

Figure 2.8: *Python extension in search result*

The Python extension automatically installs the **Pylance** and **Jupyter** extensions to simplify programming and improve the coding experience.

Note: Pylance is an optional dependency, which means the Python extension will function even it is uninstalled later.

Code Runner extension

Chapter 3, Top Extensions in VS Code, is dedicated to installing extensions, but we will install two important extensions before we run any program: Code Runner extension and Pylint extension. Code Runner is necessary to avoid going to the terminal again and again to run a Python program. It is designed to support all the most widely used programming languages, like Javascript, HTML, C, C++, Java, and Python; these are among the 25 languages that it supports. Additional languages can also be supported. Search for Code Runner in the extension search box and install it. It had almost 16 million installations at the time of writing this chapter. *Figure 2.9* shows the CodeRunner extension preview as shown in VS Code:

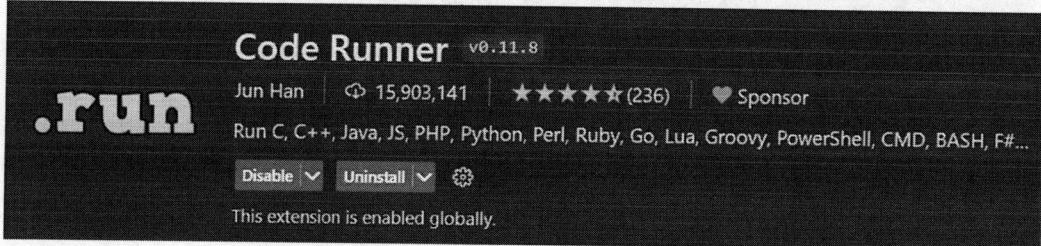

Figure 2.9: *CodeRunner Extension installation*

Successful installation of Code Runner will make a play button (▷) appear in the top-right corner of your VS Code editor. This button can be used to run the code.

The second important extension is Pylint (preview shown in *Figure 2.10*). Pylint is a linting tool for Python that helps developers identify and fix code issues quickly and easily. The Pylint extension in VS Code provides an excellent linting experience for Python in VS Code, enabling you to quickly see problems with your code and take corrective action. The extension provides enhanced linting features, such as checking code for PEP8 compliance and quickly identifying issues. It also includes support for running Pylint from the command line. With this extension, you can efficiently write better Python code, save time, and get more productive.

Figure 2.10: Pylint Extension Preview

Linting tools are programming tools that help ensure that a program's code adheres to coding standards and is correctly formatted. It can detect and flag potential programming errors, such as undefined variables, inconsistent formatting, errors in logic, and unclosed loops. Linting tools are often used to detect and eliminate programming errors before the code is compiled and run.

Project Work: Design a Simple Battleship Game

Let us look at the following problem statement and solve using Python in VS Code:

Design a simple battleship game: Let us develop a simple strategic guessing game between humans and computers. The program creates a 5*5 board, and the computer conceals its battleship in a row and column (generated using a random number). Human users call shots by guessing where the computer has concealed its battleship. If the guess is right, the computer's fleet is destroyed, and the user wins. *Figure 2.11* shows the sample output:

```
Battleship Challenge - GAME ON!
O   O   O   O   O
O   O   O   O   O
O   O   O   O   O
O   O   O   O   O
O   O   O   O   O
hint: row=0, col=4
Enter Guess Row (Starts with 0):1
Enter Guess Col (Starts with 0):1
You totally missed my battleship!
Attempt : 1
```

Figure 2.11: Sample output

Random module

We need to use the **random** module to develop this simple battleship application. This is a built-in module that can help create random numbers. Some of its popular methods are listed in *Table 2.1*:

Method	Description
seed()	Initialize the random number generator
randrange()	Returns a random number between the given range
randint()	Returns a random number between the given range
choice()	Returns a random element from the given sequence
choices()	Returns a list with a random selection from the given sequence
random()	Returns a float number randomly between 0 and 1

Table 2.1: List of commonly used methods of random module

Let us look at the complete code:

```python
import random

battle_pattern = []

for i in range(5):
    battle_pattern.append(['O '] * 5)

def display(pattern):
    for p in pattern:
        print(" ".join(p))

print("Battleship Challenge - GAME ON!")
display(battle_pattern)

def get_random_row(pattern):
    return random.randint(0, len(pattern) - 1)

def get_random_col(pattern):
    return random.randint(0, len(pattern[0]) - 1)

ship_row = get_random_row(battle_pattern)
ship_col = get_random_col(battle_pattern)
print(f"hint: row={ship_row}, col={ship_col}")

for option in range(4):
```

```
input_row = int(input("Enter Guess Row (Starts with 0):"))
input_col = int(input("Enter Guess Col (Starts with 0):"))

if input_row == ship_row and input_col == ship_col:
    print("You Win! You sunk my battleship!")
    break
else:
    if option == 3:
        battle_pattern[input_row][input_col] = "X "
        display(battle_pattern)
        print("Sorry Player... Game Over!")
        print("\nShip is here: [" + str(ship_row) + "]["+
str(ship_col) + "]")
    else:
        if (input_row < 0 or input_row > 4) or (input_col <0 or
input_col > 4):
            print("Where did you fire ? Over the ocean.")
        elif (battle_pattern[input_row][input_col] == "X"):
            print("You have already got that wrong.")
        else:
            print("You totally missed my battleship!")
            battle_pattern[input_row][input_col] = "X "
    print("Attempt : ",option + 1)
    display(battle_pattern)
```

Here is how to execute the preceding program in VS Code editor:

- Click on file and then on new file.

- Type a file name without any spaces and give it the **py** extension, for example, **battleready.py**.

- Now, hit enter. It will open the file browser to select a location to save your file. Browse to a folder location and save the file there.

- New code editor will open. Type the preceding program in the editor. Be careful about the indentation. Indentation is critical to writing Python programs.

- Now, click on the **Play** button to begin the execution of the program. Output can be seen on the terminal screen below the editor. Snapshot of the program code is shown in Figure 2.12:

```
D: > PythonFiles > 🐍 battleready.py > ...
1    import random
2
3    battle_pattern = []
4
5    for i in range(5):
6        battle_pattern.append(['O '] * 5)
7
8    def display(pattern):
9        for p in pattern:
10           print(" ".join(p))
11
12   print("Battleship Challenge - GAME ON!")
13   display(battle_pattern)
```

Figure 2.12: Screenshot of the code and the highlighted play button

The preceding code generates multiple O-shaped battleship patterns, as shown in *Figure 2.13*:

```
Battleship Challenge - GAME ON!
O  O  O  O  O
O  O  O  O  O
O  O  O  O  O
O  O  O  O  O
O  O  O  O  O
hint: row=0, col=0
Enter Guess Row (Starts with 0):3
Enter Guess Col (Starts with 0):3
You totally missed my battleship!
Attempt :  1
O  O  O  O  O
O  O  O  O  O
O  O  O  O  O
O  O  O  X  O
O  O  O  O  O
Enter Guess Row (Starts with 0):1
Enter Guess Col (Starts with 0):1
You totally missed my battleship!
Attempt :  2
```

Figure 2.13: Screenshot of the output below the screen

Autocomplete extension helps improve the coding speed by suggesting the complete code based on the characters entered and allowing the programmer to select the suggested code. IntelliSense Python extension supports code completion based on the current interpreter version. Linting extension analyses the completed Python code and looks for potential errors. This makes navigation in the lines of code easy and helps correct the different problems. We have successfully executed our first program. Let us understand a few components of Python that we have used in this program. Apart from using the random module, we have also done the following:

- Using a List **battle_board** to store the locations

- Using **for** loop and **if-elif-else** to build the logic

- Declaring and using user-defined functions: **get_random_row** and **get_random_col**

Conditional statements for decision-making (if – elif - else):

Let us say the code needs to greet the user of your application based on the time of the day. For example, good morning if it's morning (after midnight to before noon) and good evening from noon till midnight. Good Evening and Good Morning, both options are present in the code, but based on a certain condition, the code needs to print only one of them at a given time. That is possible using conditional statements.

If-blocks are logic statements used to control the flow of a program. They are used to test conditions and execute different code depending on the result of the test. An if-block consists of an if statement, followed by one or more optional elif (else if) statements and an optional else statement.

Generally, the syntax for an if-block in Python is as follows:

```
if condition1:
    statement1
elif condition2:
    statement2
...
else:
    statementN
```

The **if** statement contains a condition (condition1). If the condition evaluates to True, the associated statement (statement1) is executed.

If the condition evaluates to False, the statement is not executed, and the **elif** or **else** statement is tested. If the condition in the **elif** statement evaluates to True, the associated statement (statement2) is executed. This process is repeated until a condition is found to be True or the else statement is reached.

The **else** statement is optional and is used to execute code when no other condition evaluates to True. If no conditions are found to be True, the code in the else block is executed.

An if-block can contain any valid Python statements, including loops, function calls, and variable assignments. It is also possible to nest if-blocks, enabling more complex logic.

To check a single condition, only the **if** statement is used; **elif** and **else** are used for multiple conditions.

Let us look at an example to find the highest value among the three numbers. The algorithm is explained with the comments added within the code:

```python
#Finding the highest value among 3 variables
a,b,c = 55,44,33

if a >= b:
    if a >= c:
        #A is either equal to or greater than all the given values
        print("A variable is greatest!")
    else:
        #C is greater hence C is the highest
        print("C variable is greatest!")
else:
    #Means B is greater than A
    if b >=c:
        #B is highest
        print("B variable is greatest!")
    else:
        #C is higher than C
        print("C variable is greatest!")

print("Thank you for using our program")
```

In the preceding example, we used **Nested-IF** condition. Nested if statements are if statements that are the target of another if statement. They are useful when you want to check multiple conditions at the same time. Nested if conditions are a frequently used piece of code where the evaluation of one condition is necessary before a decision can be made on another condition. In other words, nested if conditions are used when a certain condition needs to be met before a certain action happens.

Here is how you can handle nested if conditions step-by-step:

1. First, create an If-Else statement and determine the condition you will be evaluating.

2. Next, inside the body of the If-Else statement, include an additional If-Else statement. This nested If-Else statement should contain a second condition you need to evaluate, which depends on the result of the first If-Else statement.

3. Then, add the code that will be executed if both Conditions 1 and 2 are met.

4. Next, include the necessary Else statements for Condition 1 and Condition 2, which will be executed if either Condition 1 or Condition 2 is not met.

5. Finally, end the nested If-Else statement, and end the containing code block with an end statement.

After these steps, the nested if condition should be fully functional and set up correctly, and the block of code should execute correctly.

Iterating using Loop

There would be a situation while developing a logic where there is a requirement of iterating over a sequence of code multiple times. This is called a loop in programming terminology and Python, and it is achieved using keywords *WHILE* and *FOR*. The **while** loop statement is when we do not know how many times the statements need to be repeated but we have a condition until which we need to execute the same block of code. A while state can sometimes have an else clause, but that is not mandatory.

When the number of times statements need to be repeated is known, we prefer the **for.. in** statement. The **range()** function can be used to generate sequence to repeat. Range(5) will generate values: 0,1,2,3,4 (0 is the starting value when not mentioned, the default increment value is 1, and ending value always excludes the given number).

BREAK: Both **For** and **While** have defined ways to stop the iteration when work is done, but at times, we have to stop the loop before that assigned value. This is where the **break** statement comes into the picture. When the **break** statement is encountered, the loop stops execution even if the while loop condition has not become false or the for loop has not yet completed iteration over the sequences.

CONTINUE: The **continue** statement is used where there is a need to inform Python to skip executing the rest of the statements in the current loop and go back to the beginning of the loop.

EXIT: The program will **exit** when it encounters the exit function without continuing.

Let us practice a program that uses the while loop to check the size of the entered text:

```
while True:
    #Directly using True instead of a conditional statement
    #  will make it an infinite running loop
    s= input('Enter something: ')
    if s.lower()=='quit':
        #lower() will convert s content into lowercase break
        break
```

```
    print("Length of the given text is ", len(s))
print("Goodbye")
```

The preceding program will continue to print the size of the text entered until it encounters the quit statement. The lower function will convert the input variable into a small case irrespective of what the user entered.

User-Defined Functions (UDFs)

Functions are written once but are used in multiple places, so we call them reusable pieces of programs. First, the function must be defined and named to a block of statements. The **def** keyword is placed before the function name, followed by an identifier name. Identifier is followed by a pair of parentheses that may enclose some variables' names (optional), and it ends with a colon. Next comes the block of statements that are part of this function. Defining alone does not make a function work; we need to call the function by name to run that block. We have already seen the workings of many built-in functions, such as **print()** and **range()**. In the battleship program, we created the **get_random_row()** and **get_random_col()** user-defined functions to get values from the user. Let us see an example:

```
    #Define the function
    def greet(name):
        print("Hello, " + name + ". Have a good day!")

    #calling the function
    greet("Sachin Tendulkar")
```

The preceding function is used to greet a person. This function greets the person whose name is passed in as parameter to the **greet()** function.

Using list in Python

A list is a data structure that holds an ordered collection of items, that is, you can store a sequence of items in a list. The values are separated by **,** (comma) and enclosed within a pair of square braces **[ ]**. Consider this example:

```
    var1 = [5,10,15,20]   #List
```

Some of the popular list methods are listed in the following table:

Method	Description	Example
append()	Adds an element at the end of the list	thislist.append("orange")
extend()	Add the elements of a list (or any iterable), to the end of the current list	fruits.extend(cars)
clear()	Removes all the elements from the list	thislist.clear()
index()	Returns the index of the first element with the specified value	x = fruits.index("cherry")
copy()	Returns a copy of the list	x = fruits.copy()

Method	Description	Example
insert()	Adds an element at the specified position	fruits.insert(1, "orange")
count()	Returns the number of elements in the list	x = fruits.count("cherry")
pop()	Removes the element at the specified position	fruits.pop(1)
remove()	Removes the item with the specified value	fruits.remove("banana")
reverse()	Reverses the order of the list	fruits.reverse()
sort()	Sorts the list	fruits.sort()

Table 2.2: Important methods of List datastructure

Let us write a program and understand the list concepts:

```
months = [
    'January', 'February','March',
    'April','May','June',
    'July','August','September',
    'October','November','December'
    ]
endings = ['st', 'nd', 'rd'] + 17 * ['th'] + ['st', 'nd', 'rd'] + \
        7 * ['th'] + ['st']

year = input("Enter Year: ")
month = int(input("Enter Month: "))

day = int(input("Enter the Day: "))
month_no = months[month - 1]

days = str(day) + endings[day - 1]

print("The date you have entered is ", days, " ", month_no, " ",
year)
```

The preceding program reads the date in year, month and day format then returns it in a combined format, with the month number converted to words.

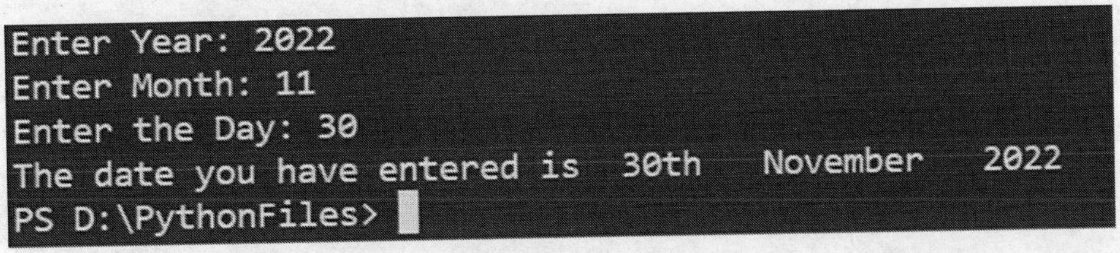

```
Enter Year: 2022
Enter Month: 11
Enter the Day: 30
The date you have entered is  30th   November   2022
PS D:\PythonFiles>
```

Figure 2.14: Output of List Program

Since we are not covering the basic programming concepts in detail in this book, readers are encouraged to refer to the basic programming textbook to understand these concepts.

We recommend *Learn and Practice Python* by *Swapnil Saurav*, but you can choose any other as well.

Setting and configuring the editor

VS Code can be customized to the core. It allows almost every component of the user interface and functional behavior to be customized to the programmer's preferences through its various setting options. There are two important settings that one notices when the workspace is opened:

- **User settings**: Settings that care for users' preferences are applied globally to any instance of VS Code the same user opens.

- **Workspace settings**: Settings specific to the particular workspace are stored inside the workspace, which are applied when the workspace is opened.

Let us see how one can customize these settings.

User setting

User settings are customized by editing the settings editor settings. Here are the steps you can follow to open the settings editor:

Windows/Linux: Goto **File** | **Preferences** | **Settings**

macOS: Goto **Code** | **Preferences** | **Settings**

A screen similar to *Figure 2.15* will open:

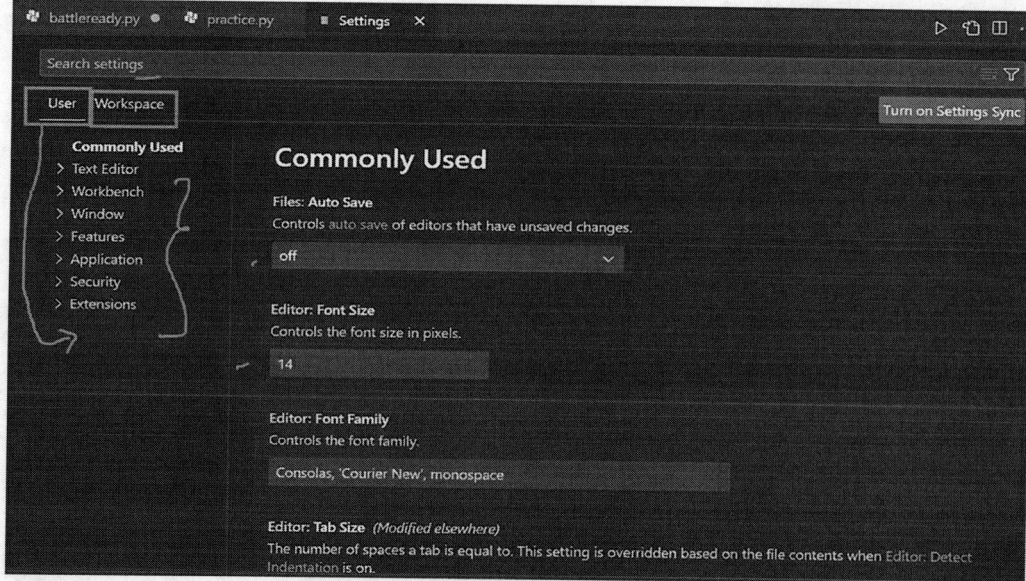

Figure 2.15: Screenshot of User Settings

One can also use the keyboard shortcut to open the settings editor by typing: (**Ctrl+,**) in Windows and **Command + ,** (comma) in Mac.

In the search bar, one can discover the settings they want. While searching in the bar, one will notice that it will not only show and highlight the settings matching the criteria but also apply a filter to remove those not matching. This makes the search quick and easy to use.

All the editor-related settings, such as settings groups, search, and filtering behave the same for user and workspace settings. For a given project workspace editor-related settings are given preference over user settings. Still, some application-related settings, such as updates and security, cannot be overridden by workspace settings. For this reason, one will not even be able to access these settings in workspace settings but are very much available in the user settings. One can see the list of settings available by clicking on the respective tabs for user and workspace, as shown in *Figure 2.15*.

Figure 2.16 shows all the options for font search results. When one changes here, it is applied to the VS Code immediately. One can also see all the settings that have been modified as they are indicated with a blue color box.

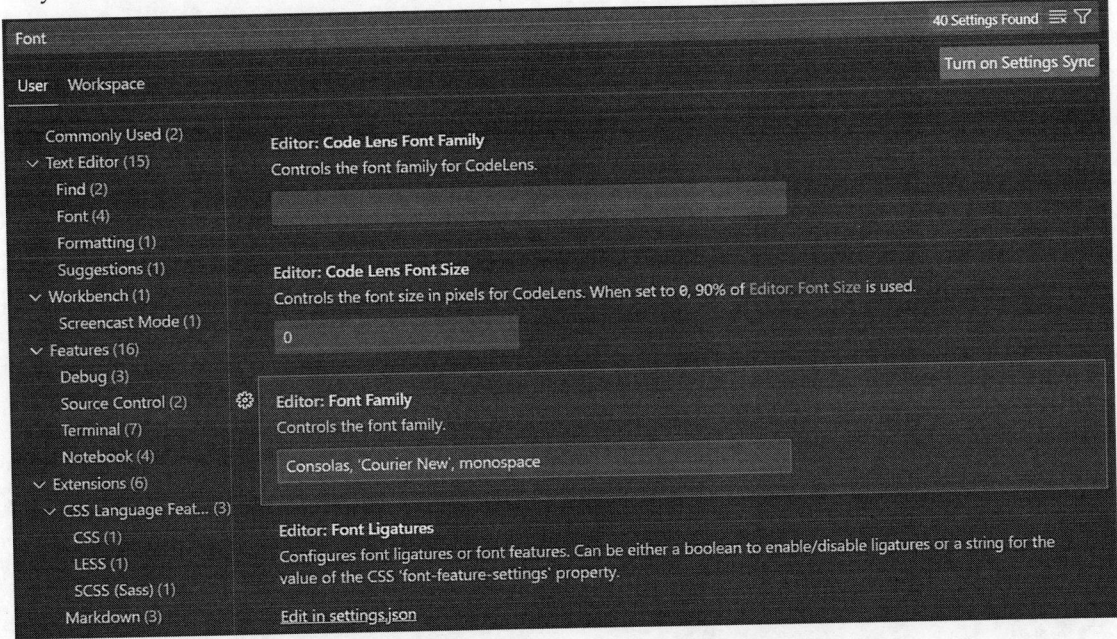

Figure 2.16: Search result for Font in User Settings

Clicking on the gear icon (**More Actions**...*Shift+F9*) will open a context menu with the option to reset the setting to its default value. This will undo all the changes made to the settings. This can also be used to copy the setting ID or JSON name-value pair.

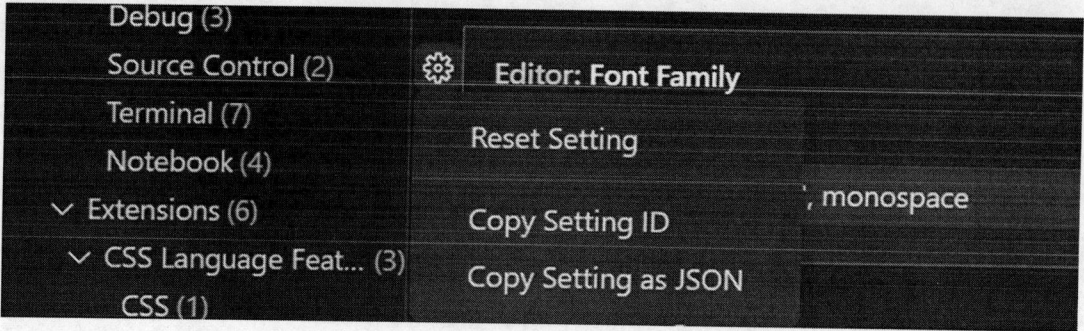

Figure 2.17: Gear icon presents reset setting to default and other options

Settings generally have three options using which edits can be made. Settings can be edited by selecting given values from a checkbox or a dropdown or even entering the value using an input to change to the desired settings. Related settings are added together in groups and presented in a tree view so that it is easy to find and navigate to. Groups that show popular customizations are generally at the top. To the right of the search bar, one can see a funnel and filter buttons. Users can add several filters to the search bar to manage settings easier, as shown in *Figure 2.18*:

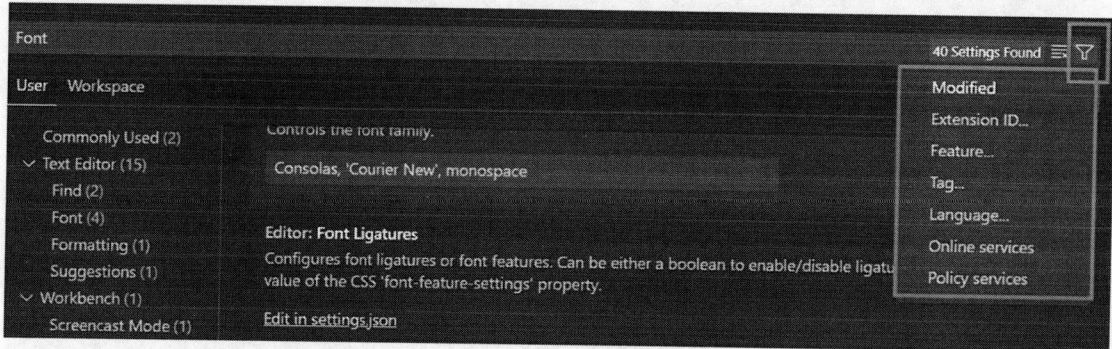

Figure 2.18: Different filter options added to search bar

The **@modified** filter is added in the **Search** bar shows the settings that have been configured. If the editor is not behaving as expected and the developer wants to check if this is because of customization or wrong configuration, this filter is useful.

The following is the list of other VS Code filters:

- **@ext**: Edit settings specific to any extension

- **@feature**: Edit settings specific to a features subgroup, for example, File explorer

- **@id**: Find a setting based on the setting ID, for example, **@id:workbench. activityBar.visible**

- **@lang**: Apply a language filter. *Figure 2.19* shows the **Filters** in the **Search** bar:

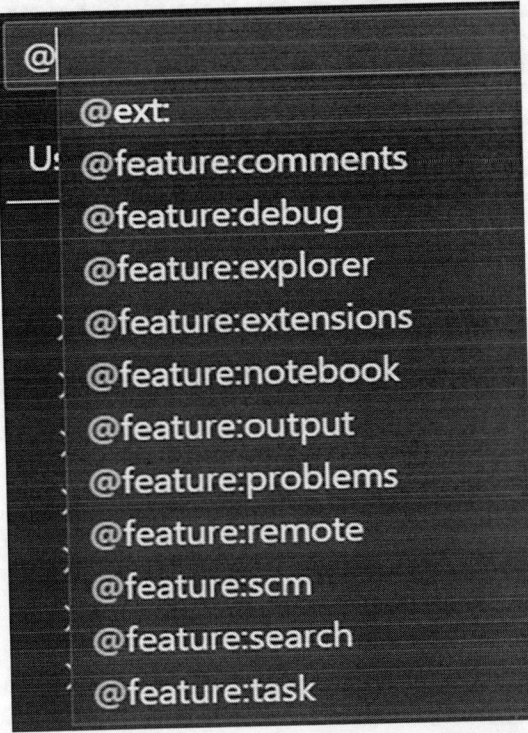

Figure 2.19: Filters included in the search bar

VS Code extensions can also be edited with custom settings. These settings are visible under an extensions section. One can also review an extension's settings. This can be done from the extensions view (*Ctrl+Shift+X*), by selecting the extension and clicking on reviewing the feature contributions tab.

So far, we are trying to edit the settings in UI, but there is a settings file where we can edit the values directly. The file is called **settings.json**. To open the **settings.json** file, go to Preferences: Open Settings (JSON) command in the **Command Palette (Ctrl+Shift+P).** This is shown in *Figure 2.20*:

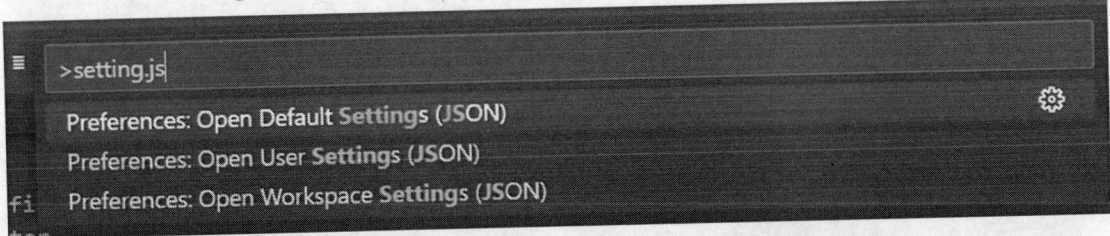

Figure 2.20: How to open JSON Settings in the Command Palette (Ctrl+Shift+P)

One can review and edit this file. *Figure 2.21* shows a sample **settings.json** file:

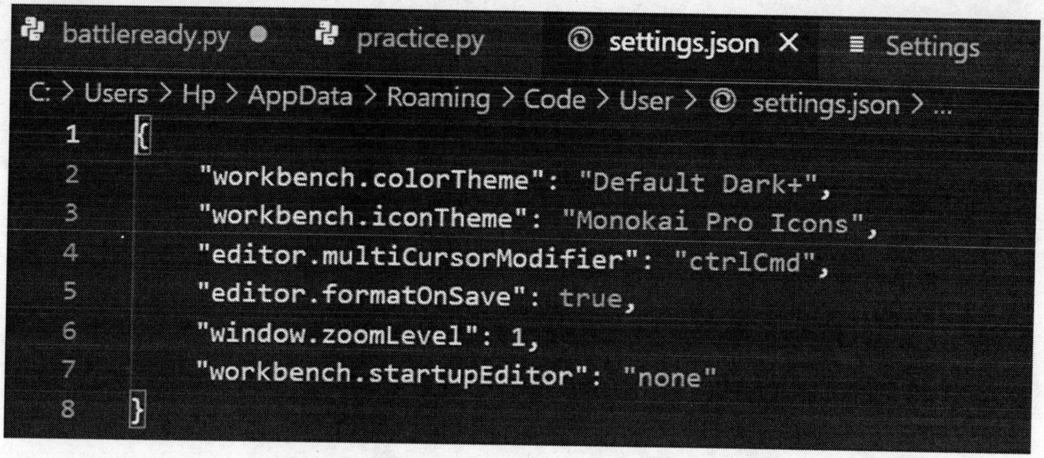

Figure 2.21: Sample Settings (JSON) file

Once the file is open in an editor, settings can be written in the JSON format. The JSON format has setting ID and its corresponding value. For example, *Figure 2.20* shows the applied theme in **Monokai**. One can edit/delete/add a new ID and corresponding value to the settings. VS Code can return to the default settings when all the content between the two curly braces {} is deleted and the file is saved. Like code editor, the **settings.json** file also has full IntelliSense with smart completions settings. If any error creeps in due to an incorrect JSON style, the portion of the code also gets highlighted, just like a Python code. Some settings, such as **Workbench: Color Customizations**, can only be edited in **settings.json**. In *Figure 2.22*, **colorCustomization** has been set to #4000ff, making line numbers appear in blue (hex equivalent color code).

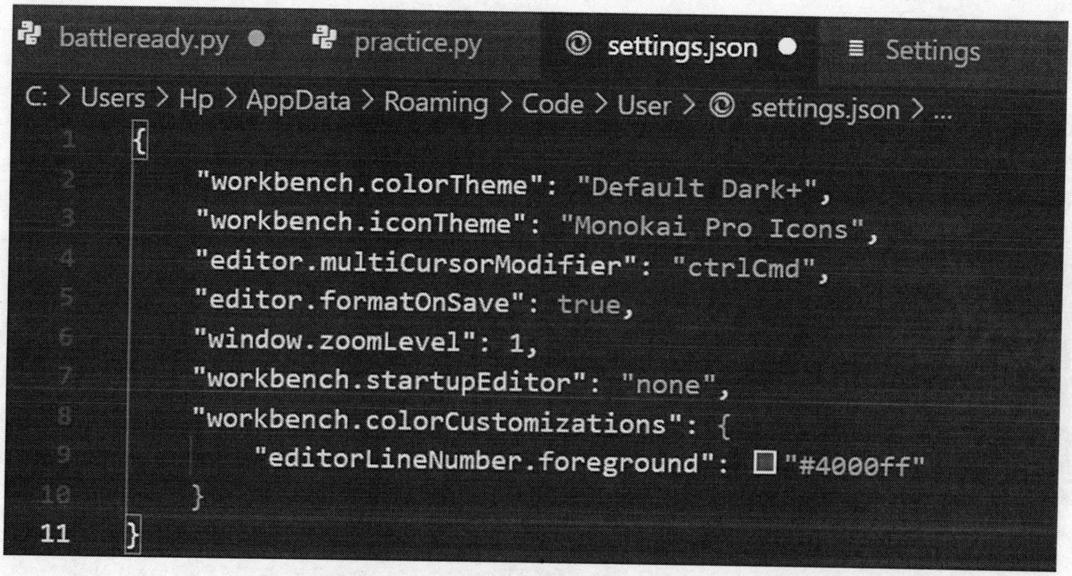

Figure 2.22: colorCustomizations in Settings (JSON) file

Earlier, we discussed that **File| Preferences| Settings** will open the settings editor UI, but those who prefer to always work directly with the `settings.json` file can set the `workbench.settings.editor: json` option so that **Preferences| Settings** and `keybinding Ctrl+` will always take you to the `settings.json` file.

You can look for user settings file here:

> On Windows platform: `%APPDATA%\Code\User\settings.json`
>
> On macOS platform: `$HOME/Library/Application\ Support/Code/User/settings.json`
>
> On Linux platform: `$HOME/.config/Code/User/settings.json`

Workspace settings

Workspace settings, unlike user settings, are not global; they are specific to a project. This allows settings to be shared across developers working on the same project. Workspace settings are always designed to override user settings. You can edit via the settings editor **Workspace** tab or open that tab directly with the preferences: open **Workspace Settings** command.

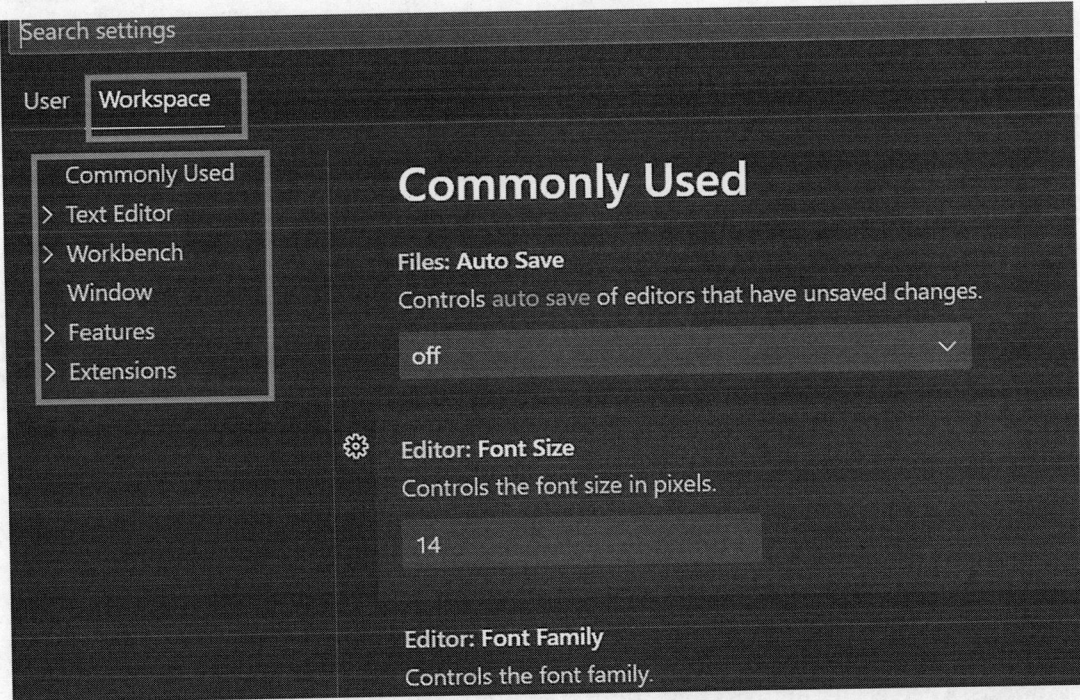

Figure 2.23: Workspace settings

Workspace Settings are stored in a `settings.json` file, just like user settings. This can be edited directly via the **Preferences: Open Workspace Settings (JSON)** command. If you are looking for the workspace settings file, you can find it in the **.vscode** folder in your root location. When a workspace settings **settings.json** file is added to the project or the source control, the settings for the project are shared with all the users of that project.

We have been talking about workspace, but what is it? Workspace in VS Code is usually just your project root folder. All the workspace settings and configurations, like debugging and task configurations, are also stored at the root itself, in the **.vscode** folder. It is possible to have more than one root folder in a VS Code workspace through a feature called multi-root workspaces.

Let us now turn our discussion toward language-specific editor settings. There are two different ways to open language-specific editor settings and customize them:

- The first method is opening the settings editor, clicking the **Filter** button, and selecting the **language option** to add a language filter based on the programming languages.

- The second available option is to directly type a language filter of the **@ lang:languageId** form into the search widget option.

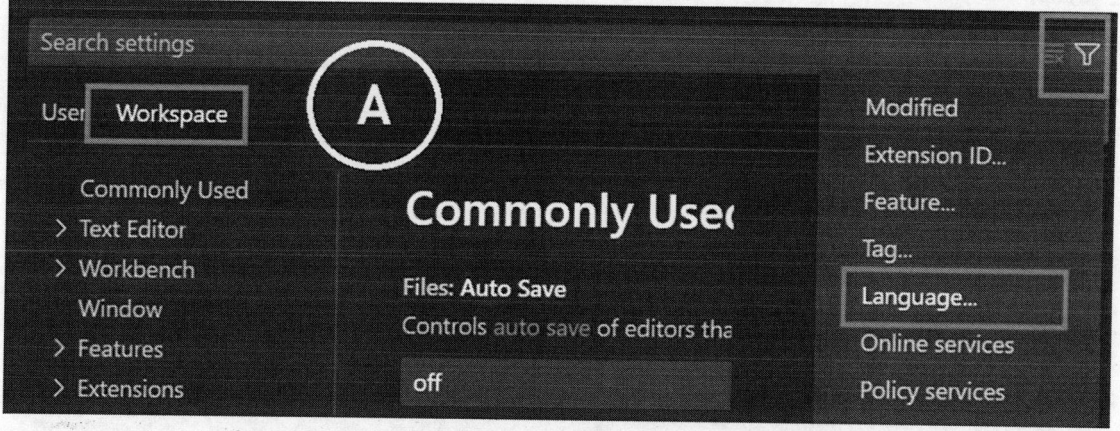

Figure 2.24: Opening language-specific settings

The language-specific settings will show only the configurable options for that specific language. We will look at Python-specific settings in *Chapter 3, Top Extensions in VS Code*.

Settings and security

Some settings allow specifying an executable VS Code that can run to perform certain operations. The setting allows choosing the shell that the integrated terminal would use. Understandably, for various security reasons, such settings can be defined only in the user settings and not in the workspace scope that multiple users can use. A few other settings are not available in the workspace scope, like **git.path**, **terminal.external.windowsExec**, **terminal.external.osxExec**, and **terminal.external.linuxExec**.

Keyboard arguments

Intuitive keyboard shortcuts, easy customization, and community-contributed keyboard shortcut mappings let you easily navigate your code. VS Code provides rich, customized and easy-to-edit keyboard shortcuts. After displaying the options, one can easily change, remove, and reset their keybindings using the available actions. Displaying a list of keybindings is also easy; it can be done using a search box on the top. The search box helps find commands or keybindings and directly navigate to them. Those using VS Code on Windows platform can open this editor by going straight to the menu under **File | Preferences | Keyboard Shortcuts**. (macOS users can do so by going to **Code | Preferences | Keyboard Shortcuts**).

Keymap extensions are a great feature that will help the users of other editors to start using VS Code editor quickly. Anyone who wants to see the list of popular keymap extensions can go to **File | Preferences | Migrate Keyboard Shortcuts from...** This will bring up the list of popular keymap extensions. These extensions modify the VS Code shortcuts to match those of other editors, so you do not need to learn new keyboard shortcuts while switching to VS Code.

Figure 2.25*: List of a few editors from which keyboard shortcut migration is supported*

A printable version of the keyboard shortcuts can be downloaded from **Help | Keyboard Shortcut reference** (Refer *Figure 2.25*). It gives a condensed PDF document generated specific to the platform you are using. This document can be printed and stuck near your monitor for easy reference.

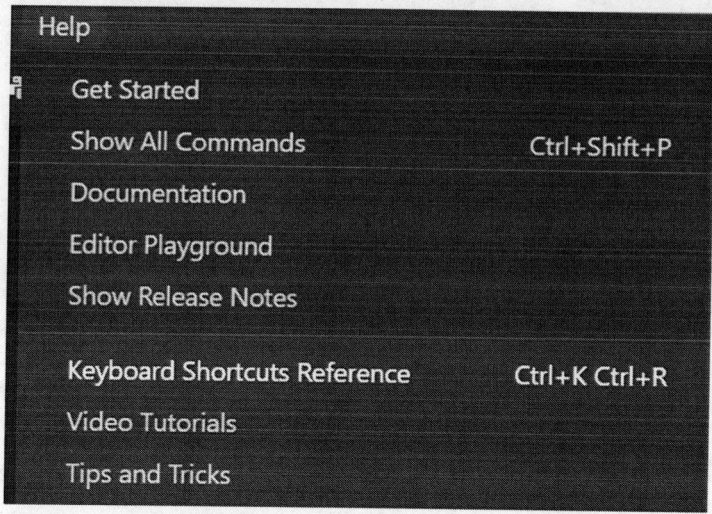

Figure 2.26: Help | Keyboard Shortcut Reference: to get a condensed PDF list of keyboard shortcuts

Conclusion

We are at the end of the chapter and have done a great job writing and building our first Python program. Whenever we move to a new environment, it always makes sense to spend some time trying to understand the nuts and bolts of the environment; that was our goal for this chapter. We have successfully installed Python and VS Code, set up Python environment using Python extension, installed default extensions along with it, and learned about editing settings. Spend some more time working with settings, edit your font to your liking, and get the theme of your choice so that you love working with the editor.

Now, it is time to move on to the next chapter. In the next chapter, we will learn about more useful Python extensions and edit Python-related settings.

## CHAPTER 3

Top Extensions in VS Code for Python

Technology is nothing. What's important is that you have a faith in people, that they're basically good and smart, and if you give them tools, they'll do wonderful things with them.

— Steve Jobs

Introduction

Extensions to VS Code editor are invaluable. They help improve code quality and speed up the development work too. We will look at some general-purpose extensions that are must-haves. Two big areas where Python programming is used are data science and web development. We will also look at the popular extensions that apply to data scientists and web developers. In this chapter, we will explain the functionality of popular extensions and how to find them in the VS Code marketplace, and we will install and manage these extensions. No doubt, these extensions are what make VS Code the most popular IDE, so we added this chapter to benefit all. Apart from that, we will discuss functions, modules, and packages in Python. These concepts help us manage lengthy code easily and efficiently.

Structure

We are going to cover the following topics in this chapter:

- Top VS Code extensions
- Python-specific settings

- Installing and using Python packages
- Functions, modules, and packages in Python

Now, let us dive deep into these topics.

Objectives

The objective of this chapter is to provide an overview of the top extensions for Python programming in Visual Studio Code and explain how to install and use these extensions. We will also talk about their purpose and characteristics. Extensions add more functionality to VS Code for Python, such as linting, debugging, and code formatting. Additionally, many popular extensions provide IntelliSense, which provides smarter code completion based on variable types, function definitions, and imported modules. This makes it easier and faster to write and understand code. We will also learn about functions, classes and modules and look at the implementation of these concepts in Python.

Top VS Code extensions

So, you have installed VS Code now and maybe even created your first program if you have followed our chapters. There are a few extensions that will simply increase the power of your VS Code. Using VS Code extensions, you can add different language support (we did that in *Chapter 2, Setting Up the Environment*), debuggers, and various other tools to make your development experience better. By creating extensions, developers take advantage of VS Code's rich extensibility, which allows them to plug their extensions directly into the VS Code UI, making it available to VS Code users. To start using the extensions, take the following steps to download any extension:

Step 1: Browse for extensions

The first step is to find these extensions in the marketplace. One can easily browse and install extensions from VS Code itself. Clicking on the extension's icon in the activity bar or by typing the extensions command (*Ctrl+Shift+X*) will bring up the extensions view, which looks like the icon shown in *Figure 3.1*:

Figure 3.1: Extensions icon

You can filter the search results using the **filter** option available at the top-left of the screen, as shown in *Figure 3.2*:

Figure 3.2: *Extension search result with filter option*

A popular list of extensions can be seen in *Figure 3.3*:

Figure 3.3: *Popular extensions list*

Each result in the list will include a brief description of the extension, the publisher of that extension, the total number of downloads, and the rating on a 5-star scale. When the extension is selected, the extension's details page is displayed, where one can learn more.

Step 2: Search for an extension

One can search for an extension by typing the extension name in the search box at the top of the extensions view. Clear the existing text if any and type in the complete or part of the extension name you are looking for. So, if you type Python, it will bring up a list of Python language extensions. Knowing the extension ID can help if there are many extensions with similar names. For example, `wayou.vscode-todo-highlight` is the ID for the TODO Highlight extension. One can directly type the ID in the search box as well.

Step 3: Install the extension

To install the extension of your choice, click the **install** button. It will transform into the manage gear button after the installation is complete. In *Figure 3.3*, the Python extension has a gearbox indicating that it is already installed on the local machine, whereas the C/C++ option has the **install** option, which means it has not been installed. Clicking the **install** button will install the C/C++ extension to run C/C++ programs on VS Code.

Step 4: Manage extensions

It is easy to manage the extensions in VS Code. VS Code allows the users to install/enable/disable/update or uninstall extensions through the extensions view, the command palette, or command-line switches. Commands have the **Extensions:** as a prefix in the command palette.

1. How to list installed extensions

   When a user launches VS Code, by default, the extensions view is presented with the extensions that are currently installed and enabled, all recommended extensions, and a collapsed view of the extensions disabled by the user.

2. How to uninstall an extension

   Users can select the **manage** gear button of an extension and then choose the **uninstall** option from the dropdown menu to uninstall an existing extension. This action will also prompt the user to reload VS Code.

3. How to disable an extension

   Uninstalling permanently removes the extension, but in case a user wants to remove the extension temporarily, they can choose the **disable** option in the **gear** button. The user has the option to disable an extension globally or for the current workspace, as shown in *Figure 3.4*. Disable extension will also prompt to reload VS Code. There is also an option named **disable all installed extensions** command available under **more actions** in the command palette dropdown menu.

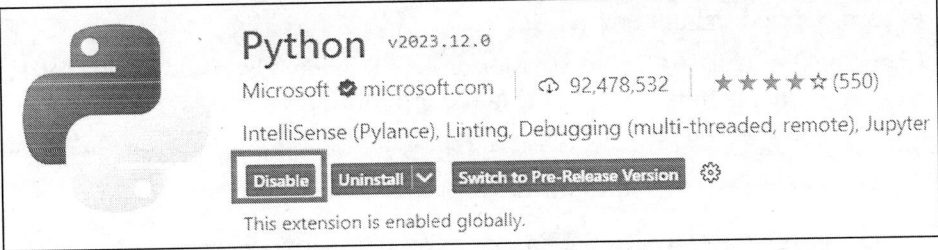

Figure 3.4: Disable option in the each extension

4. Enable an extension

   All disabled extensions remain disabled until the users choose to enable them. Users can re-enable the extensions with the enable or enable (workspace) commands available in the dropdown menu. To enable all extensions, you can choose the option from the command palette or from **more actions (...)**, which provides a dropdown menu. This is the quickest way to enable all the extensions.

5. Extension auto-update

   VS Code constantly checks for extension updates and installs them automatically if the auto-update option is checked. Users are asked to reload VS Code if any extension has been updated. Some users prefer to update the extensions manually, in which case they have to disable the auto-update option with the **disable auto-updating** extensions command that sets the **extensions.autoUpdate** setting to false. Auto-update is shown in *Figure 3.5*:

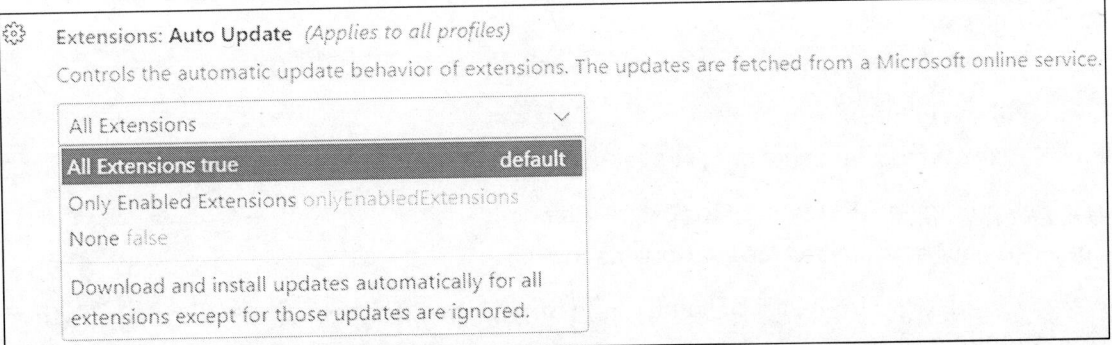

Figure 3.5: Auto update option for extensions

6. Update an extension manually

   Users can look for the extensions that have updates available by using the show outdated extensions command that uses the outdated filter. Then, by clicking the **update** button for the outdated extension, the update will be installed. The update all extensions command can be used to update all your outdated extensions at the same time.

7. Recommended extensions

    Users also see a list of recommended extensions by default or can look for recommended extensions by setting recommended filter active. Recommendations can be based on the following:

    • **Workspace recommendations**: Based on other users of the workspace

    • **Other recommendations**: Based on recently opened files

Users can list, install, and uninstall extensions from the command line, which helps in automation. One has to keep in mind that to find an extension, one has to provide the full name, along with its **publisher.extension**, for example, **ms-python.python**.

Here is an example:

Setting the root path for an extension:

```
code --extensions-dir <dir>
```

Listing the already installed extensions:

```
code –list-extensions
```

To see the versions of already installed extensions use:

```
 --list-extension
```

Show versions:

```
code --show-versions
```

Installs an extension:

```
code --install-extension (<extension-id> | <extension-vsix-path>)
```

Uninstalls an extension:

```
code --uninstall-extension (<extension-id> | <extension-vsix-path>)
```

Enables proposed API features for extensions:

```
code --enable-proposed-api (<extension-id>)
```

Now we will move to the list of some of the important extensions that will help in Python programming.

Pylance

Pylance by Microsoft can massively enhance your productivity. Pylance is a Python language server, offering enhancements to IntelliSense, syntax highlighting, and a host of other features for an amazing development experience for Python developers. IntelliSense is more like a generic name for various code editing features that would include code completion, parameter info, quick info, and member lists. IntelliSense features are also known by names like code completion, content assist, and code hinting. ntelliSense quickly shows the probable methods, class members, and documentation you may want to use as you type. One can trigger completions at any time with Ctrl+Space. Pylance enhances the help provided by IntelliSense. Some of the features provided by Pylance are as follows:

- Docstrings
- Signature help and type information
- Parameter suggestions
- Code completion
- Auto-imports (add and remove import)
- As-you-type reporting of code errors and warnings
- Code outline
- Code navigation
- Type checking mode
- Native multi-root workspace support
- IntelliCode compatibility
- Jupyter notebooks compatibility
- Semantic highlighting

Let us move to see the top three most popular features in the next section.

Auto-imports

The Pylance extension has a feature that automatically adds imports to the top of the Python files whenever a reference to a dependency is made in the environment. It does not install the dependency, but if it is already installed and available in the Python environment, then it adds it. At the same time, it removes the reference if it is no longer used in the program. One can see a lightbulb icon with suggestions to add or remove imports depending on the scenario.

Semantic highlighting

Semantic highlighting highlights (that is, colors) classes, functions, properties, and other Python object types to make them more readable.

Type checking

There is a new concept called type hinting, which is the practice of specifying expected data types for variables or functions or even for classes. Type hinting is new to Python, and even though Python does not enforce it, most programmers consider it as a best practice. Pylance helps developers to understand if their code violates any documented type hints if it has a type-checking setting enabled.

One has to make the required settings change to make this enabled. *Figure 3.6* shows the steps to edit the settings:

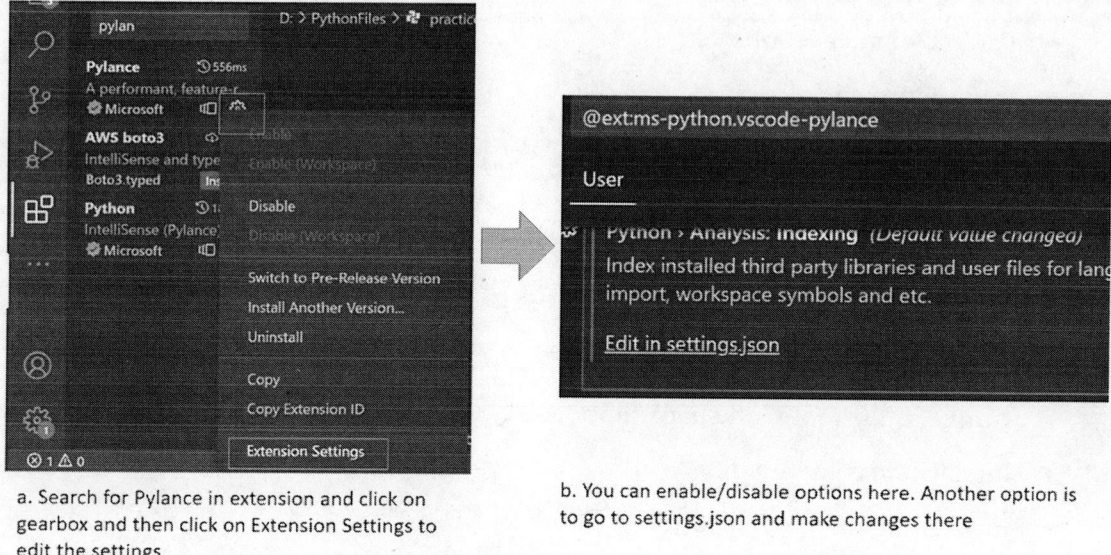

a. Search for Pylance in extension and click on gearbox and then click on Extension Settings to edit the settings

b. You can enable/disable options here. Another option is to go to settings.json and make changes there

Figure 3.6: *Steps to edit the settings for Pylance extension*

The following text can be added to **settings.json** to enable the type hinting:
```
{
        "python.analysis.typeCheckingMode": "basic"
}
```

Type-checking mode can take either basic or strict:

- **Basic:** Checking basic datatype
- **Strict:** Highest error severity, all type checking rules

It is recommended to have a basic setting at the moment.

Figure 3.7 shows the implementation. Look at the error message, it says the **Expression of the type is incompatible**, and it also refers to the Pylance extension.

```
D: > PythonFiles > 🐍 practicePy.py > ...
  1     greeting:str = "Good Morning"
  2     greeting = 34
  3     print(greet Expression of type "Literal[34]" cannot be assigned to
               declared type "str"
                 "Literal[34]" is incompatible with
             "str" Pylance(reportGeneralTypeIssues)

             View Problem (Alt+F8)   Quick Fix... (Ctrl+.)
```

Figure 3.7: Type error when trying to assign an integer value to a string variable

Code Runner

The second must-have extension based on our recommendation is Code Runner. It runs the code instantaneously and supports multiple programming languages. The view of Code Runner extension is shown in *Figure 3.8*:

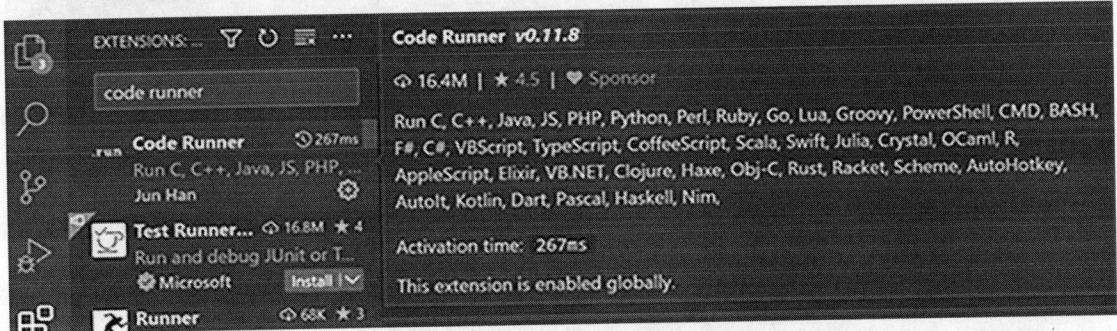

Figure 3.8: Installing Code Runner extension

Code Runner, by default, is set to use its panel for showing the results of the Python script. It is recommended to be set up in a way that will show the results of the integrated terminal. Follow these steps to change the settings so that the results can be displayed in the terminal:

1. Press ctrl+ or click on the **gearbox** located in the bottom-left corner of the screen to open the **settings** panel.

2. To open the settings, type **code runner terminal** on the search bar.

3. You will now see an option, **Code-runner: Run In Terminal**.

4. Tick the option to enable it, and you are done. This looks very much like the option shown in *Figure 3.9*:

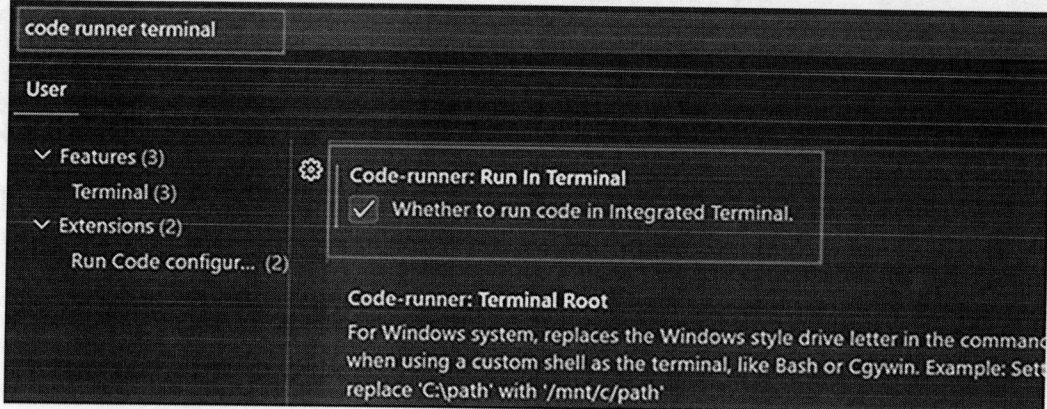

Figure 3.9: *Change the settings of Code Runner so that the results can be displayed in the terminal*

Let us run a program and see the output in the Terminal, as shown in *Figure 3.10*:

```python
class Learn:
    def welcome(self):
        print("Learn to use VS Code Extensions")



lesson1 = Learn()
print(f'Object Created: {lesson1}')
lesson1.welcome()
```

```
PROBLEMS    OUTPUT    DEBUG CONSOLE    TERMINAL    JUPYTER

PS C:\Users\Hp> python -u "d:\PythonFiles\practicePy.py"
Object Created: <__main__.Learn object at 0x000001CBC5939300>
Learn to use VS Code Extensions
PS C:\Users\Hp>
```

Figure 3.10: *Program running in the terminal*

Indent Rainbow

Indent Rainbow is a simple yet powerful extension that colorizes each tab space to make **indentation** more visible and readable for the programmers. The image of the extension is shown in *Figure 3.11*:

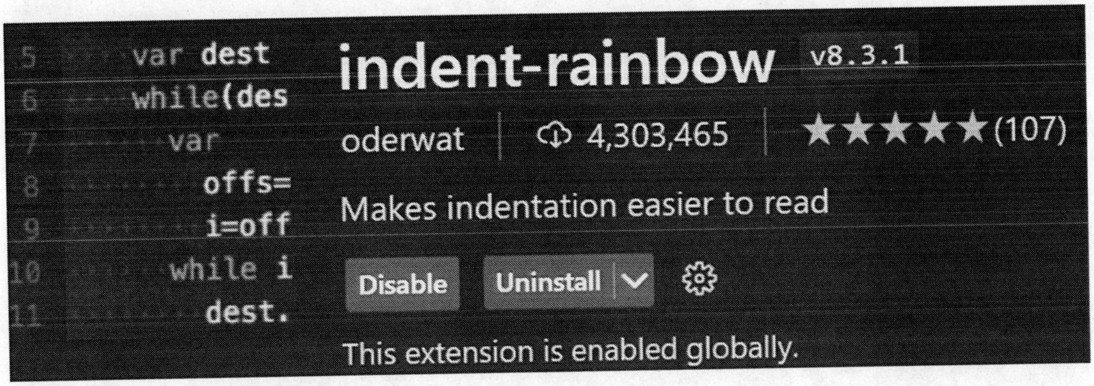

Figure 3.11: Indent Rainbow extension

Indent Rainbow helps make code more readable by displaying different indentation levels with different colors. It helps you spot indentation errors and visualize the structure of the code, as shown in *Figure 3.12*:

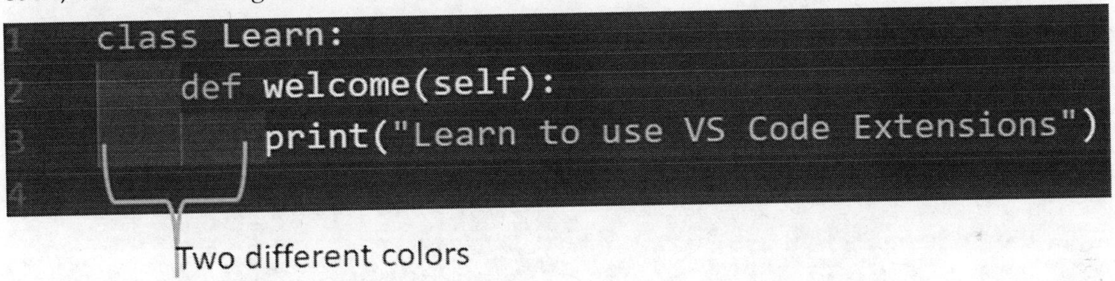

Two different colors

Figure 3.12: Program running in the terminal

By default, Indent Rainbow uses VIBGYOR color, hence the name Rainbow; but we can always change the default settings by editing the **User Settings**. The following code is an example that shows how you can edit the **Indent Rainbow** color settings:

```
"indentRainbow.colors": [
    "rgba(245, 40, 145,0.1)",
    "rgba(245, 40, 145,0.3)",
    "rgba(245, 40, 145,0.6)",
    "rgba(245, 40, 145,0.8)",
    "rgba(245, 40, 145,0.2)"
]
```

You can pick your color from here:

https://rgbacolorpicker.com/

Path Intellisense

Path Intellisense is a Visual Studio Code extension that autocompletes filenames for you when you are typing in file paths. *Figure 3.13* shows the view of the extension. It helps you save time and increase productivity by providing you with the ability to quickly find, open, and insert the right files in your project. It also provides an easy way to quickly add new files to your project.

Figure 3.13: Path Intellisense extension

Path Intellisense is the VS Code plugin that autocompletes filenames. *Figure 3.14* shows the suggestions made by Path Intellisense when we select a folder:

```
D: > PythonFiles > practicePy.py > ...
    1   # A Python program to read a text file and displays
    2   # first 300 characters on the screen
    3   # Opening a file "Poem1.txt"
    4   file1 = open("Poems/")
    5                          📄 Poem1.txt
    6   print("Reading first  📄 Poem2.txt
    7   print(file1.read(300))
    8   print()
    9   # Closing the file
   10   file1.close()
   11
```

Figure 3.14: Suggestions are shown by Path Intellisense extension

VS Code supports both relative and absolute paths. The absolute path is the complete path, including the drive name. The relative path takes the path from the location mentioned in the terminal. Here is an example of how a terminal might look:

```
C:\Users\hp
```

Tabnine AI Autocomplete

Tabnine AI Autocomplete in VSCode is a powerful code autocompletion tool powered by artificial intelligence. This extension uses **machine learning (ML)** algorithms to understand the context in which the code is used and suggest the best code completion options. It integrates seamlessly with Visual Studio Code and can help developers quickly complete their code with fewer errors. The extension looks as shown in *Figure 3.15*:

Figure 3.15: *Tabnine AI Autocomplete extension*

Tabnine is better than most of the other autocomplete extensions because it can predict and complete the whole line based on context and syntax and also suggest your next lines of code. *Figure 3.16* shows the difference between suggestions made with and without Tabnine:

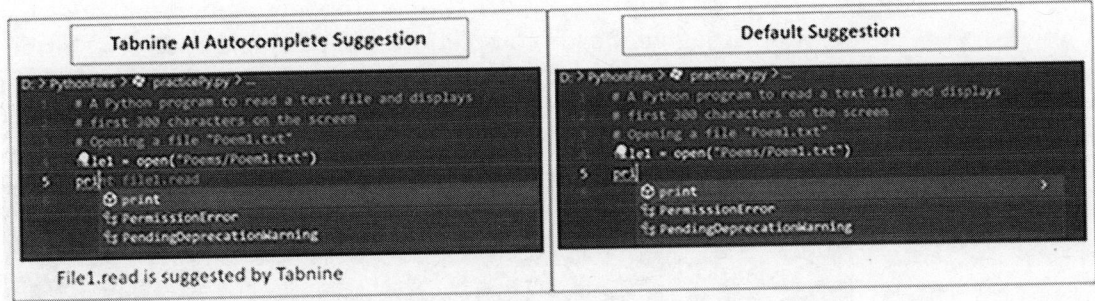

Figure 3.16: *Tabnine AI Autocomplete even adds file1.read*

Python Indent

Python indent in VSCode is a setting that gives the ability to set the number of spaces used for indenting code blocks. This is useful for keeping your code neat and organized and for making it easier to read. The extension looks as shown in *Figure 3.17*:

Figure 3.17: *Python Indent extension*

In the default settings, every time you hit the **Enter** key in a piece of Python code, the cursor will go to the beginning of the next line. The Python Indent extension parses the Python file up to the location of the cursor. As seen in *Figure 3.18*, this extension can determine exactly how much the next line should be indented and how much other lines should be un-indented.

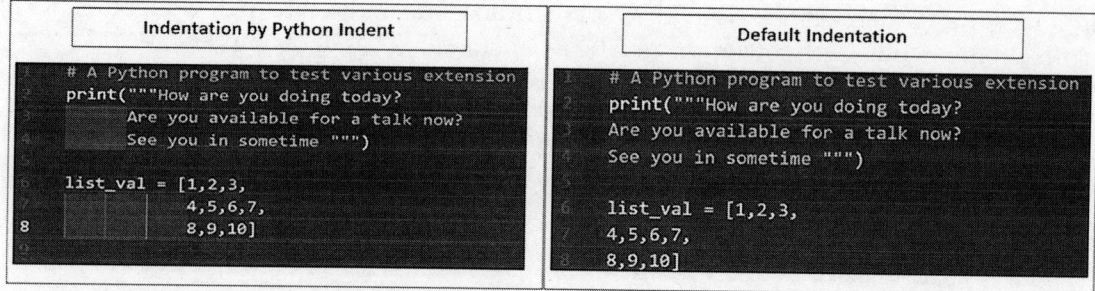

Figure 3.18: Python Indent extension indenting better than the default settings

Jupyter

Jupyter Extension in VS Code is an extension that allows you to write and execute Jupyter notebooks directly in the VS Code editor. It includes support for debugging, embedded Git Control, syntax highlighting, intelligent code completion, snippets, and code refactoring. The extension also allows you to easily switch between Python and R programming languages, and other languages such as Julia, C++, and Go. *Figure 3.19* is a screenshot of the Jupyter extension:

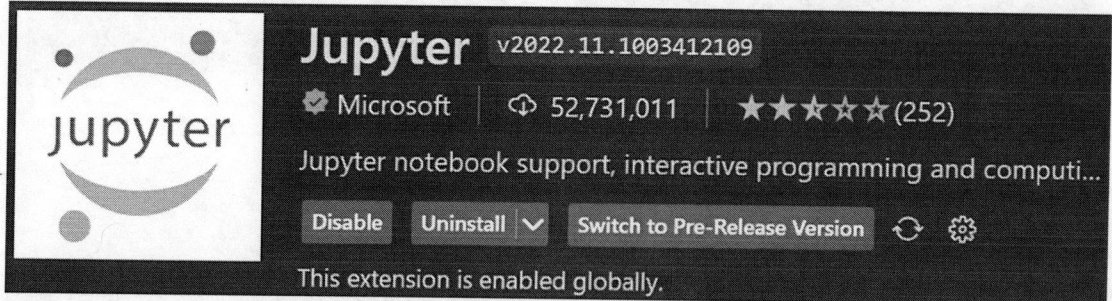

Figure 3.19: Jupyter extension

Jupyter, earlier known as IPython Notebook, is an open-source project that helps us combine markdown text and executable Python code onto a single platform called a notebook. Jupyter extension is available in VS Code, using which we can run programs in the notebook. To work with Jupyter, one has to install the Jupyter extension, and then to open or create a notebook, one has to open the command palette (*Ctrl+Shift+P*) and select **Create: New Jupyter Notebook**, as shown in *Figure 3.20*:

Figure 3.20: Creating a new file in Jupyter

Executing the **Jupyter Notebook** program:

1. Type your program code in the editor. Run your program by clicking on the run icon to the left of the code cell or by using the shortcut *Ctrl+Enter*. The output appears directly below the code cell.

2. One can run multiple cells by clicking the **Run All** option. One can even select **run all above** or **run all below**.

3. Using the **Export** option, Python code can be exported to PDF or HTML format. Export option is shown in *Figure 3.21*.

4. To save your **Jupyter Notebook**, click on the **file** option and then select the **save** option or use the shortcut *Ctrl+S*.

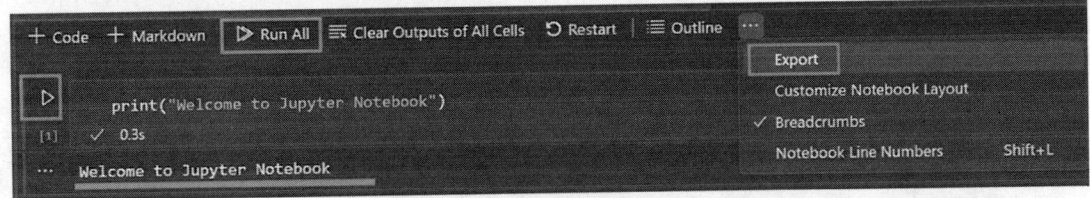

Figure 3.21: Various options available in Jupyter Notebook

Error Lens

The Error Lens Extension in VS Code displays errors and warnings in the editor's 'problem' area and in the editor gutter. It helps identify and fix errors quickly and easily. It can be used to navigate to the source of the problem. *Figure 3.22* is a screenshot of Error Lens extension:

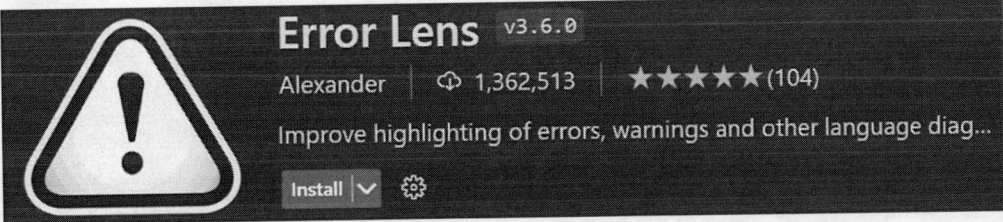

Figure 3.22: Error Lens extension

The Error Lens extension displays the error, warning, and diagnostic messages in line with the code itself. It eliminates the need for developers to hover over or click any other options or execute the code to see the error. This extension also highlights the code line with different colors to provide better visualization of errors, differentiating between errors and warnings easily. We can see the difference in *Figure 3.23*:

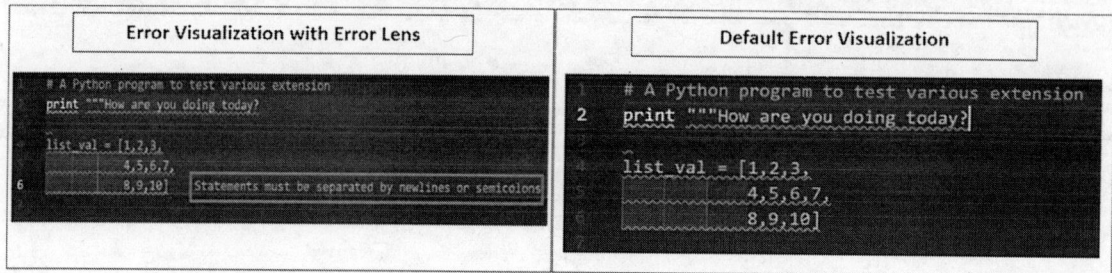

Figure 3.23: *Error message appearing along with the code with Error Lens*

Better Comments

The best comment extension for Visual Studio Code is the 'Better Comments' extension. This extension provides a variety of comment types, such as alerts, queries, todos, and highlights. It also allows you to easily adjust the colors of these comment types, making it easier to differentiate between them. *Figure 3.24* is a screenshot of the Better Comments extension:

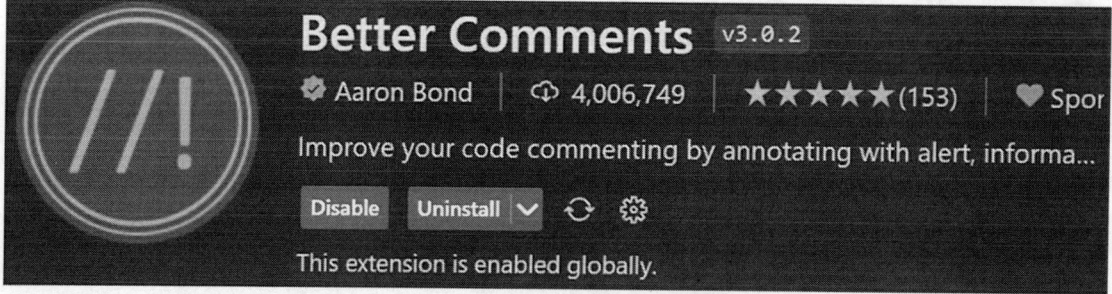

Figure 3.24: *Better Comments extension*

As the name suggests, it improves the comment by giving the capability to customize different colors for comments. Comment can be classified using the following properties:

- ! for alerts /important comments
- ? for questions
- TODO for the task

The mentioned properties of the Better Comments extension are shown in *Figure 3.25*:

```
1   #This is default way of Commenting
2   #ToDo: For task related comment
3   #?: Ask questions to this way
4   #! IMPORTANT NOTE: Do not delete this comment
5
6   """
7   ! Important Note in multi line comment
8   ? Question test in multi line comment
9   TODO: Task in multi line comment
10  """
11
```

Figure 3.25: Better Comments extension

Lightrun

Lightrun is an open-source Visual Studio Code extension that provides an easy way to run and debug programs from within the text editor. Lightrun is available for other programming languages, like Python, Java, C, C++, and Rust. With Light Runner, you can quickly test and debug code without needing to leave the editor or manually set breakpoints. *Figure 3.26* is a screenshot of the Lightrun extension:

Lightrun v1.8.4

Lightrun | 8,731 | ★★★★★ (4)

Easily observe and debug live production applications.

Disable   Uninstall ∨   ↻   ⚙

This extension is enabled globally.

Figure 3.26: Lightrun extension

We are introducing a real-time debugging platform: Lightrun. It supports multiple languages apart from Python. The reason for its popularity is that it has an intuitive interface for the developers to add logs, traces, and metrics in production for debugging the code in real time. One can debug by exploring the stack trace and variables after adding Lightrun snapshots in real time and on demand. It supports multi-instance too. The community edition of Lightrun is free to use, but its professional edition costs for the additional capabilities it provides.

Python Test Explorer

The Python Test Explorer extension in VS Code is a plugin that enables developers to quickly and easily run unit tests, check code coverage, and debug test failures in Python projects. With this extension, developers can quickly assess the quality of their code, identify areas that need improvement, and make sure their code is bug-free before pushing it to production. *Figure 3.27* is a screenshot of Python Test Explorer extension:

Figure 3.27: Python Test Explorer extension

The Python Test Explorer extension for VS Code offers various user-friendly features, such as the ability to run Unittest, Pytest, or Testplan tests. The sidebar of the extension shows a complete view of the tests and test suites with their state, which helps the developer focus on tests that failed.

Python-specific settings

The Python extension required to execute Python code is a highly configurable extension that provides users with the power to customize entire setting options. Overall, in the version that was available at the time of writing this book, there are 79 settings available. We will look at the important ones in *Table 3.1*:

Setting	Default	Description
defaultInterpreterPath	Python	It has the path to the default Python interpreter. It can get variables like ${workspaceFolder} and ${workspaceFolder}/.venv.

Setting	Default	Description
interpreter. infoVisibility	onPythonRelated	It controls when to display the selected interpreter information on the status bar. It will always show on the status bar and never hide it entirely. onPythonRelated displays only when Python-related files open in the editor.
venvFolders	[]	These are paths to folders where virtual environments are created.
logging.level	error	The level of logging extension will perform. Other possible values: off, error, warn, info, and debug.
include	[]	Paths to directories or files are to be included in analysis.
exclude	[]	Paths to directories or files are not to be included in the analysis.

Table 3.1: Python extension settings value

Installing and using Python packages

One of the main reasons why Python programming language is so popular is because it supports various packages, which can be downloaded from PyPI. Let us now write a program that will use the **matplotlib** and **numpy** packages to create a graph. Matplotlib is a standard library for creating static or animated or interactive visualizations in Python. *Figure 3.28* shows how to import packages or modules and the error if those libraries are not installed:

```
1   import matplotlib.pyplot as plt    Import "matplotlib.pyplot" could not be
2   import numpy as np    Import "numpy" could not be resolved
3   from matplotlib import colors    Import "matplotlib" could not be resolved
4   from matplotlib.ticker import PercentFormatter    Import "matplotlib.ticker
```

Figure 3.28: Error for libraries not installed

Unless you have a previously installed matplotlib package, you would get the message, **ModuleNotFoundError**: No module named matplotlib, as shown in *Figure 3.28*. This error message indicates that the required package is not available in the system. To install the matplotlib package, use the command palette to run terminal: create new terminal (*Ctrl+Shift+`*). This command opens a command prompt for your selected interpreter.

It is not recommended to avoid the packages in a global interpreter environment. One should use a project-specific virtual environment, as it helps isolate the installed packages from other environments and create version-specific conflicts. One can use the following commands to create a virtual environment and then install the required packages:

Windows:

```
py -m venv .venv
.venv\scripts\activate
```

MacOS/Linux:

```
python3 -m venv .venv
source .venv/bin/activate
```

When a new virtual environment is created, VS Code prompts you to set it as the default for the current workspace folder. Select your new environment using the **Python: Select interpreter** command from the command palette, as shown in *Figure 3.29*:

Figure 3.29: Selecting interpreter path

Here are the ways to install the packages on various operating systems:

- MacOS

  ```
  python3 -m pip install matplotlib
  ```

- Windows

  ```
  python -m pip install matplotlib
  ```

- Linux (Debian)

  ```
  apt-get install python3-tk
  python3 -m pip install matplotlib
  ```

Rerun the program now, and the errors will be resolved.

Functions, modules, and packages in Python

To begin with, we need to understand that a package is a collection of modules, and a module contains functions and classes. As depicted in *Figure 3.30*, we can say that **functions** are the subset of **Modules**, and **Modules** are the subset of **Packages**:

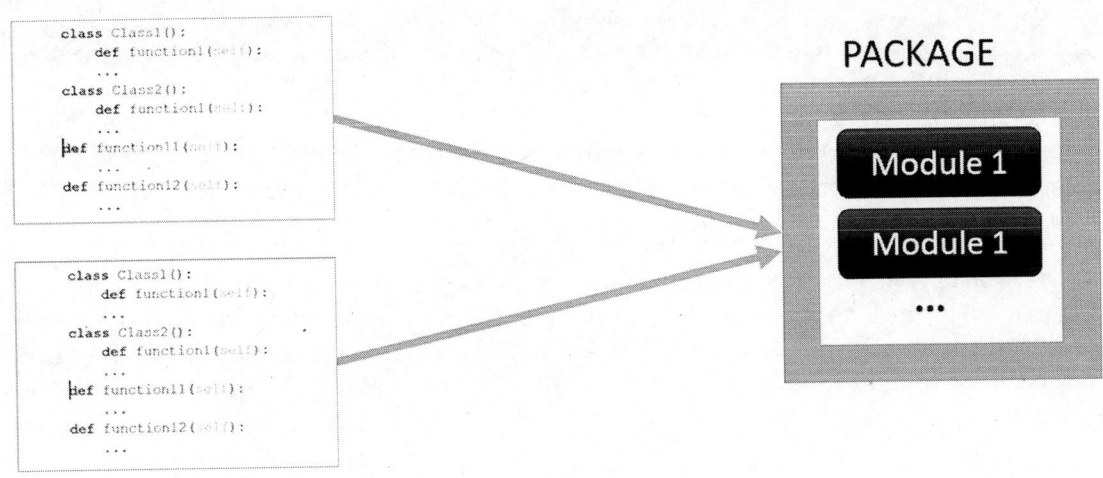

Figure 3.30: Functions, modules, and packages

Functions

A function is a block of code put together under one name, and it only runs when it is called. One can pass data (known as parameters) into a function, and the function can return data to where it is called.

Figure 3.31 shows the types of functions we come across in Python:

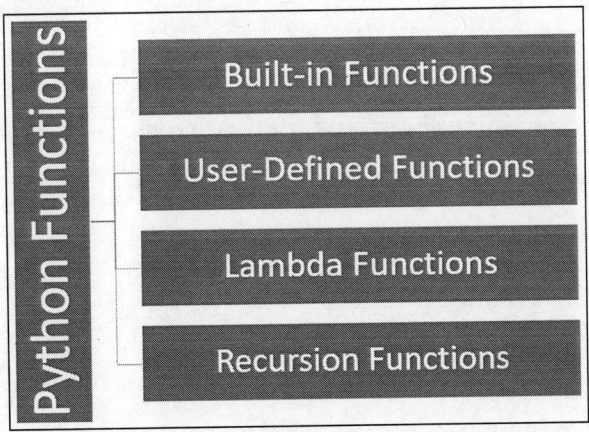

Figure 3.31: Types of Python functions

There are two types of functions: one which is already built and available for use and called Built-in functions, and the other wherein the user has to write the code for the function from scratch known as user-defined functions. Let's understand them better:

- **Built-in Functions:** There are several built-in functions in Python that are readily available for use. Listed here are a few of them:

```
print(), abs(), hash(), delattr(), set(), help(), all(), dict(), setattr(), min(), any(), dir(),
hex(), next(), slice(), ascii(), divmod(), id(), object(), sorted(), bin(), enumerate(), input(),
oct(), staticmethod(), bool(), eval(), int(), open(), str(), breakpoint(), exec(), isinstance(),
ord(), sum(), filter(), issubclass(), pow(), super(), bytes(), float(), iter(), tuple(), callable(),
format(), len(), property(), type(), chr(), frozenset(), list(), range(), vars(),classmethod(),
getattr(), locals(), repr(), zip(), compile(), globals(), map(), reversed(), __import__(),
complex(), hasattr(), max(), round()
```

The **dir(builtins)** in Python returns a list of all the names in the built-in module **builtins**. The **builtins** module contains functions and variables that are built-in in Python and can be used without being imported. The **dir()** function, in general, returns a sorted list of names in the specified namespace. The following code can help you view the list:

import builtins
print(dir(builtins))

Let us execute a few of these functions; readers are encouraged to run them and see the results:

- o   Printing on the screen:

    ```
    print("Welcome to Python World")
    ```

- o   Print the eval result:

    ```
    print(eval("4+5*2"))
    bin(50)
    a=input("Enter Your Name: ")
    abs(-789)
    ```

- **User-defined functions:** Functions that we create ourselves to perform specific tasks are referred to as user-defined functions. Functions in Python are defined using the **def** keyword, followed by an identifier with a pair of parentheses. There may be variable names enclosed within the parentheses and a colon at the end of the line; what follows under indentation is the block of statements that are added for this function. When the function is called, the values are passed as arguments; in the same way, we define parameters.

    Let's build our first user-defined function now. We will name the function **func**.

Note: The names given in the function definition are called parameters, and the values supplied to the function call are called arguments.

Code will look something like the following:

```
x=50
#Function definition
def func(x):
    print("X is ",x)
```

```
    x=2
    output = "Changed X locally to " + str(x) + " in the function"
    return output

result = func(x)
print(result)
print("X is still ",x)
```

In the preceding program example, we defined a function named **func()**, which takes one parameter **x** and returns one variable output. In this example, if the value for argument **x** is not provided while calling, it would result in an error, so the **x** is the required argument.

In the following example, we are specifying default argument values for parameters. The default value is added by appending the assignment operator (=) to the parameter name in the function definition, followed by the default value, as demonstrated in the following example:

Here is the function definition:

```
def displayinfo(name, city="Delhi"):
    # Printing a passed info in this function
    print("Name: ",name, "\nCity ", city)
    return
```

Now you can call the printinfo function:

```
displayinfo(city="Mumbai", name="Sachin")
displayinfo(name="Virat")
```

In the preceding example, at the time of call, if no value is provided to the city, it will use the default value **Delhi**. In the first function call, we are providing the value for the city, so the function will take **Mumbai**. This example also demonstrates how keyword arguments work in a function call. The calling function identifies the arguments by the parameter names in this case, that is, **city = "Mumbai"** and **name= "Sachin"**. Keyword arguments help skip arguments or place them out of order. The Python interpreter uses the keywords passed to match the values with parameters. Apart from not worrying about the order of the arguments, an advantage is that only those parameters will be given the values which we need. This is only when other parameters have default argument values.

Sometimes, we may not know exactly how many arguments the caller may pass; in such cases, we have the option to use variable length parameters, which is achieved using * (stars). When we declare a single-starred parameter, such as ***argv**, all the arguments from that point till the end are collected in a tuple format, called **argv**. And when you declare a double-starred parameter like ****argv**, then all the keyword arguments from that point till the end are collected in a dictionary format, called **argv**.

Let us implement a function total that takes a variable number of arguments both as **Tuple** and **Dictionary**. This is a simple example that accepts the arguments and prints them in the function body:

```python
def total(initial=10, *numbers, **keywords):
    count = initial
    for num in numbers:
        count+=num
    for key in keywords:
        count+=keywords[key]
    return count
print(total(10,5,10,15,twenty=20,thirty=30,fifty=50))
```

Functions have an inbuilt mechanism to handle documentation. The concept is called DocString. They are an important part of the Python language and are used to make code more readable, maintainable, and reusable.

DocString

A docstring is a string value that occurs as the first statement in a function, class, method or module definition. When a module, function, class, or method is called, the interpreter scans the definition for a docstring and, if found, it is passed as the first argument to the function. A docString is used to document a brief explanation of what a function does, though it is optional but always recommended. DocString is a comment added immediately below the function header. Generally, triple quotes are used so that the description can extend up to multiple lines. Docstring is available to us as the __doc__ attribute of the function. Let's implement docstring in a program. In the following function greet, the first line given in triple quote (""") is docstring:

```python
def greet(name):
    """ This function is used to greet a person.

    This function greets to the person passed in as parameter."""
    print("Hello, " + name + ". Have a good day!")
```

You can, at any point in time, display the docstring content of any function. Writing the code to check the doc string of the function **greet()** which we created above:

```python
print(greet.__doc__)
```

Now, let us check the doc string for built-in function **print()**:

```python
print(print.__doc__)
```

Docstrings are used to document the purpose of a function, method, class, or module and provide usage examples and other useful information.

Python also has a third type of function called the one line function or Lambda function. For cases where the entire logic can be built with just one line, this is preferred to make code short and simple:

- **Lambda functions**: Lambda operator or lambda function is used for creating small, one-time, and anonymous function objects in Python. Its basic syntax is as follows:

  lambda arguments : expression

  The lambda operator can take any number of arguments, but it can have only one expression. It cannot contain any statements and returns a function object that can be assigned to any variable; for example, in the following example, **add** represents the lambda function.

  Here is a program to demonstrate a function using the lambda operator:

  ```
  add = lambda x, y: x ** y
  a = add(2, 3)
  print(a)
  ```

  Normally, the preceding program would be written as follows:

  ```
  def power(x, y):
      return x ** y
  ```

  Call the function:

  ```
  a =power(2, 3)
  print(a)
  ```

Now, let us see how recursive functions can be implemented in Python:

- **Recursion functions:** A recursive function in Python is a function that calls itself. It is an algorithm that calls itself, with an updated version of its own input, until it reaches a solution. This type of function can be very powerful for solving complex problems that can be broken down into smaller chunks. Recursive functions can be used to traverse data structures, implement mathematical algorithms, and even solve games. Recursion is a way of coding, in which a function calls itself one or more times in its body, usually as the returning value of the function call, and the function is called a recursive function.

  A recursive function terminates if the solution of the problem is downsized and moves toward a base case. It is where the problem can be solved without further recursion. A recursion can end up in an infinite loop if the base case is not met in the calls.

  Let us take a situation where recursion is best suited, calculating the factorial of a number. A factorial of 4 would be the multiplication of all the numbers between 1 and 4. Here is an example:

  $4! = 4 * 3 * 2 * 1$

  Or, we can write this as follows:

  $4! = 4 * 3!$

  $3! = 3 * 2!$

  $2! = 2 * 1$

This is a classic scenario to use the recursion concept. The terminating condition would be when we try to find a factorial of 1 or lower value, which is called the base case.

Let us write a program to implement the factorial of a number using recursion. Intermediate steps can be tracked by adding two **print()** functions to the previous function definition:

```python
def factorial(n):
    print("factorial has been called with n = " + str(n))
    if n == 1:
        return 1
    else:
        res = n * factorial(n-1)
        print("track ", n, " * factorial(" ,n-1, "): ",res)
        return res
```

Now, test the function:

```python
print(factorial(5))
```

The output is given in *Figure 3.32*:

```
factorial has been called with n = 5
factorial has been called with n = 4
factorial has been called with n = 3
factorial has been called with n = 2
factorial has been called with n = 1
track  2  * factorial( 1 ):  2
track  3  * factorial( 2 ):  6
track  4  * factorial( 3 ):  24
track  5  * factorial( 4 ):  120
120
```

Figure 3.32: Output from the factorial recursion program

Classes

Classes are the building blocks of **Object-Oriented Programming (OOP)**. OOP in Python is a programming paradigm that uses classes and objects to create a model of real-world objects and their interactions. It is a way of organizing and structuring code to make it more readable, maintainable, and reusable. OOP in Python includes class definitions, inheritance, encapsulation, abstraction, and polymorphism. It allows developers to create objects that have specific properties and behaviors, which can then be used to create applications and programs.

Now, let us examine the terms you will encounter in discussions about OOP:

- **Object:** An object is an entity that has a state and behavior. It may be physical and logical. For example, a mouse, keyboard, chair, table, pen, etc. Everything in Python is an object, and almost everything has attributes and methods.

- **Class:** Class can be defined as a collection of objects. It is a logical entity that has specific attributes and methods. For example, if you have a student class, then it should contain an attribute and method, that is, an email ID, name, age, roll number, etc.

A class creates a new data type where objects are instances of the class. An object is defined as a real-world entity related to the problem domain, with crisply defined boundaries. Objects are encapsulated with attributes (called fields in Python) and behavior or services (called methods in Python).

Figure 3.33 shows the members of a class. Members of a class in Python include attributes, methods (services), and class variables. Attributes are used to define the properties of a class, such as its data and behavior. Methods are functions that are associated with a particular class and can be used to manipulate the data and behavior of that class. Finally, class variables are variables that are shared among all instances of a class and can be used to store information that is applicable to all the instances.

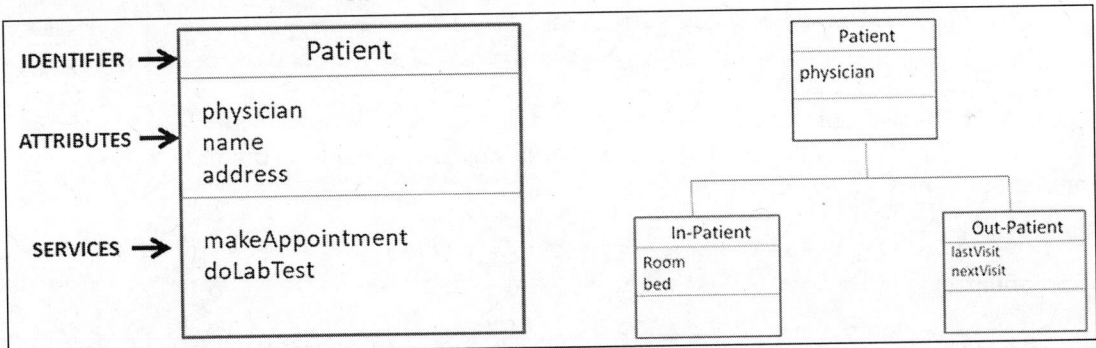

Figure 3.33: *Example of classes*

As depicted in *Figure 3.33*, the patient is a class that has its set of members. Patients can be either in-patients or out-patients.

Method

Method is a function that is associated with an object. In Python, the method is not unique to class instances. Any object type can have methods. Objects can store data using variables (also called fields) that belong to them. Objects also have functionality by using methods. Methods are the functions defined in a class. In terms of definition, functions and methods are similar, the difference being that the functions are independent, whereas methods belong to a class or object. A class is created using the class keyword. The fields and methods of the class are listed in an indented block.

Let us create an example class in Python and look at its workings:

Here is an example of declaring a class:

```python
class Book:
    """Represents a Book class example"""
    #declaring a class variable:
    book_count = 0
```
Now initialize the variable using the init
```python
    def __init__(self,title): #self keyword represents instance (object) of
the class

        ''' Initialize the data'''
        self.title = title
        print("Initializing the title of the book: ", self.title)
        #When a book is created, it should increase the total book count by
1
        Book.book_count +=1  #Since its a class variable, Class name.
variable is used


    def remove(self):
        '''Removing book from the list'''
        print("{} is being removed from the list!".format(self.title))
        Book.book_count -= 1
        if Book.book_count <= 0:
            print("It was the last book in the shelf. You don't have any
more book!")
        else:
            print("There are still {} books in the shelf!".format(Book.
book_count))


    def say_hi(self):
        """Hello from the book class"""
        print("Hello from Class Book, I am being called by ",self.title)


    @classmethod
    def how_many(cls):
        """Prints current number of books available"""
        print("Currently there are {} books in the shelf.".format(cls.
book_count))


#### Below code is used to create object of the class Book
#Creating objects and initializing the title using __init__

#Automatically called while creating objects
```

```
book1 = Book("The A to Z of Retail Management")
book2 = Book("Learn and Practice Python Programming")
book3 = Book("Boost your career")
#calling class variable using classname
print("Total number of books available in the shelf: ",Book.book_count)
#Calling functions
book1.say_hi()
book2.remove()
#calling class variable using object
print("Total number of books available in the shelf: ",book3.book_count)
```

We used the **__init__()** method in the preceding example to initialize the variables. Let's understand the significance of this method.

The init method

There are a few methods that have special significance in Python classes, including the **init** method. The **__init__** (double underscore init double underscore) method is executed as soon as an object of a class is instantiated. Since the method is automatically called, it is used to initialize the object.

Note: The double underscores are at both the beginning and the end of the init.

More about Class and Objects

Class variables (owned by class) are shared, and they can be accessed by all instances of that class. There is only one copy of the class variable, unlike object variables, which are duplicated for each object. When any one object makes a change to a class variable, the change will be seen by all the other instances as there is a single copy.

Object variables belong to each object/instance of the class. Each object has its copy of the field, i.e., they are not shared and are not related in any way to the field by the same name in a different instance.

The **classmethod()** is a built-in function in Python, which establishes ownership of the method to the given class. Class methods can be called by both class and object.

In the preceding example, **book_count** belongs to the book class and hence, is a class variable. The **title** variable belongs to the object and is assigned using **self**. The population class variable is referred to as **Book.book_count** and not as **self.book_count**. Object variable name is referred to using the **self.title** notation in the methods of the object. Instead of **Book.book_count**, it can also be referred to as **self.__class__. population** as every object can be referred to its class via the **self.__class__** attribute.

The **init** method is used to initialize the book instance with a name, and we increase the **book_count** by 1 since a book is added. In the **remove()** method, we simply decrease the **Book.book_count** by 1. All class members are public, which means they can be accessed from any class or even from the main. If data members have names with the double underscore prefixed, such as **__privatevar**, Python uses name mangling to effectively make it a private variable. Any variable that is meant to be used only within the class or the object should begin its name with an underscore, and all other names are public and can be used by other classes/objects. This is only a convention and is not enforced by Python (except for the double underscore prefix, which is to make the members private).

There are four important pillars of class and objects:

- Inheritance
- Polymorphism
- Data abstraction
- Encapsulation

Inheritance

Inheritance is a process by which objects of one class acquire the properties of the objects of another class. Inheritance provides code reusability, makes it easier to create and maintain an application. In this section, we will cover the basics of inheritance.

What is inheritance in Python?

Inheritance is a way of creating a new class (called a child class) from an existing class (called a parent class). The child class will have the same properties and behaviors as the parent class, but it can also have its own unique properties and behaviors. Inheritance provides a way to reuse code from the parent class and extend it.

Syntax of Inheritance

In Python, inheritance is specified using the following syntax:

```
class ChildClass(ParentClass):
    # code
```

Here, **ChildClass** is the name of the child class and **ParentClass** is the name of the parent class.

How does inheritance work in Python?

Inheritance works by allowing a child class to inherit the properties and behaviors of a parent class. When a child class inherits a parent class, it automatically inherits the methods and attributes of the parent class. This means the child class can use the inherited methods and attributes without having to define them again.

For example, suppose we have a class called **Animal**, which has an attribute called name and a method called **speak**(). We can create a new class called **Dog**, which inherits from **Animal**:

```python
# Example of Inheritance in Python
class Animal:
    def __init__(self, name):
        self.name = name

    def speak(self):
        print("%s says 'hello!'" % self.name)


class Dog(Animal):
    def bark(self):
        print("%s barks 'woof!'" % self.name)


# Create an instance of the Dog class
d = Dog("Fido")


# Call the speak() method
d.speak()


# Output
Fido says 'hello!'


# Call the bark() method
d.bark()
```

Output

```
Fido barks 'woof!'
```

In this example, we defined a class named **Animal**, which has an attribute called name and a method called **speak()**. We then created a class called **Dog**, which inherits from **Animal**. This means that the **Dog** class gets the methods and attributes of the **Animal** class automatically.

When we create an instance of the **Dog** class, we can call the **speak()** method inherited from the **Animal** class, as well as the **bark()** method defined in the **Dog** class. This is how inheritance works in Python.

Inheritance provides a number of advantages, including the following:

- **Code Reusability**: Inheritance allows us to reuse existing code instead of having to write it from scratch. This saves time and makes the code easier to maintain.

- **Simplicity**: Inheritance makes it easier to extend existing code instead of having to rewrite it. This makes the code simpler and easier to understand.

- **Extensibility**: Inheritance makes it possible to add new features to an existing class without having to modify any existing code. This makes it easier to extend an application as needed.

Polymorphism

Polymorphism allows programs to execute different behaviors in different contexts; for example, consider the following code:

```python
class Animal:
    def make_sound(self):
        print("This animal makes a sound!")


class Dog(Animal):
    def make_sound(self):
        print("Woof!")


class Cat(Animal):
    def make_sound(self):
        print("Meow!")


dog = Dog()
cat = Cat()


dog.make_sound()
cat.make_sound()
```

The output of this code is:
```
Woof!
Meow!
```

In this code, we defined a superclass, **Animal**, and two subclasses: **Dog** and **Cat**. The **Dog** and **Cat** classes both inherit the **make_sound()** method from the **Animal** class. However, they each override the method, so when the **make_sound()** method is called on each object, the respective sound of a dog or cat is printed. This is an example of polymorphism, as the same method (**make_sound()**) can execute different behaviors depending on the context in which it is called.

Data abstraction

Data abstraction is the process of hiding the implementation details from the user and providing only the functionality to the user. In Python, data abstraction is provided by abstract classes and interfaces. Abstract classes contain one or more abstract methods. Abstract methods must be implemented by any non-abstract subclass. An interface class contains only abstract methods.

Let us consider an example to understand data abstraction. We have a class called **Shape**, which is an abstract class. It contains three methods: **get_area()**, **get_perimeter()** and **draw()**. The **get_area()** and **get_perimeter()** methods are abstract methods, since they are not implemented in the **Shape** class. The **draw()** method is a concrete method, as it is implemented in the **Shape** class:

```
class Shape:
    def get_area(self):
        pass


    def get_perimeter(self):
        pass


    def draw(self):
        print("Drawing a shape")
```

Now, let us create a subclass of **Shape** called **Square**. It implements the **get_area()** and **get_perimeter()** methods, which are abstract methods of the Shape class:

```
class Square(Shape):
    def __init__(self, side):
        self.side = side
```

```python
def get_area(self):
    return self.side * self.side


def get_perimeter(self):
    return 4 * self.side
```

In this example, the Square class implements the abstract methods of the Shape class. The user of the Square class will only know that it is a shape and will not know how it is implemented. This is data abstraction.

Encapsulation

Encapsulation is a mechanism of wrapping the data and the functions that operate on that data within a single unit. This allows the programmer to protect the data from outside interference and misuse and to easily reuse the code.

For example, let us say we want to create a class that represents a vehicle. We can create a class called **Vehicle** and add two data members to it: one for the make and one for the model of the vehicle. We can also add a method to the class to calculate the total cost of the vehicle:

```python
class Vehicle:
    def __init__(self, make, model):
        self.make = make
        self.model = model


    def calculate_total_cost(self):
        # calculate total cost here
        return 100
```

Now that we have our class, we can create an instance of the **Vehicle** class and use it to represent a specific vehicle:

```python
my_car = Vehicle("Honda", "Civic")
total_cost = my_car.calculate_total_cost()
```

In this example, we have encapsulated the data (make and model) and the methods (**calculate_total_cost**) inside the **Vehicle** class. This allows us to easily reuse the code and protect the data from outside interference. Encapsulation is an important feature of object-oriented programming, as it allows the programmer to create a well-structured, maintainable program. It also allows the programmer to easily reuse code and protect data from outside interference.

Modules

The module is a Python file (**.py**) that contains code to perform a set of related tasks. A Python module may contain variables, functions, classes, etc. Let us say your friend has written some wonderful functions and classes, and you want to use the code from them. You can ask them for the **.py** file and put that in the same folder as your file. You can start using it by simply importing it into your code.

Let us create a dummy but working module ourselves by writing the following code in a file called **aboutme.py**:

```python
# defining a class AboutMe
class AboutMe:
    # defining the __init__ method
    def __init__(self, name, city):
        self.name = name
        self.city = city

    # defining the getCity method
    def getCity(self):
        print(self.name + " lives in the city " + self.city)


# defining the function hello
def hobbies():
    print("I love playing badminton and have my interest in"
          "Creative arts, including writing and painting.")


# creating a variable
work = 'I am a Technoculturist'


if __name__ == "__main__":
    print("Executed when invoked directly")
    # calling the function hobbies()
    hobbies()

    # creating the object captain
    captain = AboutMe('Dhoni','Ranchi')

    # calling the getCity() method for the object
    captain.getCity()

    #printing the variable work present in aboutme.py
    print(work)
```

When you execute the **aboutme.py** file, the content inside the **if** condition will be executed. **__name__** == , **__main__** will result to true because the Python interpreter reads the source file before executing and defines a few special variables. One such variable is

__name__, which is set to value **__main__** for the file that is directly called. When we execute **aboutme.py**, the condition becomes true, but when the same file is referenced from another Python file, **__name__** will be set to the module's name. The module's name is available as value to **__name__** global variable.

Now, let us use this as a module and call its member from a different file. Create another file **practicePy.py**, though the name does not matter in this case. Type the following code to call the members from the **aboutme.py** file:

```
# importing the module aboutme.py
#Class, Function and Variable all are now imported
import aboutme

# calling the function hobbies() from aboutme.py
aboutme.hobbies()

# creating the object captain of class AboutMe
captain = aboutme.AboutMe('Kapil','Chandigarh')

# calling the getCity() method for the object
captain.getCity()

#printing the variable work present in aboutme.py
print(aboutme.work)
```

The output displayed is shown in *Figure 3.34*:

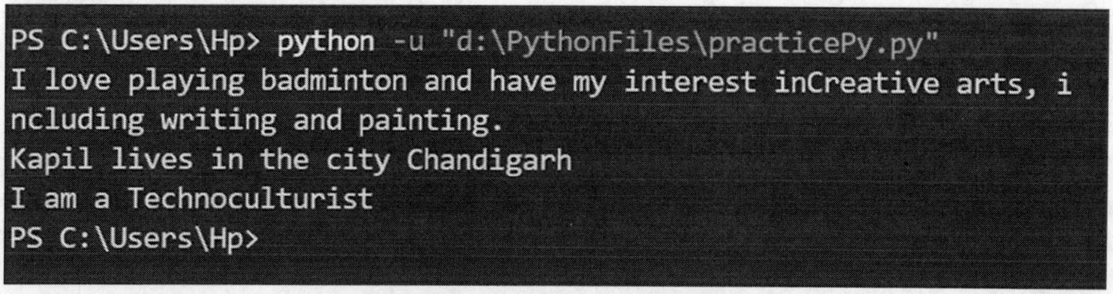

```
PS C:\Users\Hp> python -u "d:\PythonFiles\practicePy.py"
I love playing badminton and have my interest inCreative arts, i
ncluding writing and painting.
Kapil lives in the city Chandigarh
I am a Technoculturist
PS C:\Users\Hp>
```

Figure 3.34: Output of calling a module

We have seen how to add classes, variables, and functions to a module. Now, let us see how modules are added together in a package.

Packages

We all will work on big projects at some point in time, and that means dealing with large amounts of code. Writing everything together in a single file will make our code complex to handle. The recommended way is to separate the code into multiple files, keep related codes together in packages, and use the package when required in the projects. This is a great way to reuse the codes.

One possible organization of packages and modules while developing a game could look as shown in *Figure 3.35*:

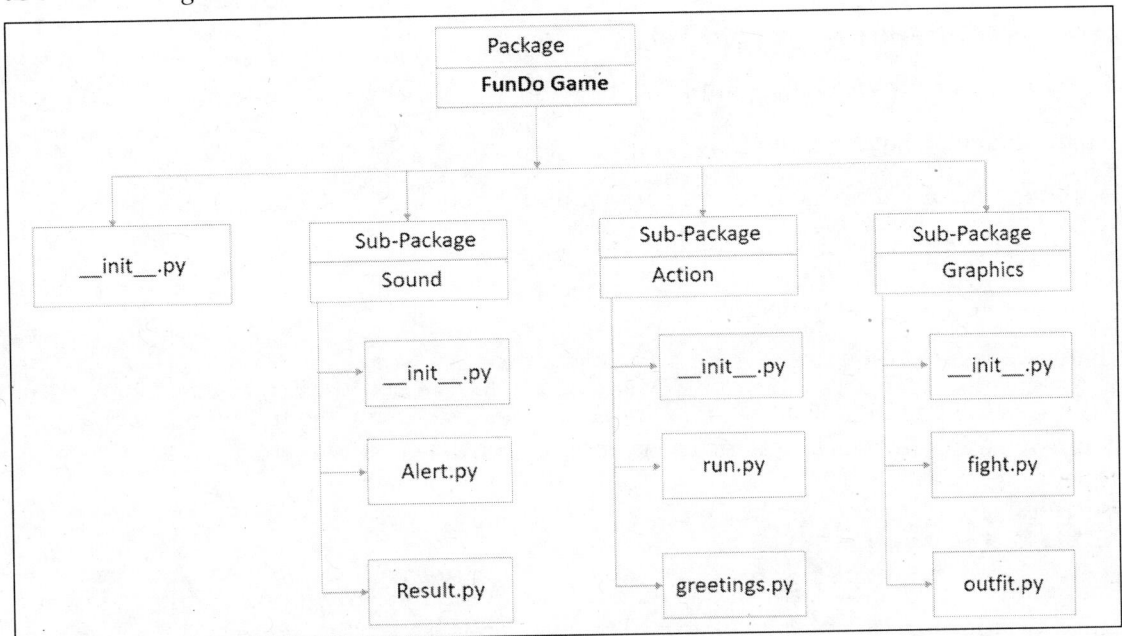

Figure 3.35: Example of a Python package

The **FunDo** game directory has a file named **__init__.py**, which is a must for Python to consider it as a package. The developer has the option to leave this file empty, but generally, they place the initialization code for the given package in the **__init__.py** file.

One can import modules from packages using the **.**(dot) operator. For example, if we want to import the outfit module (**outfit.py**) in the preceding example, it can be done as follows:

```
import FunDo.Graphics.outfit
```

Now, if this module contains a function named **change_shoes()**, we must use the full name to reference it.

```
FunDo.Graphics.outfit.change_shoes("blues")
```

There is an alternate way to call the functions without giving a lengthy name. This time, we give an alias to the import package, as follows:

```
import FunDo.Graphics.outfit as fgo
```

We now reference it as follows:

```
fgo.change_shoes("blues")
```

We can also call them differently than what we have named, so that we do not have to give the full package name while referencing, as follows:

```
from FunDo.Graphics import outfit
```

We can now call the function simply as follows:

```
outfit.change_shoes("blues")
```

Another way of importing is to call the required function from a module, as follows:

```
from FunDo.Graphics.outfit import change_shoes
```

Now we can directly call this function:

```
change_shoes("blues")
```

Although this might look easier, it is not recommended. Using the full namespace avoids confusion and prevents two same identifier names from colliding.

Conclusion

Extensions are what make VS Code efficient for Python programming. We have learned about the top 10 popular extensions used by developers across the world and the powerful features of these extensions. Python extension for VS Code is highly configurable, so it makes sense to configure it to make the development of applications easy. For that purpose, we looked at some of the Python-specific settings, which can be edited in VS Code. We learned how to install packages available in **Python Package Index (PyPI)**, which is the official third-party repository for Python packages. In the last section of the chapter, we focused on understanding how to create functions, modules, and packages for application development. We are getting closer to developing amazing applications.

In the next chapter, we will build our first Python app using all the basic concepts, but before that, we will learn to handle 2D data using numpy, scientific calculation using scipy, and table structure using pandas. We will also solve a business problem using data visualization; in the last section, we will learn to work with *github.com*.

## CHAPTER 4

Developing Visualizing Python App in VS Code

If I can't picture it, I can't understand it.
— Albert Einstein

Introduction

People like visuals and the importance of visuals, as it helps us visualize simple and complex concepts, interact with the presented data, and bring everyone on the same page, regardless of their level of expertise. Every industry wields data and analytics as competitive weapons, operational accelerants, and innovation catalysts. **Data-Driven Decision-making (DDDM)** is about using facts, metrics, and data to make strategic business decisions aligned with organizational goals, objectives, and initiatives. Based on historical and current data, businesses use predictive analytics, statistics, and modeling to determine potential outcomes and future performance. But at the same time, it is getting difficult to make sense of trillions of data rows created daily. This is where visualization is playing an increasingly key role. Experts use data visualization to tell stories that everybody in the organization can understand. They do this by curating data into an easily understood form, highlighting the trends and outliers. In this chapter, we will look at a couple of examples of visualization that tell a story by removing the noise from data and highlighting useful information, and then showing how this can help the business make decisions.

This chapter assumes that the readers have some knowledge of Python topics like Numpy, Scipy, Pandas, Matplotlib, and Seaborn. We will get an overview of these topics in this chapter, so even if you have no working knowledge, it should be fine.

We will also look at using the basics of Git version control in **Visual Studio Code (VS Code)**. We will learn about integrated Git support and understand how to work with remote repositories. We will conclude the chapter by learning how to debug the application.

Refer to the GitHub location to access the dataset.

Structure

In this chapter, we will cover the following topics:

- Virtual Environment Concept
- Python topics:
- Learning the basics of statistics
- Visualization for Data Analysis
- Working with GitHub

Now, let us dive deep into the topics.

Virtual Environment Concept

Before we get into the Python topics, let us understand the concept of virtual environment. This is the right time to discuss it. Creating a virtual environment is a great way to keep your Python projects organized and separate from each other. It allows you to install libraries and dependencies specific to a project without affecting your global Python installation. Here is how you can create a virtual environment and install libraries in it:

1. Open your command line or terminal.

2. Install the **virtualenv** package if you don't have it already. You can do this by running the **pip install virtualenv** command.

3. Once **virtualenv** is installed, navigate to the directory where you want to create your virtual environment.

4. Run the **virtualenv myenv** command to create a new virtual environment called **myenv**. You can choose any name you like. This command creates a new directory with the same name as your virtual environment within the current directory.

5. Activate the virtual environment by running the appropriate command for your operating system:

- On Windows: `myenv\Scripts\activate`

- On macOS/Linux: `source myenv/bin/activate`

6. Once the virtual environment is activated, your command-line prompt will change to indicate that you are now working within the virtual environment.

7. You can now install libraries into your virtual environment. For example, to install the `numpy` library, run the **pip install numpy** command. This will download and install the library into your virtual environment.

8. You can install multiple libraries by running additional **pip install** commands.

9. You can check the installed libraries in your virtual environment by running the **pip list** command.

10. When you are done working in your virtual environment, you can deactivate it by running the `deactivate` command. This will restore your global Python environment.

By creating and using virtual environments, you can easily manage your Python projects and their dependencies with minimal conflicts or interference between them.

Python topics

Numpy, Scipy, Pandas, Matplotlib and Seaborn are popular Python libraries used for data analysis and manipulation:

- Numpy is used for scientific computing, array manipulation, and linear algebra.

- Scipy is used for scientific and technical computing, statistics, and more.

- Pandas is used for data manipulation and analysis, data cleaning, and data wrangling.

- Matplotlib is used for data visualization and plotting.

- Seaborn is used for statistical data visualization and plotting.

These libraries are important because they make it easier to manipulate, analyze, and visualize data, which is critical for data science and machine learning applications. Let's learn about them in detail.

Numpy

Numerical Python (NumPy) is used for working with arrays in Python. It has functions for linear algebra, Fourier, and so on. NumPy arrays are stored in memory at one continuous place so that processes can access and manipulate them efficiently. Numpy is used in Python programming after installing and importing the **numpy** library in your Python applications. Numpy can be installed using **pip** command and imported in the program using the **import** keyword. In the following example, we have imported Numpy and then created an alias **np** while importing:

```
import numpy as np
```

The preceding the statement will import NumPy and make it ready to use. In the next line, we will see how to create a list to Numpy array:

```
Array1 = numpy.array([10, 20, 30, 40, 50])

print(array1)
```

ndarray is the array object of NumPy that is used to work with arrays. NumPy **ndarray** object is created using the **array()** function. Consider this example:

```
import numpy as np

array1 = np.array([2, 4, 6, 8, 10])

print(array1)

print(type(array1))
```

In the following example, let us create a 2D array with two arrays:

```
import numpy as np

array1 = np.array([[1, 3, 5], [4, 5, 6]])

print(array1)
```

NumPy Arrays provides the **ndim** attribute that tells how many dimensions the array has. Take a look at this example:

```
import numpy as np

array1 = np.array([[[1, 3, 5], [2, 4, 6]], [[3, 2, 1], [1, 2, 3]]])

print(array1.ndim)
```

Let us look at some of the important attributes of an **ndarray** object in *Table 4.1*:

`ndarray.ndim`	Gives the dimensions (axes) size of the given array
`ndarray.shape`	Gives the dimensions of the given array in a tuple format, for example, shape(n,m) implies a matrix with rows=n and columns=m
`ndarray.size`	Gives the count of elements in the given array, for example, an array (m,n) will have size of m*n
`ndarray.dtype`	Gives an object of data type of the values in the array, for example, numpy.int32, numpy.int16, and numpy.float64
`ndarray. itemsize`	Gives the size of each member of the array in bytes; performs the same operation as ndarray.dtype.itemsize; for example, an array of type float64 has itemsize 8 (=64/8)

Table 4.1: Attributes of ndarray

Let us use Numpy to solve a linear equation:

$$2x + 5y + 2z = -38$$

$$3x - 2y + 4z = 17$$

$$-6x + y - 7z = -12$$

Here is how it is solved using Numpy:

```python
import numpy as np
#A: Coefficient Matrix
A=[[2,5,2],[3,-2,4],[-6,1,-7]]
A=np.array(A)
#print(type(A))
print(A)
#B: Constant Matrix based on Solution
b=[[-38],[17],[-12]]
b=np.array(b)
#print(type(B))
print(b)
detA=np.linalg.det(A)
if detA==0:
    print("Solution is not possible!")
else:
    InvA = np.linalg.inv(A)
    C= np.matmul(InvA,b)
    print("Solution: x = {}, y= {}, z={}".format(C[[0]],C[[1]],C[[2]]))
```

The output of the preceding code is shown in *Figure 4.1*:

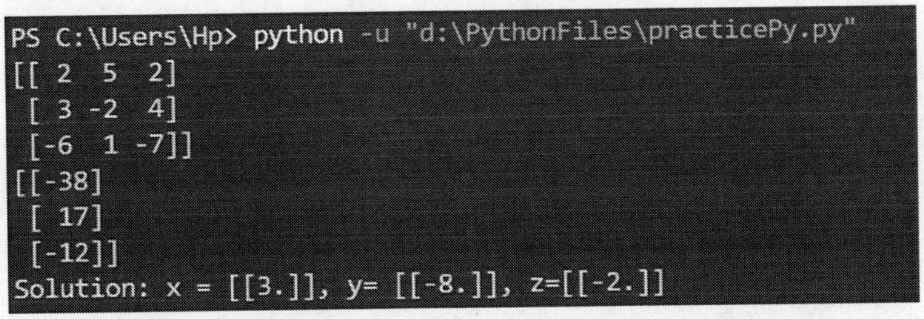

```
PS C:\Users\Hp> python -u "d:\PythonFiles\practicePy.py"
[[ 2  5  2]
 [ 3 -2  4]
 [-6  1 -7]]
[[-38]
 [ 17]
 [-12]]
Solution: x = [[3.]], y= [[-8.]], z=[[-2.]]
```

Figure 4.1: Output of linear equation

Scipy

The **scipy** library is used for scientific computing and is free and open source. To use the **scipy** library in Python, follow these steps:

1. **Install Scipy**: Run the following command in your terminal or command prompt:

   pip install scipy

2. Import the necessary **functions/classes** from **scipy**:

```
from scipy import function/class
```

Replace **function/class** with the specific function or class you want to use from **scipy**. Important subpackages available in **scipy** are listed in *Table 4.2*:

Subpackage	Description
cluster	Algorithms for clustering
constants	List of constants for physical and mathematical metrics
fftpack	Provides a list of methods for Fast Fourier Transform
integrate	Provides methods for integration and ordinary differential equation solvers
interpolate	Useful for interpolation and smoothing splines
io	Useful for input and output operations
linalg	Tools for linear algebra
ndimage	Capabilities to perform N-dimensional image processing
odr	Capabilities for orthogonal distance regression
optimize	List of optimization and root-finding routines
signal	Capabilities for performing signal processing
sparse	Capabilities to work with sparse matrices and associated routines
spatial	Capabilities to work with spatial data structures and algorithms

Table 4.2: Subpackages under Scipy

Example 4.1

Let us look at how to solve a combination problem using Scipy.

Let us take an example where we have a group of 4 girls and 6 boys; 4 children are to be selected to chair a college committee. How many ways can we select the group such that at least one boy should be in all the possibilities?

Solution: We have four options:

o   Selecting all 4 boys: 6C4

o   Selecting 3 boys and 1 girl: 6C3 × 4C1

o   Selecting 2 boys and 2 girls: 6C2 × 4C2

o   Selecting 1 boy and 3 girls: 6C1 × 4C3

It can be solved using the **Scipy.special.comb** package as follows:

```python
from scipy.special import comb

sum=0
#find combinations of 5, 2 values using comb(N, k)
#selecting 4 boys: 6C4
com = comb(6, 4, exact = False, repetition=False)
sum+=com
#selecting 3 boys and 1 girl: 6C3 × 4C1
com = comb(6, 3) * comb(4, 1)
sum+=com
#selecting 2 boys and 2 girls: 6C2 × 4C2
com = comb(6, 2) * comb(4,2)
sum+=com
#selecting 1 boy and 3 girls: 6C1 × 4C3
com = comb(6, 1) * comb(4, 3)
sum+=com
print("Total combination possible: ",sum)
```

The preceding code will generate the total combination, and the output is represented as shown in *Figure 4.2*:

```
PS C:\Users\Hp> python -u "d:\PythonFiles\practicePy.py"
Total combination possible:  209.0
```

Figure 4.2: Output of combination problem

Pandas

The Pandas package is for data extraction and preparation. Pandas is a very popular library that provides high-level data structures, which are simple to use and intuitive. It provides data structures like dataframes for handling tabular data and a wide range of functions for data manipulation.

Here is a basic guide to using Pandas in Python:

1. **Install Pandas**: Use pip or conda to install Pandas if you have not already. Open your terminal or command prompt and run the following command:

   ```
   pip install pandas
   ```

   or

   ```
   conda install pandas
   ```

2. **Import Pandas**: Import the Pandas library in your Python script or notebook using the following line of code:

```
import pandas as pd
```

3. **Reading Data**: Pandas can read data from various file formats, such as CSV, Excel, and SQL databases. Use the appropriate function, like **read_csv()**, **read_excel()**, or **read_sql()** to read the data into a dataframe. Consider this example:

```
df = pd.read_csv('data.csv')
```

Pandas has many inbuilt methods for grouping, combining data and filtering, and performing time series analysis. Pandas can easily fetch data from different sources like SQL databases, CSV, Excel, and JSON files, and manipulate the data to perform operations on it.

Example 4.2

Let us look at a demonstration of reading three datasets from GitHub and merging them:

- o **user_usage.csv**: Contains users' monthly mobile usage statistics

- o **user_device.csv**: Contains details of 'use' of the system by individuals, with dates and data from the device

- o **android_devices.csv**: Dataset with device and manufacturer data, listing all Android devices and their model codes

1. **Read CSV**: In the following code, we will use the **read_csv**() method provided by Pandas to read the CSV files from the GitHub location directly:

```
import pandas as pd
#Read the 3 csv files
d1 = pd.read_csv(r'https://raw.githubusercontent.com/swapnilsaurav/
Dataset/master/user_usage.csv')
# monthly mobile usage statistics
print(d1.head(5))
d2 = pd.read_csv(r'https://raw.githubusercontent.com/swapnilsaurav/
Dataset/master/user_device.csv')
#check the device and OS version for each user
print(d2.head(5))
d3 = pd.read_csv(r'https://raw.githubusercontent.com/swapnilsaurav/
Dataset/master/android_devices.csv')
#contains details of all Android devices with model number and
manufacturer
print(d3.head(5))
```

2. Let us look at the linking attributes between these datasets. We see that **use_id** is a common column in **user_usage** and **user_device** dataframes. Model column

of the devices and device column of the **user_device** dataset contain common codes. Now, let us form a single dataframe with columns for user usage figures (like *calls per month, sms per month, and so on*) and device information (*model, manufacturer,* and so on). Let us **merge** (or join) our sample datasets into a single dataset before performing analysis.

Let us add the device and platform columns to the **user_usage** dataframe using the merge command of Pandas:

```
#adding device and platform columns to the user_usage
result = pd.merge(d1,
                  d2[['use_id', 'platform', 'device']],
                  on='use_id')
print(result.head())
```

3. Merging requires parameters like a left dataset, a right dataset, and a common column to merge on. By default, **merge()** performs an inner merge operation. Let us start the analysis and check the sizes or shapes of inputs and outputs:

```
#Analyze the dimensions of the dataframes
print("user_usage Dimensions: ",d1.shape)
print("user_device Dimensions: ", d2[['use_id', 'platform',
                                        'device']].shape)
print("result Dimensions: ",result.shape)
```

The preceding code will give the output shown in *Figure 4.3*. It shows that final number of rows is 159 and columns is 6:

```
user_usage Dimensions:  (240, 4)
user_device Dimensions:  (272, 3)
result Dimensions:  (159, 6)
```

Figure 4.3: Output of Combination dataset

We started with 240 rows in **user_usage** and 272 rows in **user_device**, but the resultant dataframe has only 159 rows, as shown in *Figure 4.3*. Why do we see that the result differs in size from the original dataframes?

An inner merge/join keeps only the common values in the result's left and right dataframes. In this example, only the rows that contain **use_id** values that are common between **user_usage** and **user_device** remain in the result dataset. Let us validate what we just said by looking at how many values are common between the left and right datasets. The following code will display the common rows as **True**, and no match will return **False**.

```
#how many values are common
print(d1['use_id'].isin(d2['use_id']).value_counts())
```

The output of the preceding code is shown in *Figure 4.4*; we see that only 159 rows are common:

```
True        159
False        81
Name: use_id, dtype: int64
```

Figure 4.4: True indicates the number of datapoints that are common

Other Merge types

Apart from Inner Merge/ Join, other types of joins are as follows:

- **Left Merge / Left outer join**: Keep every row in the left dataframe even if the corresponding values are in the right dataset. Adds NaN/empty values for missing values of the on variable in the right dataframe.

- **Right Merge / Right outer join**: Keep every row in the right dataframe and add empty / NaN values in the output for any missing values in the left dataframe.

- **Outer Merge / Full outer join**: An outer merge or full outer join returns all the rows from the left and right dataframes, and matches up rows where possible, with NaNs elsewhere.

We can change the merge to a left-merge with the *how* parameter in merge command, as shown in the following code:

```python
#Changing the merge to a left-merge with the "how" parameter
result = pd.merge(d1,
                  d2[['use_id', 'platform', 'device']],
                  on='use_id',
                  how='left',
                  indicator =True)
result.head()
print("user_usage Dimensions: ",d1.shape)
print("result Dimensions: ",result.shape)
print(f"There are {result['device'].isnull().sum()} missing values in the
result.")
```

Let's see how to use **left_on** and **right_on** to merge with different columns.

Now, let us add the third dataframe. We will redo the first merge to get back to inner merge and then merge devices dataframe. The code is presented here:

```python
# Adding platform and device to the user usage
result = pd.merge(d1,
                  d2[['use_id', 'platform', 'device']],
                  on='use_id',
                  how='left')
# Merging on the "device" column in result
# match the "Model" column in devices (d3)
d3.rename(columns={"Retail Branding": "manufacturer"},inplace=True)
```

```
result = pd.merge(result,
                  d3[['manufacturer', 'Model']],
                  left_on='device',
                  right_on='Model',
                  how='left')
print(result.head())
```

MatPlotLib

Matplotlib is the basic plotting library for the Python programming. It is also an extension of numerical NumPy. It provides an object-oriented API for embedding plots into applications using general-purpose GUI toolkits like Tkinter.

Seaborn

The Seaborn library uses Matplotlib underneath to plot graphs. Matplotlib is preferred for basic plots, while Seaborn is used for more advanced statistical plots and provides more attractive default color palettes.

We will see MatPlotLib and Seaborn in action while building the application.

Learning the Basics of Statistics

We always have to fight for the right and useful datasets to solve business problems. Let us understand the components of a dataset. A dataset is a set of data from a study or experiment. An instance is a single row of data, and the collection of instances that share a common attribute is called dataset. Data can come in many forms, but our analysis in this chapter will rely on two primary data types: numerical and categorical. Numerical or quantitative data is any measurable data, for example, height, weight, or the phone bill cost. You should be able to perform arithmetic operations like multiplication, average, and so on. Numerical data can be of two types: discrete and continuous.

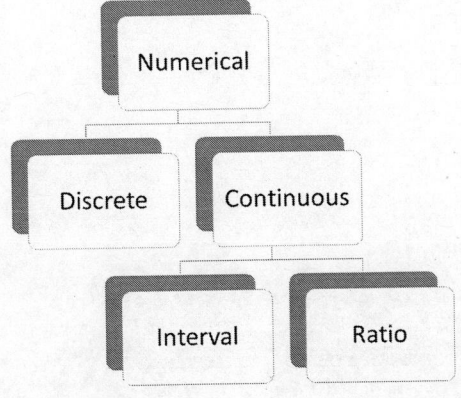

Figure 4.5: Types of numerical data

Discrete data

Discrete data is information broken up into smaller units or discrete variables. Each variable can only take on certain values (for example, 0, 1, 2, 3, 4, 5). A more practical example will be counting the cups of water required to empty a bucket.

Data can be represented using various charts. The following is an example where a stacked bar chart captures the quarterly average collection of GST from 5 cities. Let us learn to plot such a chart. Refer to *Figure 4.6* to see how a stacked bar graph looks:

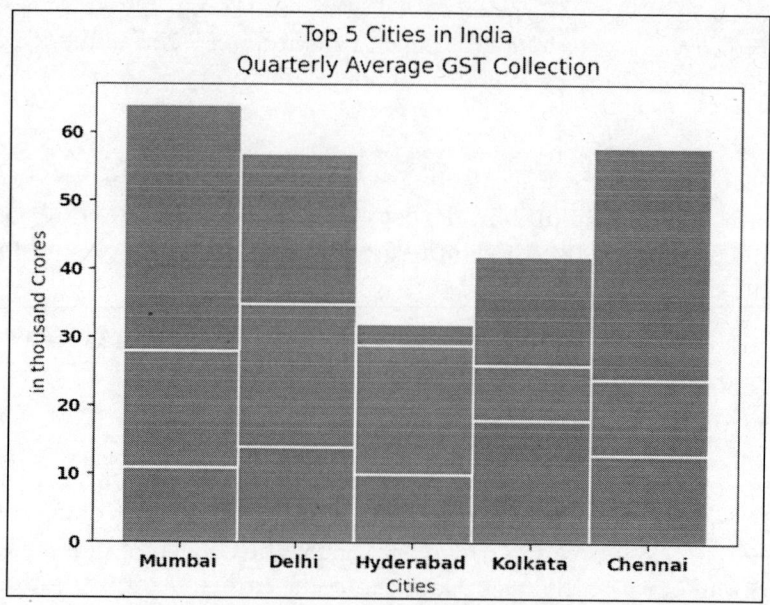

Figure 4.6: Example of stacked bar chart

Here is the Python code to generate the plot shown in *Figure 4.6*:

```python
import matplotlib.pyplot as plt
from matplotlib import rc

import numpy as np
import pandas as pd
# put y-axis in bold
rc('font', weight='bold')
# Values of each group
Y22Q1 = [11, 14, 10, 18, 13]
Y22Q2 = [17, 21, 19, 8, 11]
Y22Q3 = [36, 22, 3, 16, 34]
# Heights of bars1 + bars2
bars = np.add(Y22Q1, Y22Q2).tolist()
# Creating 5 positions for the bars on x-axis
r = [0, 1, 2, 3, 4]
```

```
# Names of group and bar width
names = ['Mumbai', 'Delhi', 'Hyderabad', 'Kolkata', 'Chennai']
barWidth = 1
# Create brown bars
plt.bar(r, Y22Q1, color='#7f6d5f', edgecolor='white', width=barWidth)
# Creating green bars (middle), on top of the first bar
plt.bar(r, Y22Q2, bottom=Y22Q1, color='#557f2d',
        edgecolor='white', width=barWidth)
# Create green bars (top)
plt.bar(r, Y22Q3, bottom=bars, color='#2d7f5e',
        edgecolor='white', width=barWidth)
# Custom X axis

plt.xticks(r, names, fontweight='bold')
plt.xlabel("Cities")
plt.ylabel("in thousand Crores")
plt.title("Quarterly Average GST Collection")
plt.suptitle("Top 5 Cities in India")
# Show graphic
plt.show()
```

Continuous data

Continuous data can take on any value within a range. Examples of continuous data include weight, temperature, time, and speed. They are measured and not counted, often represented by a continuous line graph. An example is the Cumulative Grade Point Average (CGPA) in a 5-point grading system that defines first-class students as those whose CGPA falls under 4.5 - 5.0, upper second-class as 3.50 - 4.49, lower second-class as 2.50 - 3.49, third class as 1.5 - 2.49, pass class as 1.00 - 1.49 and fails as 0.00 - 0.9. Continuous data is uncountable finite.

Continuous data can be subdivided into two types: interval and ratio data.

Interval data

Interval data is continuous quantitative data where the difference between two values has meaning. This data type is measured on an equal interval scale, meaning the difference between each set of values is consistently equal across the data set. Examples of interval data include temperature, height, and time. Interval data is numerical values that can take up only addition and subtraction operations.

For example, the temperature measured in degrees Celsius (or Fahrenheit) is considered interval data, and this temperature does not have a zero point.

Trend analysis on interval data is conducted by capturing data using an interval scale survey using the same question. It is one of the most popular analysis techniques to plot trends and insights by presenting data over a certain period. In *Figure 4.7*, let us see the 5-year percentage trend in revenue (in USD) for Infosys:

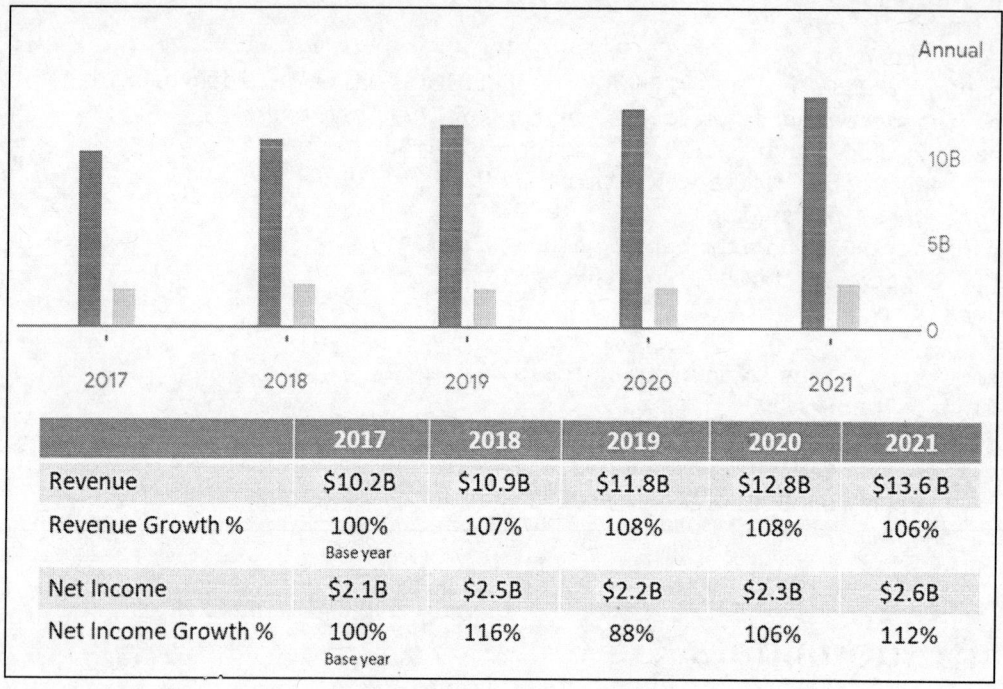

	2017	2018	2019	2020	2021
Revenue	$10.2B	$10.9B	$11.8B	$12.8B	$13.6 B
Revenue Growth %	100% Base year	107%	108%	108%	106%
Net Income	$2.1B	$2.5B	$2.2B	$2.3B	$2.6B
Net Income Growth %	100% Base year	116%	88%	106%	112%

Figure 4.7: 5-year trend example

Ratio data

Ratio data is continuous data with a zero point, for example, the temperature measured in Kelvin. Suppose we measure the temperature of two things as 10°C and 20°C, respectively; it doesn't mean that the second thing has two times higher temperature than the first one because 0°C doesn't mean the absence of temperature.

Cross-tabulation analysis technique can be a method to understand the relationship between multiple variables. The contingency table (or a crosstab) is used to establish a correlation between multiple ratio data variables in a tabular format. An example of a crosstab is shown in *Figure 4.8*. Crosstab can be used with any data level: ordinal or nominal; and it treats all data as nominal data (nominal data is not measured but categorized). For example, you can analyze the relation between two categorical variables like age and purchase made.

Figure 4.8 shows a crosstab analysis based on two questions:

- What is the age of the respondent?

- Which electronic gadgets are they likely to buy in the next 1 month?

Age	Laptop	Phone	Tablet	Digital Camera
20-25	38%	29%	31%	12%
25-30	19%	15%	24%	17%
30-35	23%	19%	11%	27%
35-40	19%	12%	9%	30%
above 40	12%	17%	5%	31%

Figure 4.8: Example of Cross Tabulation

General characteristics/features of numerical data:

- Numerical data is quantitative in nature.

- You can perform arithmetic operations like addition and multiplication.

- They can be both estimated and precise.

- The difference between each interval on a numerical data scale is equal.

- Numerical data can be visualized in different ways, depending on scatter plots, dot plots, stacked dot plots, histograms, and so on.

Categorical data (or Qualitative data)

Categorical data can be classified into distinct categories or groups, for example, gender, social class, ethnicity, and hometown. It is non-quantitative and great for grouping individuals or ideas with similar attributes, helping machine-learning models streamline data analysis.

This can be further classified as nominal and ordinal data.

Nominal data

Nominal data represents values (or categories) that can be put in any order. It represents only the individual category or name and only represents quality and not information about the size of the difference. Values have no specific order and can be written in any order. Examples of such data are as follows:

{Male, Female}

{North Zone, South Zone, East Zone, West Zone}

{Maruti, Tata Motors, Mahindra, Toyota, Ford}

Ordinal data

Ordinals are categorical where the value follows some order and we can determine the direction of the difference of a variable, but we cannot determine the size of the difference.

There is a meaning in the order, like Very Good would be greater than Good, but these are categorical because we do not know by how many times Very Good is greater than Good.

For examples, refer to the various options mentioned here:

Poor	Fair	Good	Very Good	Excellent

Table 4.3: Rating options for a training course

E	D	C	B	A

Table 4.4: Students' grade

First-Choice	Second Choice	Third Choice

Table 4.5: Preferences

We know the order in the ordinal data is like this:

Excellent > Good

The order is maintained no matter what value we assign to them. Categorical data can be summarized in a table that lists individual categories and their respective frequency count, for example, frequency distribution.

One can also use a relative frequency distribution that lists the categories and proportion with which each occurs. *Figure 4.9* depicts the frequency and relative frequency of the placement data of a business school. For example, it indicates that 73 students were placed in an accounting role, which constituted 28.9% of the entire student population.

EXAMPLE: STUDENT PLACEMENT

Area	Frequency	Relative Frequency
Accounting	73	28.9%
Finance	52	20.6%
General Management	36	14.2%
Marketing / Sales	64	25.3%
Other	28	11.1%
Total	**253**	**100%**

Figure 4.9: Frequency Distribution Table

Frequency and relative frequency distributions can also be summarized as bar and pie charts, respectively. Refer to *Figure 4.10* for the visualization:

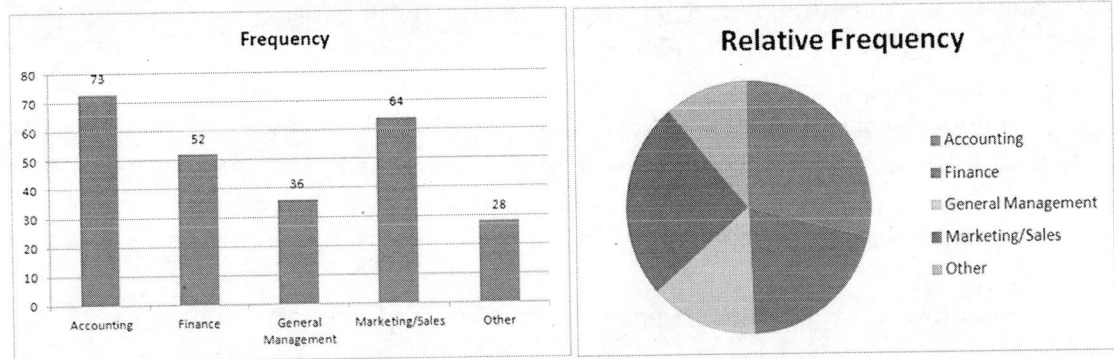

Figure 4.10: Bar graph and pie chart from frequency distribution table

Visualization for Data Analysis

In this section, we will learn to use Matplotlib and Seaborn to visualize the data. The first plot we will discuss is scatter plot. A scatter plot shows the relationship between two datasets represented on the X and Y axes. They can be used to show trends, clusters, patterns, and relationships in a cloud of data points, especially a very large one.

Problem: What causes Job Stress for Managers in Software Industry?

Software engineers experience psychosocial work stress that may negatively affect physical and mental health over time. A researcher wants to study the impact of various factors on job stress for managers working in the software industry. They have identified three factors, family support, work-family conflict, and sleep, that can impact stress levels. They worked with 3683 respondents and documented the findings in **JobStressData. csv**. They want to check if these factors can help us predict software engineers' stress levels. Let us analyze the data using Python. Refer to the following steps:

1. **Define the problem**

   Presented here are a few examples of the problem statement. You can develop your problem statements based on questions like the following:

   a. Which factors help us influence the stress levels of managers in the software industry?

   b. Can we predict the stress levels of managers working in the software industry based on family support, work-family conflict and sleep as factors?

2. **Get the data**

   We are going to use the **JobStressData.csv** file. You can download the file from the given GitHub location. First, let us understand which libraries we need to use. If you do not have them, you can install them using the **pip** command. Refer to *Chapter 3, Top Extensions in VS Code for Python*, for more details.

The code shows the libraries that are required to plot, including **numpy**, **pandas**, **scipy**, **matplotlib** and **seaborn**:

```python
import numpy as np
import pandas as pd

from scipy import stats
import matplotlib.pyplot as plt
import seaborn as sns


from scipy.stats import pearsonr
```

Let us read the data into the Pandas dataframe:

```python
data = pd.read_csv("dataset/JobStressData.csv")
print(data.shape)  # shows number of rows, columns
```

The **JobStressData.csv** dataset is on GitHub to download.

3. **Data cleaning**

The next step would be to clean and read the relevant data. The given dataset has data for both managers and non-managers, so let us filter to get only the manager-relevant data.

Let us summarize the data to find the types of data we have. If the DataFrame contains numerical data, the description contains this information for each column:

   a. **count**: The number of not-empty values

   b. **mean**: The average (mean) value

   c. **std**: The standard deviation

   d. **min**: the minimum value

   e. **25%**: The 25% percentile*

   f. **50%**: The 50% percentile*

   g. **75%**: The 75% percentile*

   h. **max**: The maximum value

The following code will summarize the data after filtering based on role value of **Manager**:

```python
summary = data.describe()
print(summary)

# Filter the data for job role = MANAGER
manager_df = data.loc[data['Role'] == "MANAGER"]

manager_df = manager_df.drop('Role',axis=1)
```

```
print(manager_df.corr())
```

Figure 4.11 shows the correlation coefficient between all the columns. This is the output from the preceding code:

	FamilySupportScore	WorkFamilyConflict	Sleep	JobStress
FamilySupportScore	1.000000	0.263975	-0.029655	0.340277
WorkFamilyConflict	0.263975	1.000000	-0.118527	0.588248
Sleep	-0.029655	-0.118527	1.000000	-0.013498
JobStress	0.340277	0.588248	-0.013498	1.000000

Figure 4.11: *Correlation coefficient between various factors*

The last line prints the correlation coefficient between all the columns. The coefficient of correlation is a statistical metric to find the strength of a linear relationship between two variables. Coefficient values can range from -1 to 1. When the correlation coefficient is -1, it describes a perfect negative, inverse correlation, with values in one series rising as those in the other decline, and vice versa. A coefficient of 1 shows a perfect positive correlation or a direct relationship, and a coefficient value of 0 means there is no linear relationship.

In the dataset we have, most of the values are between -0.5 and +0.5, indicating there is no or very little correlation between these factors.

4. **Analyze the data**

   We can represent the preceding data using **heatmap**. A **heatmap** is a plot that shows the magnitude of a phenomenon as color in two dimensions. The color variation may be by hue or intensity. The following code shows how to plot a heatmap using the **seaborn** library.

   ```
   # plotting the heatmap for correlation
   ax = sns.heatmap(manager_df.corr(), annot=True)
   plt.show()
   ```

   The heatmap output from the preceding code is plotted in *Figure 4.12*:

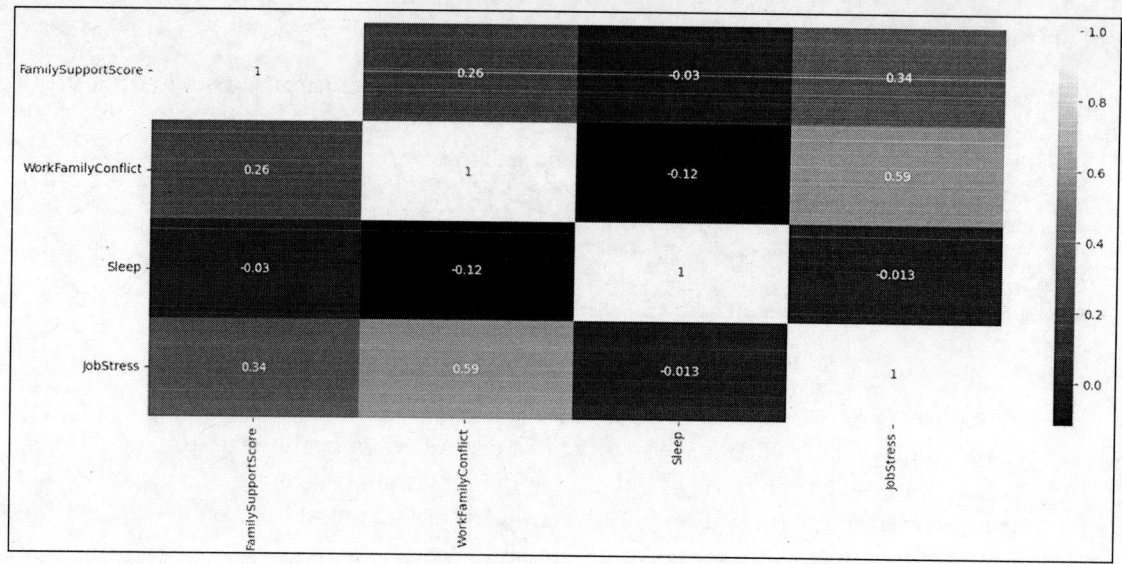

Figure 4.12: Heat map of correlation values

In a **scatter plot**, the independent variable is plotted on the x-axis, and the dependent variable is plotted on the y-axis. Scatter plots show the extent of correlation, if it exists, between the attributes. Let's plot using the following code:

```
# Scatterplot
ax = sns.scatterplot(x="WorkFamilyConflict", y="JobStress",
data=manager_df)
ax.set_title("Job Stress vs. Work-Family Conflict")
ax.set_xlabel("Work-Family Conflict")
plt.show()
```

The preceding code generates the scatter plot shown in *Figure 4.13*:

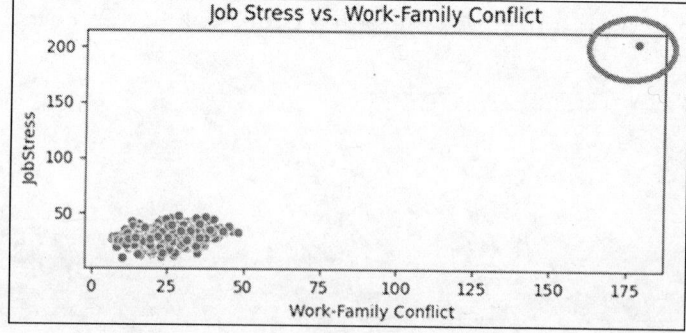

Figure 4.13: Scatter plot of Job Stress versus Work family Conflict

In *Figure 4.13*, we can see that there is one very high value that is not giving us a good view of the entire data. This is an outlier value. Let us remove this value and plot the values again. There will be an impact on the correlation value; we will see that later in this section:

```
# Let's use .loc to restrict values of 'WorkFamilyConflict' displayed
manager_df = manager_df.loc[manager_df['WorkFamilyConflict'].
between(0, 70)]
ax = sns.scatterplot(x="WorkFamilyConflict", y="JobStress",
data=manager_df)
ax.set_title("Job Stress vs. Work-Family Conflict")
ax.set_xlabel("Work-Family Conflict")
plt.show()
```

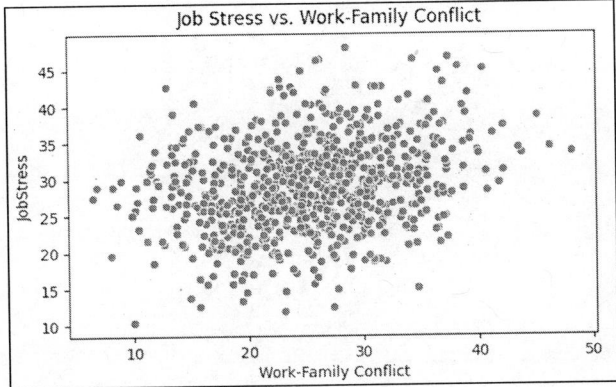

Figure 4.14: *Scatter plot of Job Stress versus Work family Conflict after removing the outlier value*

Figure 4.14 shows the updated scatter plot. We can see a slightly positive trend but not big enough to conclude that there is a high positive correlation value. Later, we will calculate the Pearson Correlation constant to check the value, as indicated in *Figure 4.18*. Before that, we will also learn to plot the best-fit line and see the trend.

5. **Visualize the data**

    As discussed earlier, a scatter plot visualizes the correlation concept. Let us see the possible types of correlation shown by a scatter plot. Refer to *Figure 4.15* to know the behavior of correlation:

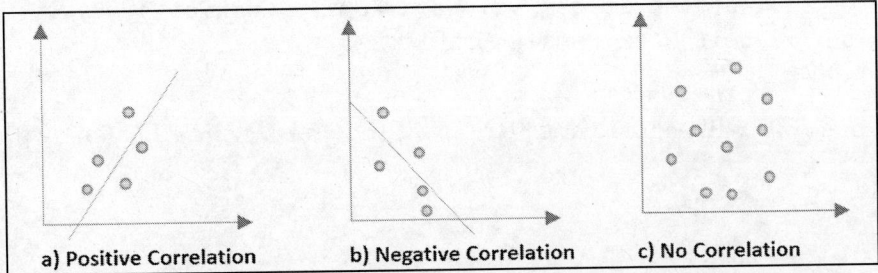

Figure 4.15: *Types of Correlation shown by Scatter plots*

Best-fit line gives a trend based on all the scatter plot points. Let us see the Python code for plotting the scatter plot along with the best-fit line below:

```
# Adding a best fit line
sns.lmplot(x="WorkFamilyConflict", y="JobStress", data=manager_df)
ax.set_title("Job Stress vs. Work-Family Conflict")
ax.set_xlabel("Work-Family Conflict")
plt.show()
```

Figure 4.16 shows the scatter plot with the best-fit line:

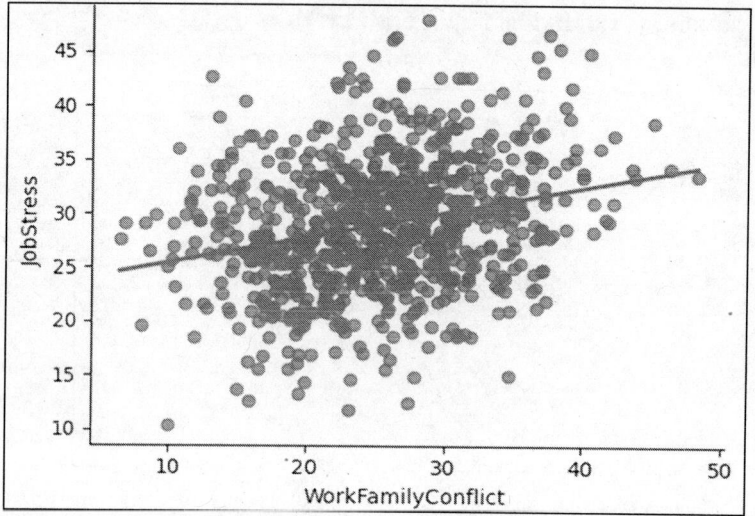

Figure 4.16: *Scatter plot with best-fit line for WorkFamilyConflict v JobStress*

There is a small positive trend visible in the best-fit line shown in the scatter plot in figure 4.16. Let us add a third dimension as a hue to the scatter plot. Hue is to group similar attributes and represent them in the same color. The following code use Hue concept to group similar values using this Python code:

```
# Adding FamilySupportScore as a third dimension
sns.lmplot(x="WorkFamilyConflict", y="JobStress",
           hue="FamilySupportScore", data=manager_df)
ax.set_title("Job Stress vs. Work-Family Conflict")
ax.set_xlabel("Work-Family Conflict")
plt.show()
```

The preceding code will result in a scatter plot as shown in *Figure 4.17* along with the Hue value:

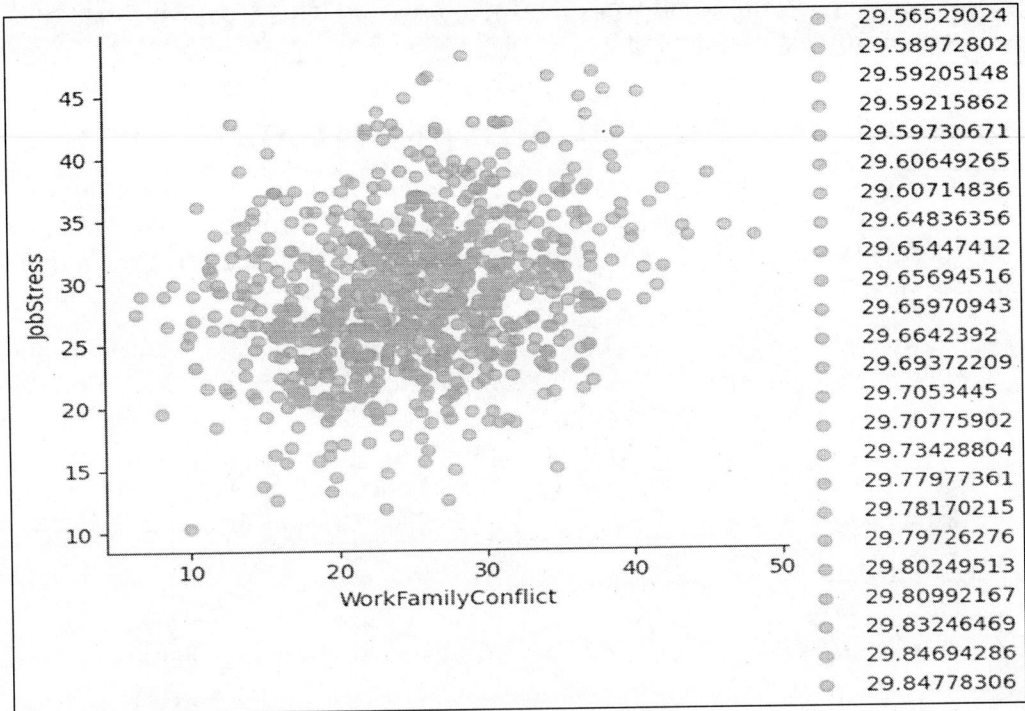

Figure 4.17: Scatter plot with Hue

6. **Summarize the outcome**

   Pearson correlation coefficient is also known as Pearson's r. It is a measure of linear correlation between two given variables. Calculated as the ratio between the covariance of two variables and the product of their standard deviations, it is essentially a normalized measurement of the covariance. The result will always have a value between −1 and 1. Let us calculate the Pearson's correlation of our dataset:

```
# Coefficient of correlation
from scipy.stats import pearsonr
corr, _ = pearsonr(manager_df['JobStress'], manager_df['WorkFamilyConflict'])
print('Pearsons correlation: %.3f' % corr)
```

Figure 4.18 shows the correlation value to be around 0.265:

```
Pearsons correlation: 0.265
```

Figure 4.18: Correlation value for WorkFamilyConflict v JobStress

Earlier while plotting the heatmap, it was 0.588 but removing that one outlier value reduced the correlation value to 0.265. Such a low value (less than 0.5) indicates an extremely weak correlation between job stress and work-family conflict and it is not possible to predict job stress based on work-family conflict.

Data analysis and Business outcome

In the previous example, we created and analyzed a problem with a scatter plot. Another plot that is widely used in data analytics is histogram. We discussed frequency distribution and seen a small example in demonstrated in the plot in *Figure 4.9*. Let us simulate a business problem where we will use a histogram to solve it:

1. Let us assume you are the marketing manager of a large telephone service provider. You want to analyze your customers' international call charges, so you randomly select 200 customers and note their monthly bill amount. You want to extract meaningful data to help you make strategic decisions for the company. Let us look at the data by reading through Python code and later analyze my approach for the analysis.

2. **Get the data**

   The dataset has been uploaded to the GitHub location mentioned earlier. The numbers are in US$. Let's use Python code to read the dataset as Pandas dataframe:

```python
import numpy as np
arr = np.loadtxt("D:/dataset/HistogramData.csv",
                delimiter=",", dtype=float)
print(arr)
```

Figure 4.19 shows a part of the dataset:

```
[ 42.19   38.45   29.23   89.35 118.04 110.46    0.     72.88   83.05   95.73
 103.15   94.52   26.84   93.93   90.26   72.78 101.36 104.8    74.01   56.01
  39.21   48.54   93.31 104.88   30.61   22.57   63.7  104.84    6.45   16.47
  89.5    13.36   44.16   92.97   99.56   92.62   78.89   87.71   93.57    0.
   8.37    7.18   11.07    1.47   26.4    13.26   21.13   95.03   29.04    5.42
  77.21   72.47    0.      5.64    6.48    6.95   19.6     8.11    9.01   84.77
  75.71   88.62   99.5    85.      0.      8.41    3.2     1.62   91.1    10.88
```

Figure 4.19: Sample from the dataset

3. **Exploratory data analysis**

   There is very little information we can get by reading 200 observations. You will probably notice that the highest value is $119.63 and the lowest is 0.0, but this is not enough to make any meaningful decision. You can construct a frequency distribution and then a histogram plot from it. Let's look at the code for constructing the histogram:

```python
import matplotlib.pyplot as plt
#create bin
```

```
bin = [10 * i for i in range(13)]
# plot histogram
plt.hist(arr, bin)
plt.show()
```

Refer to *Figure 4.20* for how the histogram would look with the data we have:

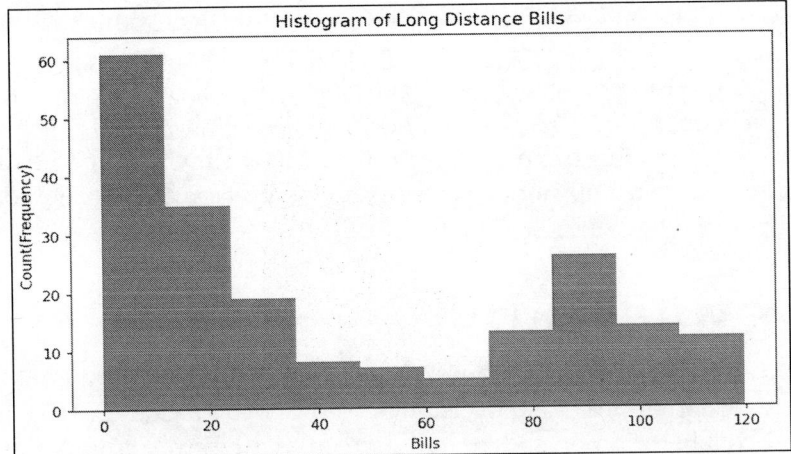

Figure 4.20: Histogram

4. **Observation**

Histogram gives a clear view of how observations are distributed. Let us divide the customers into three groups: i) small – those whose bill is less than $30, ii) medium – those whose bill is between $30 and $90, and iii) high – those whose bill is above $90. Refer to *Figure 4.21* to see the different groups we have created:

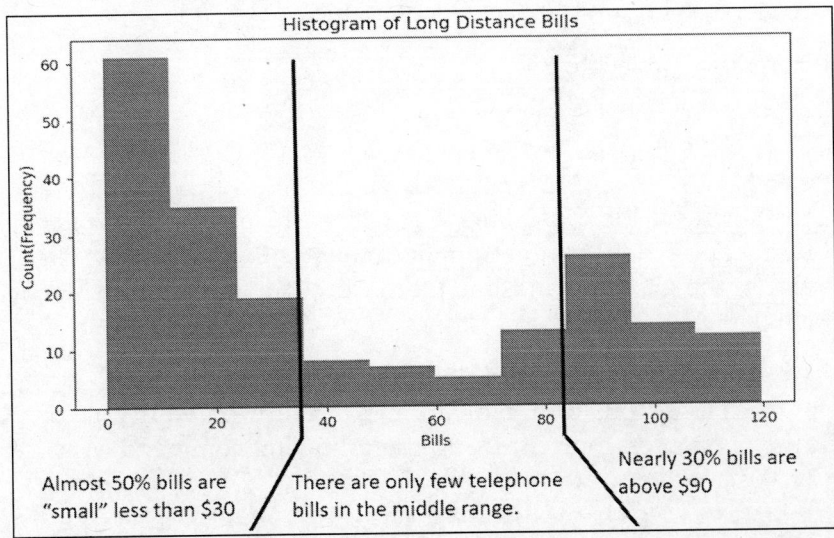

Figure 4.21: Observation of data points from Histogram plot

5. **Interpretation**

It requires domain knowledge to interpret such results. Let us suppose the same data was being analyzed by the marketing manager of a retail store; they would be disappointed to know that only 30% of their customers shop big. They would make plans like **Buy One Get One** (**BOGO**) to encourage customers to move from small to medium and to high-value purchases. But since in this case we are talking about a telephone service provider, their focus will be these high customers. These high-paying customers are easy targets for their competitors to snatch away by offering cheaper plans. So, for a telecom provider, the priority is to move these high bills payers into the medium group to retain them in the business. That is precisely why you will notice so many plans by companies; the goal is to offer something for everyone.

Working with GitHub

GitHub is a cloud-based application providing services for storing and sharing source code with fellow programmers. Using Visual Studio Code (VS Code) with GitHub allows for sharing and collaboration on source code directly within the editor. One can interact with GitHub in multiple ways, for example, via their website at **github.com** or the Git **Command-Line Interface** (**CLI**). But by using the GitHub pull requests and issues extension, one can directly work with GitHub from the editor. In this section, we will learn the following:

- How to add an existing VS Code project to git and GitHub

- How to do commit and push whenever changes happen

- How to clone an existing project from GitHub to VS Code

- How to remove project to git

Let us get started:

1. **Install Git**

VS Code leverages local installation of Git, so the users need to install Git before performing any action. Minimum requirement is to have at least Git 2.0.0 version. We will use the git command-line interface, which can be downloaded from the following:

https://git-scm.com/book/en/v2/Getting-Started-Installing-Git

Follow the instructions to download and install it on your Mac or PC. You can check the version of your Git using the following command. Any version more than 2.0.0 is good for us to continue:

```
C:\Users\Hp>git --version
git version 2.39.0.windows.1
```

Figure 4.22: Check the Git version

2. **Create a GitHub account**

   Go to *github.com* and sign up if you do not have an account already:

Figure 4.23: Creating new account on Github

3. **Create a repository on GitHub**

   Now we create a repository for our project. On the top left, you will see the **New** button; click on it. You can do the same by clicking on the + sign in the top-right corner and then clicking **New repository**.

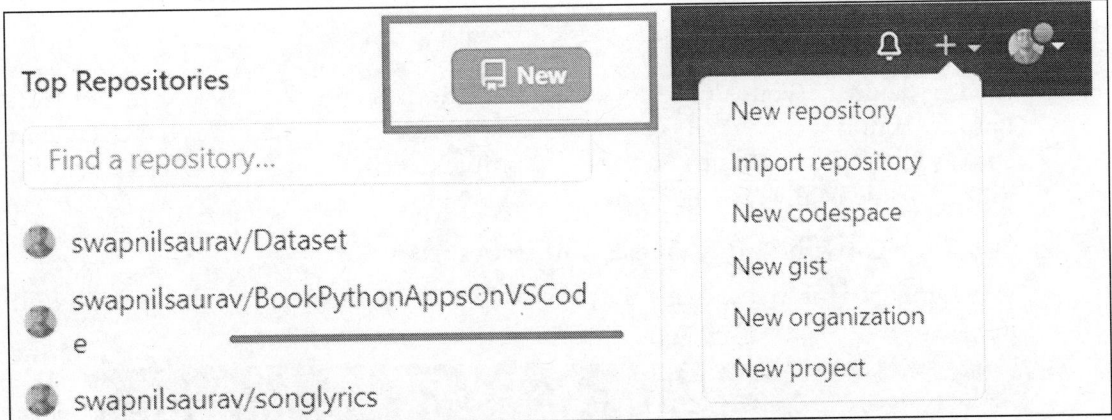

Figure 4.24: Showing two options to create a new repository

This will open the form to add values to create the repository, as shown in *Figure 4.25*:

Create a new repository

A repository contains all project files, including the revision history. Already have a project repository elsewhere? Import a repository.

Owner *   Repository name *

   swapnilsaurav ▾   /

Great repository names are short and memorable. Need inspiration? How about crispy-train?

Description (optional)

⦿ 🖥 **Public**
    Anyone on the internet can see this repository. You choose who can commit.

○ 🔒 **Private**
    You choose who can see and commit to this repository.

Initialize this repository with:
Skip this step if you're importing an existing repository.

☐ **Add a README file**
    This is where you can write a long description for your project. Learn more.

Figure 4.25: Add details to create a new repository

Give a name to your repository; a description is optional. Select the default **Public** option so that it can be shared with everyone. We have created **BookPythonAppsOnVSCode** for our examples. Initializing the project with a README file is always a good practice.

4. Install the **GitHub Pull Requests and Issues** extension:

Accessing GitHub without leaving VS Code becomes easier with the GitHub Pull Requests and Issues extension.

Figure 4.26: Github Pull Requests and Issues Extension

We already discussed how to install extensions in the previous chapter. Follow the same steps that we discussed in *Chapter 3, Top Extensions in VS Code for Python*, for installing extensions for VS Code, and install the **GitHub Pull Requests** and **Issues** extension on your VS Code editor.

First, one has to sign into the **GitHub Pull Requests and Issues** extension. You can log in by following the prompts to authenticate with GitHub in the browser and return to VS Code. Authentication can also be done by adding an authorization token manually. The authorization token can be in the browser window; copy this token and switch back to VS Code. Select **Signing into github.com** in the status bar, paste the token, and hit **Enter**.

How to set up a repository?

A user can set up a repository by searching for and cloning a repository from GitHub using the **Git: Clone** command in the Command Palette (*Ctrl+Shift+P*). It can also be done by clicking the **Clone Repository** button in the **source control** view. The **source control** view will show up only when you have no folder open. Refer to *Figure 4.27*:

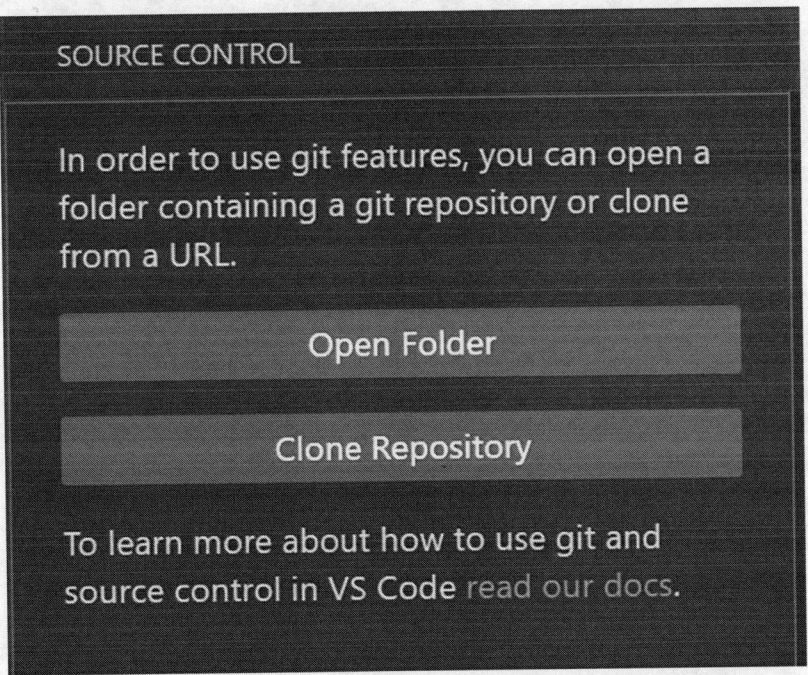

Figure 4.27: Connecting to Github repository

Filter and pick the repository cloned locally from the GitHub repository dropdown or directly type the path. If you have not logged into GitHub from VS Code earlier, you will be prompted to authenticate with your GitHub account before proceeding. You can provide the repository URL directly or search GitHub for the repository you want by typing in the text box. *Figure 4.27* indicates the place where you need to add the repository location:

Figure 4.28: Typing the Github repository location

The VS Code window will reload the repository once you have selected a repository or made a pull request. You will see the repository contents in the **File Explorer**. Now, you can open files (with full syntax highlighting and bracket matching), make edits if required, and commit changes, much like you would working on a local repository clone. Refer to the following figure:

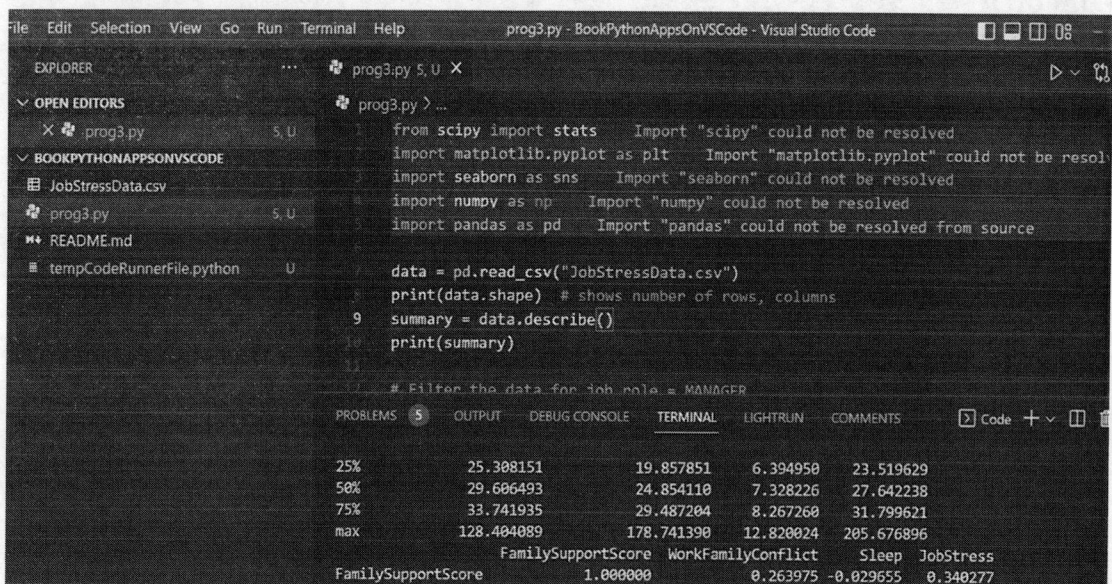

Figure 4.29: Saving program directly to the Github remote repository

However, there is one difference you will notice here. When a change is committed with the GitHub repository extension installed in VS Code, the changes are pushed directly to the remote repository, similar to working in the GitHub web interface. Another feature of the GitHub repositories extension is that every time you open a repository or branch, you are presented with the up-to-date sources available from GitHub. This eliminates the need to remember to make a pull to refresh, as we would do with a local repository. Refer to *Figure 4.30*:

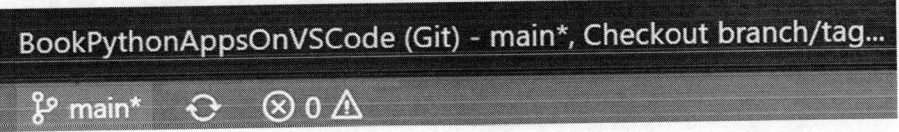

Figure 4.30: *Github branch indication*

VS Code provides another advantage: we can easily switch between branches by clicking on the branch indicator in the status bar, without needing to stash uncommitted changes. The extension remembers the changes and reapplies them when you switch branches.

Sometimes you will want to switch to working on a repository in a development environment with support for a local file system and full language and development tooling. The GitHub repositories extension makes it easy for you to do the following:

- Clone the repository locally

- Create a GitHub codespace, if there is the GitHub codespaces extension

- Clone the repository into a Docker container, if you have Docker and the Microsoft Docker extension installed

Conclusion

We have come to the end of the chapter! We found it interesting to write this chapter as we love working through data and making sense of it. We reviewed some Python concepts, like Numpy, Scipy, Pandas, and Matplotlib. We also introduced you to basic statistical concepts and helped you learn to plot using Matplotlib. We analyzed sample datasets to practice two important data analytics concepts: scatter plot and histogram. In the last section, you learned to use GitHub with VS Code.

In the next chapter, we will see how to connect to Databases from Python and develop a desktop-based application. You will also be introduced to MYSQL concepts and learn to debug a Python program on VS Code.

Join our book's Discord space

Join the book's Discord Workspace for Latest updates, Offers, Tech happenings around the world, New Release and Sessions with the Authors:

https://discord.bpbonline.com

## CHAPTER 5

Developing Desktop Application using Database

Errors using inadequate data are much less than those using no data at all.
— Charles Babbage

Introduction

This chapter will teach us to develop an application using database skills. Databases are an important part of any application and provide a way of storing and managing efficient and secure data. This chapter will explore the fundamentals of working with a database application.

Database design is the process of creating a detailed data model of a database. It defines the logical structure of a database and determines how data will be stored, organized, and accessed. Database design involves classifying data and identifying relationships among the data items. The goal of database design is to produce a model that correctly represents the data and is flexible, efficient, and easy to maintain.

We will look at the different types of databases, the different ways of accessing them using Python, and the tools Python provides to manage the database. We will also examine the basics of designing and implementing a database application. Finally, we will discuss the importance of testing and maintaining a database application.

Structure

In this chapter, we will discuss the following topics:

- Database introduction and RDBMS

- Problem statement: Developing an application

- Working with MYSQL

- Executing the Project: Performing CRUD operations

- Debugging in VS Code

Database introduction and RDBMS

A database is a data collection organized for easy storage, access, and manipulation. It is usually managed by a **Database Management System** (**DBMS**), which provides users with a systematic way to create, retrieve, update, and manage data. The data in a database is typically organized into tables, fields, and records.

There are different types of databases in use; some of them are as follows:

- **Relational database**: This type of database stores data in structured tables with rows and columns. It follows a predefined schema and uses **Structured Query Language** (**SQL**) for querying and managing data. Examples include Oracle, MySQL, and SQL Server.

- **Object-oriented database**: This type of database stores data in objects, which can contain both data and behavior. It is useful for storing complex, interconnected data structures and supports inheritance and polymorphism. Examples include MongoDB and Couchbase.

- **Hierarchical database**: This type of database organizes data in a tree-like structure, with parent-child relationships between data elements. It is mainly used for storing hierarchical data, such as file systems. Examples include IBM's **Information Management System** (**IMS**) and Windows Registry.

- **Network database**: This type of database stores data with complex relationships, using a network data model. It is similar to the hierarchical database but enables more flexible relationships between data elements. Examples include **Integrated Data Store** (**IDS**) and **Integrated Definition Language** (**IDL**).

- **NoSQL database**: This term refers to a class of databases that do not adhere to a strict tabular structure, like in relational databases. NoSQL databases are designed for scalability, high performance, and handling unstructured and semi-structured data. Some popular types of NoSQL databases are document databases (example,

MongoDB), key-value stores (example, Redis), columnar databases (example, Cassandra), and graph databases (example, Neo4j).

- **Time-series database**: This type of database is optimized for handling time series data, which is data that is recorded with a timestamp. It is commonly used in fields like financial services, IoT, and log analysis to store and analyze large volumes of time-stamped data efficiently. Examples include InfluxDB and TimescaleDB.

- **Graph database**: This type of database is designed to store and analyze highly interconnected data, such as social networks, recommendation engines, and fraud detection systems. It stores data as nodes (entities) and edges (relationships), allowing efficient traversal and querying of complex relationships. Examples include Neo4j and Amazon Neptune.

- **Spatial database**: This type of database is specialized for storing and querying spatial or geographic data. It supports indexing and analysis of 2D and 3D data types, such as points, lines, polygons, and spatial relationships. Examples include PostGIS and Oracle Spatial.

- **In-memory database**: This type of database stores data entirely in memory, rather than on disk, for faster access and processing. It is used in situations where speed is crucial, such as real-time analytics and high-speed trading. Examples include SAP HANA and VoltDB.

- **Cloud database**: This term refers to databases that are hosted and provided as a service through a cloud computing platform. These databases are scalable, highly available, and accessible from anywhere via the internet. Popular examples include **Amazon Web Services (AWS)** RDS, Microsoft Azure Cosmos DB, and Google Cloud Firestore.

In this chapter, we will develop an application with **Relational Database Management Systems (RDBMS)**. RDBMSes are used to store and manage data in structured tables. They are popular because they offer the ability to easily query data, join data from multiple tables, and enforce data integrity. They also offer features such as transactions, data security, and scalability. Relational databases are used in many applications, such as financial systems, customer relationship management systems, and e-commerce sites.

Some of the popular RDBMS databases are as follows:

- Oracle

- MySQL

- Microsoft SQL Server

- PostgreSQL

- IBM DB2

- MariaDB

- Sybase

- Informix

- Firebird

- Apache Derby

In this chapter, we will develop a working **Library Management System (LibMS)**, with MYSQL database as the back end. MySQL is an open-source **Relational Database Management System (RDBMS)** that uses **Structured Query Language (SQL)** to add, access, and manage data. It is one of the most popular databases in the world and is used in a wide range of applications, from small web applications to large enterprise applications. Many popular websites, including Facebook, Google, Twitter, and YouTube, also use MySQL.

Problem statement: Developing an application

Before we begin building the application, let us understand the requirements. A **Library Management System (LMS)** is software used to track items in a library, such as books, periodicals, audio-visual materials, and electronic documents. It provides a centralized system for cataloguing, organizing, and tracking library materials and managing library materials' circulation to library patrons. Library management systems automate library activities and processes, such as cataloguing and circulating materials. In this example, we will develop a mini LMS system with the following options:

- BOOK ISSUE

- BOOK DEPOSIT

- ADMINISTRATION MENU

    o CREATE STUDENT RECORD

    o DISPLAY ALL STUDENTS RECORD

    o DISPLAY SPECIFIC STUDENT RECORD

    o MODIFY STUDENT RECORD

    o DELETE STUDENT RECORD

    o CREATE BOOK

    o DISPLAY ALL BOOKS

    o DISPLAY SPECIFIC BOOK

o   MODIFY BOOK

o   DELETE BOOK RECORD

- EXIT

Let us build an application to implement these features. This is a comparatively large application to build. We must follow a standard practice to ensure that we develop the application within the given timeline and cost and also ensure good quality.

We will follow these steps:

1. **Break the application into components**: Start by breaking it into parts and understanding how they interact. This will help you map out the application's structure and identify which parts require the most development effort. In this application, we will break the design into the following subcomponents:

    a. Create the menu for the user.

    b. Create the database objects required to handle the back end of the system.

    c. Create the required classes and modules that will implement the features.

2. **Identify user scenarios**: Consider how users interact with the application and identify key user scenarios. This will help you understand which features will be the most important for your application and help you prioritize development efforts. We have already created this for our example in the problem statement section.

3. **Design the architecture**: Design an architecture for the application that will scale and be easy to maintain. This includes making design decisions about technology, hosting, databases, and other core components. In our example, database design becomes important, so we will spend some time doing that in the next section.

4. **Develop the application**: Once the architecture is designed, start developing the application in stages. This will help you identify any problems early on and make changes as needed. Write the code for each of the features identified.

5. **Test the application**: Test the application thoroughly before releasing it to users. This will help ensure that the application is stable and any bugs are identified and fixed.

6. **Monitor and maintain the application**: Monitor the application regularly and make changes as necessary. This will help keep the application running smoothly and ensure that any new features or changes are implemented correctly.

Now that we understand the various steps, let us dive into them.

Developing the solution

We have created a file named **MyLMS.py**, which will be our main file. Let us first build the **Menu**, and then we will connect the different functions and methods to them. We will use the infinite loop concept (**while==True**) till the user wants to keep running the menu:

```python
def adminmenu():
    print("\n\nADMIN MENU")
    print("Select the Option from below:")
    print("\n\tAdmin 1. CREATE STUDENT")
    print("\tAdmin 2. DISPLAY ALL STUDENTS")
    print("\tAdmin 3. DISPLAY SPECIFIC STUDENT")
    print("\tAdmin 4. MODIFY STUDENT RECORD")
    print("\tAdmin 5. DELETE STUDENT RECORD")
    print("\n\tAdmin 6. CREATE BOOK")
    print("\tAdmin 7. DISPLAY ALL BOOKS")
    print("\tAdmin 8. DISPLAY SPECIFIC BOOK")
    print("\tAdmin 9. MODIFY BOOK RECORD")
    print("\tAdmin 10. DELETE BOOK RECORD")
    print("\tAdmin 11. TAKE BACK TO THE MAIN MENU")
    adminchoice = input("Enter your choice from the above: ")
    if adminchoice == "1":
        return True
    elif adminchoice == "2":
        return True
    elif adminchoice == "3":
        return True
    elif adminchoice == "4":
        return True
    elif adminchoice == "5":
        return True
    elif adminchoice == "6":
        return True
    elif adminchoice == "7":
        return True
    elif adminchoice == "8":
        return True
    elif adminchoice == "9":
        return True
    elif adminchoice == "10":
        return True
    elif adminchoice == "11":
        return False
    else:
        print("Invalid Choice. Try again!")
        return True
```

```python
def menu():
    print("\n\n\n LIBRARY MANAGEMENT SYSTEM")
    print("Select the Option from below:")
    print("\n\tOption 1. BOOK ISSUE")
    print("\tOption 2. BOOK DEPOSIT")
    print("\tOption 3. ADMIN MENU")
    print("\tOption 4. DISPLAY OUT BOOKS")
    print("\tOption 5. EXIT")
    mainchoice = input("Enter your choice from the above: ")
    if mainchoice == "1":
        return True
    elif mainchoice == "2":
        return True
    elif mainchoice == "3":
        adm_cont = True
        while adm_cont:
            adm_cont = adminmenu()
        # Admin menu exited but still in main menu
        menu()
    elif mainchoice == "4":
        return True
    elif mainchoice == "5":
        return False
    else:
        print("Invalid Option Try Agin!")
        return True


# calling mainmenu
cont = True
while cont:
    cont = menu()
```

Database design

Database design includes the organization of data according to the business requirement. The database designer determines what data must be stored and how these elements interrelate. One of the widely used tools for database design is the **Entity Relationship (ER) diagram**. An **Entity-Relationship Diagram (ERD)** visually represents different data using standardized symbols and connectors. It illustrates the relationships between entities, which are used to describe the structure of a database. ERDs are used to model and design relational databases, which organize data into tables that can be linked through relationships.

Here is how to create an ERD:

- **Identify the entities and their relationships**: Start by brainstorming for a list of all the major entities involved in the problem domain. These could include people, places, organizations, or other things. For each entity, identify the related entities and their relationships.

- **Determine the attributes of the entities**: For each entity, determine the attributes that describe it and the data that needs to be stored.

- **Create a diagram**: Once the entities and their relationships have been identified, draw the diagram using a tool like Microsoft Visio.

- **Validate the diagram**: Check it to ensure that it accurately reflects the entities, attributes, and relationships identified.

- **Refine the diagram**: Make any changes to the diagram based on feedback from stakeholders or other domain experts.

Let us build ERD for our example:

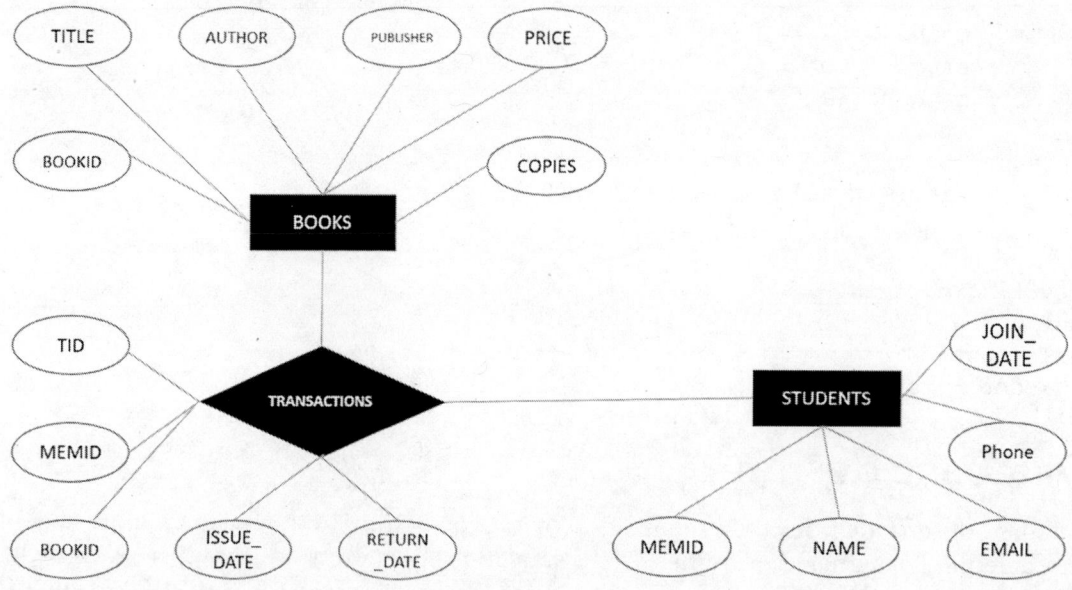

Figure 5.1: ER diagram for a simple Library Management System

Creating tables and adding Constraints

Now, convert ER diagram to table objects by following the given steps:

1. Identify the entities in the diagram

We need to create three tables:

    a. A table to store books information

    b. A table to store students' information

    c. A table to store transaction details to record who borrowed or returned the book and when

2. Create a table for each entity and assign appropriate data types to the columns.

Let us create three tables, as shown here:

BOOKS	STUDENTS	TRANSACTIONS
BOOKID - Integer	MEMER ID – Integer	TID – Integer
TITLE - Text	NAME – Text	BOOKID – Integer
AUTHOR - Text	EMAIL – Text	MEMBER ID – Integer
PUBLISHER - Text	PHONE – Text	ISSUE_DATE – Date
PRICE - Real	JOIN_DATE - DATE	RETURN_DATE - Date
COPIES - Smallint		

Table 5.1: List of tables and their columns

These are the minimum set of columns to design our database effectively.

3. Identify the relationships in the diagram.

Tables BOOKS and STUDENTS may not be directly related here, but the TRANSACTIONS table needs to connect to BOOKS and STUDENTS to make sure relevant information is only saved as transactions.

4. Create foreign keys in the appropriate tables to represent the relationships.

In this example, only TRANSACTIONS table will have foreign keys. BOOKID should be linked to BOOKS.BOOKID, and MEMBERID should be linked to STUDENTS.MEMBERID.

5. Generate the table objects in your database using the appropriate SQL commands.

Table 1: To store students' information.

Name: STUDENTS

Columns: MemberID, Name, Email, Phone, **JOIN_DATE** (Default today's)

SQL Query to **Create Table STUDENTS**:

```
CREATE TABLE STUDENTS(MEMID INTEGER PRIMARY KEY,
NAME VARCHAR2(30),
EMAIL VARCHAR2(25),
PHONE VARCHAR2(12),
JOIN_DATE DATE DEFAULT (CURRENT_DATE))
```

6. Add initial set of data if available.

Let us add some data to both the **STUDENTS** and **BOOKS** tables so that we have some data to begin working with:

```
INSERT INTO STUDENTS(NAME,EMAIL,PHONE) VALUES('Sachin','sachin@
email.com','346377');

INSERT INTO STUDENTS(NAME,EMAIL,PHONE) VALUES('Virat','virat@email.
com','544343466');

INSERT INTO STUDENTS(NAME,EMAIL,PHONE) VALUES('Dhoni','dhoni@email.
com','5645654');

INSERT INTO STUDENTS(NAME,EMAIL,PHONE) VALUES('Kapil','kapil@email.
com','4576457');


INSERT INTO BOOKS(TITLE,AUTHOR,COPIES) VALUES('Learn and Practice
Python','Swapnil Saurav',3);

INSERT INTO BOOKS(TITLE,AUTHOR,COPIES) VALUES('Learn and Practice
SQL','Swapnil Saurav',3);

INSERT INTO BOOKS(TITLE,AUTHOR,COPIES) VALUES('Learn and Practice
Data Visualization','Swapnil Saurav',3);

INSERT INTO BOOKS(TITLE,AUTHOR,COPIES) VALUES('Learn and Practice
Machine Learning','Swapnil Saurav',3);
```

Working with MYSQL

MySQL is a **relational database management system** (**RDBMS**) used for accessing and managing records in a database. In this section, we will understand how MYSQL can be installed with VS Code, connecting from VS Code to MySQL using Python, and running the tables and insert queries we created in the previous section.

Let us look at the steps to download and install MySQL server on your local machine running on Microsoft:

1. Download MySQL installer from **https://dev.mysql.com/downloads/installer/** and execute it.

2. Choose the appropriate setup type for your system. Typically, you will choose **Developer Default** to install MySQL server and other MySQL tools related to MySQL development, helpful tools like MySQL workbench.

3. Complete the installation process by following the instructions. This will install several MySQL products and start the MySQL server.

4. Get more details from **https://dev.mysql.com/doc/mysql-windows-excerpt/5.7/ en/windows-installation.html**.

5. Here are the details we have used:

    Servername: MySQLServer 8.0.17

    Username: root

    Password: learnSQL

6. MYSQL Workbench is one of the tools that would be very helpful to us. *Figure 5.2* shows how the MYSQL workbench looks:

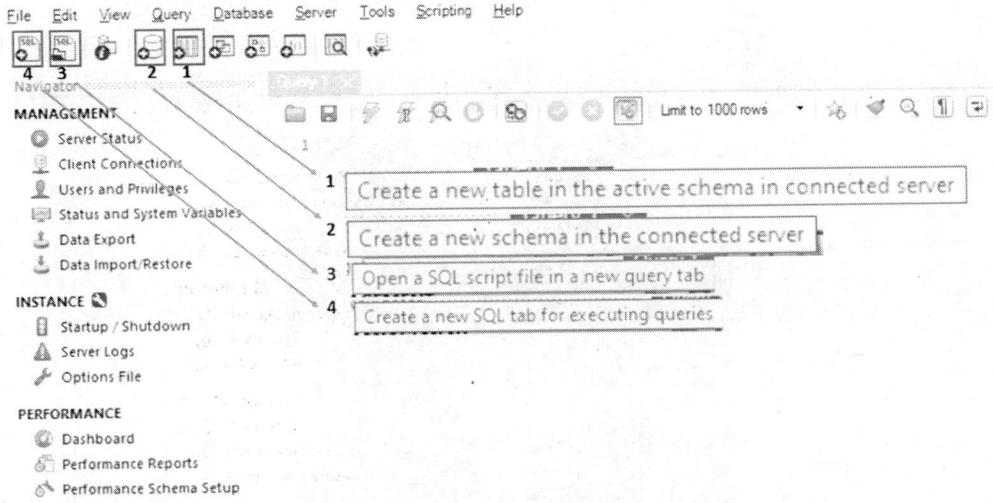

Figure 5.2: Important options in MySQL Workbench

7. Let us create a Schema titled **libraryms**, where we will create all our database objects. This can be done by clicking the **Create a new Schema in the connected server** option, as shown in *Figure 5.2*.

MYSQL server is installed and database schema is created, so we are all set from the MYSQL side. Now, let us focus on VS Code. Refer to the following steps to connect to MySQL Server using VSCode:

1. In the VS Code, Go to **Extensions** and search for the **MySQL** extension. Open the extension called **MySQL Management Tool** and install it, as shown in the following figure:

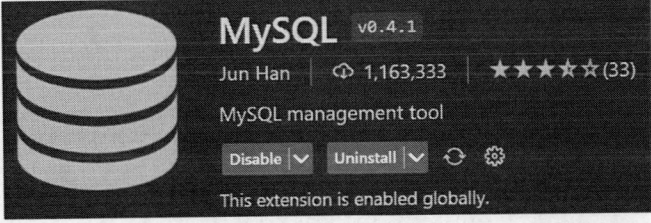

Figure 5.3: MySQL Management tool

2. MYSQL is now added to explorer. You can check by clicking on **explorer** option (first option on the left of your VS Code screen or by clicking Ctrl + Shift + E). Now, navigate to the MYSQL section and click on the + sign. It will ask you to enter the following details:

host: **localhost**

user: root

password: learnSQL

port: 3306

certificate file path: *leave it blank*

All the information is now saved and would appear as shown in *Figure 5.4*:

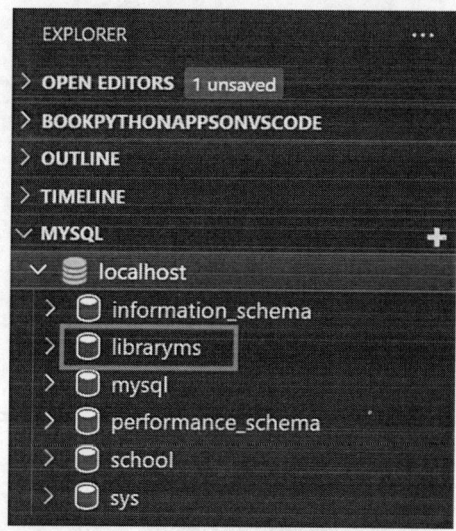

Figure 5.4: MySQL connected to VS Code

We can see the **libraryms** schema in the list when we expand; it is the same schema we created in the last section. Schema in MySQL is a logical collection of database objects such as tables, views, stored routines, and triggers. A schema is associated with a single database and contains all tables and other objects for that particular database. MySQL allows multiple users to have their schema, and each user is allowed to have their schema that is completely isolated from other schemas. As a root user, we can access all databases.

You can directly manage MYSQL as a root user, but we intend to execute SQL commands using Python code. We will create another file called *sql.py* and perform all the database-related queries from here.

We need to install and import **pymysql** library. PyMySQL is a pure-Python MySQL client library that provides us with functions to connect to the database. Also, we will declare a global variable with a database name as **libraryms**.

To use the **pymysql** library in Python, you need to follow these steps:

1. Install the **pymysql** library using pip:

    ```
    $ pip install pymysql
    ```

2. Import the **pymysql** module in your Python script:

    ```
    import pymysql
    ```

3. Establish a connection to the MySQL database by specifying the host, user, password, and database:

    ```
    connection = pymysql.connect(host='localhost', user='root',
    password='password', database='mydatabase')
    ```

    Replace **localhost** with the hostname of your MySQL server, **root** with the MySQL username, **password** with the MySQL password, and **mydatabase** with the name of your database.

4. Create a cursor object to execute SQL queries:

    ```
    cursor = connection.cursor()
    ```

5. Execute SQL queries using the cursor object:

    ```
    cursor.execute("SELECT * FROM mytable")
    ```

6. Fetch the results of the query in case of SELECT:

    ```
    results = cursor.fetchall()
    ```

    You can access the rows of the query result using the **results** variable.

7. Close the cursor and connection:

    ```
    cursor.close()
    connection.close()
    ```

It's important to close the cursor and connection to free up resources. Now, let us see the code relevant to us:

```
import pymysql

db_name = "libraryms"
```

We will add the first function, **perform_db_actions()**, to this file. This function will also call for database interaction from all other files. This file will take the database name, query and values, which would be for holding dynamic query values in tuple format. Dynamic query in SQL is a type of query that is generated at runtime based on program variables or user input. It enables generating different SQL statements on the fly rather than being pre-defined in the code. This makes building applications that can respond to changing requirements or user input easier. Let us look at an example of how dynamic query is implemented in MYSQL:

```
sql = "SELECT 'id', 'password' FROM 'users' WHERE 'email'=%s and id=%d"
cursor.execute(sql, ('contact@mysite.com',121))
```

In the preceding query, **id** and **password** will be displayed for dynamic values of **id** and **email**. Since email is of string type, we say **email = %s**, whereas we say **id=%d** because it is of integer type. Values in a tuple are then passed as separate parameters in the execute method.

The following is the complete code for **perform_db_actions()**:

```
from datetime import datetime
import pymysql

def perform_db_actions(db_name, query):
    '''This function will be called for any kinds of
    database interaction from all other files as well.
    @db_name: the name of the database
    @query: the query to be executed
    @values: the values for dynamic query in tuple format
    returns: Select query will return the recordset, other queries will
return none
    '''
    connect = pymysql.connect(host="localhost",
                              user="root",
                              password="learnSQL",
                              database=db_name)
    cursorobj = connect.cursor()
    data = []
    data = cursorobj.execute(query)
    data = cursorobj.fetchall()
    connect.commit()
    cursorobj.close()
    return data
```

Now, we create another function that will execute the **CREATE** table and the **INSERT** commands we created earlier during database design:

```
from datetime import datetime
def create_db(db_name):
    '''One time create database queries'''
    # Table 1 Students getting created
    t1 = '''Create table STUDENTS(
    MEMID INTEGER   PRIMARY KEY  AUTO_INCREMENT,
    NAME VARCHAR(30),
    EMAIL VARCHAR(15),
    PHONE VARCHAR(12),
    JOIN_DATE DATE DEFAULT (CURRENT_DATE))'''
    # call DB action
```

```python
    perform_db_actions(db_name, t1)
    t2 = '''Create table BOOKS(
BOOKID INTEGER   PRIMARY KEY AUTO_INCREMENT,
TITLE VARCHAR(30),
AUTHOR VARCHAR(15),
PUBLISHER VARCHAR(15),
PRICE REAL,
COPIES SMALLINT)'''
    perform_db_actions(db_name, t2)

    t3 = '''Create table TRANSACTIONS(
TID INTEGER   PRIMARY KEY AUTO_INCREMENT,
BOOKID INTEGER REFERENCES BOOKS(BOOKID),
MEMID INTEGER REFERENCES STUDENTS(MEMID),
ISSUE_DATE DATE,
RETURN_DATE DATE)'''
    perform_db_actions(db_name, t3)

    add_students = ['''INSERT INTO STUDENTS(NAME,EMAIL,PHONE)
VALUES('Sachin','sachin@em.com','346377')''',
                '''INSERT INTO STUDENTS(NAME,EMAIL,PHONE)
VALUES('Virat','virat@em.com','544343466')''',
                '''INSERT INTO STUDENTS(NAME,EMAIL,PHONE)
VALUES('Dhoni','dhoni@ema.com','5645654')''',
                '''INSERT INTO STUDENTS(NAME,EMAIL,PHONE)
VALUES('Kapil','kapil@ema.com','4576457')''']
    for q in add_students:
        perform_db_actions(db_name, q)
    add_books = ['''INSERT INTO BOOKS(TITLE,AUTHOR,COPIES) VALUES('Practice
Python','Swapnil Saurav',3)''',
                '''INSERT INTO BOOKS(TITLE,AUTHOR,COPIES) VALUES('Practice
SQL','Swapnil Saurav',3)''',
                '''INSERT INTO BOOKS(TITLE,AUTHOR,COPIES) VALUES('Practice
Data Visualization','Swapnil Saurav',3)''',
                '''INSERT INTO BOOKS(TITLE,AUTHOR,COPIES) VALUES('Practice
Machine Learning','Swapnil Saurav',3)''']

    for q in add_books:
        perform_db_actions(db_name, q)

    print("Your data has been created successfully!")

if __name__ == "__main__":
    create_db("libraryms")   #Onetime
```

We will return to it later and add main menu functions for ISSUE_BOOKS and RETURN_BOOKS. For now, we will move to creating **Students** and **Books** classes.

Students class

Let's create another Python file titled **ClassStudents.py**, and we will implement methods specific to **Students** like **add student, display student info, display specific student info, update student record** and **delete student record**.

In the **create_student** method, we will get all the information from the user, form a dynamic query, and pass it on to the **perform_db_actions()** to create a new student record. That is why we need to **import sql**.

The **Display_all()** and **Display_specific()** functions will display all the data about students. The only difference is that **display_specific()** will ask for the member ID before firing the **select** command.

Modify_student() is little tricky as we do not know beforehand which column value to change, so it has been implemented to display all the values one by one, and then the user can choose specific columns to change and provide new values.

Delete_student() is another simple function that deletes the given record from the **Students** table.

The following is the complete code for your reference:

```python
""" Students Example"""
import sql
import datetime as dt

class Students:
    """"Class for Students Example"""
    def __init__(self, dbname):
        """ Initialize the class """
        self.dbname = dbname

    def create_student(self):
        """ Create a new student record """
        name = input("Enter the name of the student: ")
        email = input("Enter the email id of the student: ")
        phone = input("Enter the phone of the student: ")
        query = f'''INSERT INTO STUDENTS(NAME, EMAIL, PHONE)
        VALUES('{name}', '{email}', '{phone}')'''
        sql.perform_db_actions(self.dbname, query)
        print("Successfully added Student record to the database")

    def display_all(self):
        """ Display all the student records in the database"""
        query = '''SELECT * FROM STUDENTS'''
        rows = sql.perform_db_actions(self.dbname, query)
```

```python
        print("Students in the database:")
        for student in rows:
            print(student)

    def display_specific(self):
        """ Display the details of a specific student record """
        memid = int(input("Enter the Membership ID of the the student: "))
        query = f'''SELECT * FROM STUDENTS WHERE memid = {memid}'''
        rows = sql.perform_db_actions(self.dbname, query)
        print("Details are:")
        for student in rows:
            print(student)

    def modify_student(self):
        """Modify the details of a specific student record"""
        memid = int(input("Enter the Membership ID of the student record to
be updated: "))
        query = f"SELECT name, email, phone FROM STUDENTS WHERE memid =
{memid}"
        rows = sql.perform_db_actions(self.dbname, query)

        if rows:
            cols = ["Name", "Email", "Phone"]
            update_query = "UPDATE STUDENTS SET"

            if len(rows[0]) > 1:
                for i, col in enumerate(cols):
                    print(f"Current {col} is {rows[0][i]}")
                    ch = input("Enter y to modify: ")
                    if ch.lower() == 'y':
                        inp = input(f"Enter the new {col}: ")
                        update_query += f" {col} = '{inp}',"

                if len(update_query) > 17:
                    update_query = update_query[:-1] + f" WHERE memid =
{memid}"
                    rows = sql.perform_db_actions(self.dbname, update_
query)
                    print("Data has been updated")
                else:
                    print("Nothing to update!")
        else:
            print("No such data available!")

    def delete_student(self):
        """ Delete a specific student record """
        memid = int(
```

```
        input("Enter the Membership ID of the student record to be
deleted: "))
        query = f'''SELECT memid FROM STUDENTS where memid = {memid}'''
        rows = sql.perform_db_actions(self.dbname, query)
        if len(rows) == 0:
            print("No such data available!")
        else:
            query = f'''DELETE FROM STUDENTS WHERE memid = {memid}'''
            sql.perform_db_actions(self.dbname, query)
            print("Deleted student record")
```

Books class

Let us create another Python file titled **ClassBooks.py**, and we will implement methods specific to **books**, like add books, display books, display specific book, update books, and delete books.

In the **create_book** method, we will get all the information from the user, form a dynamic query and pass it on to the **perform_db_actions()** to create the record. That is why we need to **import sql**.

The **Display_all()** and **Display_specific()** functions will display all the data about books. The only difference is that **display_specific()** will ask for the Book ID before firing the select command.

Modify_book() is little tricky as we do not know beforehand which column value to change, so it has been implemented to display all the values one by one, and then the user can choose specific columns to change and provide new values.

Delete_book() is another simple function that deletes the given record from books table.

The following is the complete code for your reference:

```
""" Books Example"""
import sql

class Books:
    """ Books Class"""
    def __init__(self, dbname):
        """ Initialize books class"""
        self.dbname = dbname

    def create_book(self):
        """ Create a new book record """
        title = input("Enter the Title of the Book: ")
        author = input("Enter the Author name of the Book: ")
        publisher = input("Enter the Publisher of the Book: ")
        price = float(input("Enter the Price id of the Book: "))
        copies = int(input("Enter the Copies of the Book: "))
```

```
        query = f'''INSERT INTO BOOKS(title, author, publisher, price,
copies)
        VALUES('{title}', '{author}', '{publisher}', {price}, {copies})'''

        sql.perform_db_actions(self.dbname, query)
        print("Successfully added book record to the database")

    def display_all(self):
        """ Display all the books in the database """
        query = '''SELECT * FROM BOOKS'''
        rows = sql.perform_db_actions(self.dbname, query)
        print("Books available in the Library are:")
        for book in rows:
            print(book)

    def display_specific(self):
        """ Display a specific book record """
        book_id = int(input("Enter the ID of the Book: "))
        query = f'''SELECT * FROM BOOKS WHERE bookid = {book_id}'''
        rows = sql.perform_db_actions(self.dbname, query)
        print("Details are:")
        for book in rows:
            print(book)

    def modify_book(self):
        """Modify the details of a specific book record"""
        bid = int(input("Enter the ID of the book record to be updated: "))
        query = f"SELECT title, author, publisher, price, copies FROM BOOKS
WHERE bookid = {bid}"
        rows = sql.perform_db_actions(self.dbname, query)

        if rows:
            cols = ['title', 'author', 'publisher', 'price', 'copies']
            update_query = "UPDATE BOOKS SET"

            if len(rows[0]) > 1:
                for col, value in zip(cols, rows[0]):
                    print(f"Current {col} is {value}")
                    ch = input("Enter y to modify: ")
                    if ch.lower() == 'y':
                        if col in ['title', 'author', 'publisher']:  #
string values
                            inp = input(f"Enter the new {col}: ")
                            update_query += f" {col} = '{inp}',"
                        elif col in ['price', 'copies']:  # numeric values
                            inp = int(input(f"Enter the new {col}: "))
                            update_query += f" {col} = {inp},"
```

```python
                    if len(update_query) > 16:
                        update_query = update_query[:-1] + f" WHERE bookid =
{bid}"
                        rows = sql.perform_db_actions(self.dbname, update_
query)
                        print("Data has been updated")
                    else:
                        print("Nothing to update!")
                else:
                    print("No such data available!")


    def delete_book(self):
        """ Delete a specific book record"""
        book_id = int(input("Enter the ID of the Book record to be deleted:
"))
        query = f'''SELECT bookid FROM BOOKS WHERE bookid = {book_id}'''
        rows = sql.perform_db_actions(self.dbname, query)
        if len(rows) == 0:
            print("No such data available!")
        else :
            query = f'''DELETE FROM BOOKS WHERE bookid = {book_id}'''
            rows = sql.perform_db_actions(self.dbname, query)
            print("Data deleted")
```

Executing the project: Performing CRUD operations

CRUD stands for Create, Read, Update, and Delete. It is a set of operations that are commonly used in database management systems to manipulate data. CRUD operations are the fundamental operations used in database systems:

- **Create**: The **Create** operation enables users to create new records in the database. This operation can be used to add new data to existing tables or create new tables. In order to successfully create records, users must be aware of the database structure and must have the appropriate permissions to add new records.

- **Read**: The **Read** operation enables users to retrieve existing records from the database. This operation is used to access existing data and can be used to search for specific records or display all records in a table.

- **Update**: The **Update** operation enables users to modify existing records in the database. This operation can be used to modify existing data or to add new data to existing records. In order to successfully update records, users must be aware of the database structure and must have the appropriate permissions to modify existing records.

- **Delete**: The **Delete** operation enables users to delete existing records from the database. This operation can be used to delete existing data or to remove records from a table. In order to successfully delete records, users must be aware of the database structure and must have the appropriate permissions to delete existing records.

CRUD operations are essential for database systems as they enable users to create, read, update, and delete data. These operations are the basic building blocks for database operations and are used by developers and administrators to manage data.

Before we execute, let's add three more functions to the SQL module, which we will use to perform CRUD operations.

The **check_outbooks()** function will check the transactions table in the database and pick up the ones that do not have return dates and then display them. Return value **null** indicates that the book has still not been returned to the library. Let's implement the **check_outbooks()** function now:

```
def check_outbooks(db_name):
    print("Borrowed list of books:")
    heading = ('TransactionID', 'Member ID', 'Book ID', 'Issue Date')
    print(heading)
    q1 = '''Select tid,memid,bookid,issue_date from transactions where
return_date is null'''
    rows = perform_db_actions(db_name, q1)
    if rows == 0:
        print("No books is pending for returning")
    else:
        for r1 in rows:
            print(r1)
```

The **issue_book()** function will take the **MemberID** and the **BookID**, and if there are enough copies of the book left in the library, it will update the **Transaction** table to indicate that the book has been issued to the student. This will decrease the count of total number of copies by one:

```
def issue_book(db_name):
    memid = int(input("Enter the Member ID: "))
    bookid = int(input("Enter the Book ID: "))
    book_count = -1

    # checking if MEMID in the database
    q1 = '''Select MEMID from Students where MEMID = %d''' % (memid)
    row1 = perform_db_actions(db_name, q1)

    # checking if BOOKID in the database and if yes then get the count
    q1 = '''Select Copies from Books where bookid = %d''' % (bookid)
    row2 = perform_db_actions(db_name, q1)
```

```
    if len(row1) < 1 or len(row2) < 1:
        print("Error: Either BookID or Membership ID is missing, please
check and re-try again!")
    elif row2[0][0] < 1:
        print("Error: There are no more copies left in the library!")

    else:
        print("Adding data....")
        #print("   ========   ", datetime.now().strftime('%d-%m-%Y'))
        book_count = row2[0][0]
        q2 = '''INSERT INTO TRANSACTIONS(MEMID,BOOKID,ISSUE_DATE)
        VALUES(%d,%d,'%s')''' % (memid, bookid, str(datetime.now().
strftime('%Y-%m-%d')))
        perform_db_actions(db_name, q2)

        # update the copies
        q2 = '''Update Books Set Copies = %d where BookID=%d''' % (
            book_count-1, bookid)
        perform_db_actions(db_name, q2)

        print("Successfully issued the book")
```

The **return_book()** function will update the database as the book is returned. It will add the return date to the database and update the number of copies in the books table:

```
def return_book(db_name):
    check_outbooks(db_name)
    given_id = input("Above are the list of transactions for borrowed book.
"
                    "Enter the transaction id alone or Membership ID,Book
ID: ")
    val1 = 0
    tid = -1
    bookid = -1
    try:
        if ',' in given_id:
            print("Membership ID and Books ID entered")
            val1 = given_id.split(",")
            val1[0] = int(val1[0])
            val1[1] = int(val1[1])
            val1 = tuple(val1)

            q1 = '''Select tid from Transactions where memid=%d and bookid=
%d
            and return_date is null ''' % (val1[0], val1[1])
            rows = perform_db_actions(db_name, q1)

            if len(rows) >= 1:
```

```
                    tid = rows[0][0]
                    bookid = val1[1]
                else:
                    print("Error: Could not find the given transaction!")

            else:
                print("Transaction ID entered")
                val1 = int(given_id)
                q1 = "Select tid, bookid from Transactions where return_date is
null and tid=%d" % (
                    val1)
                rows = perform_db_actions(db_name, q1)
                if len(rows) >= 1:
                    tid = val1
                    bookid = rows[0][1]
                else:
                    print("Error: Could not find the given transaction!")
    except Exception:
        print("Error: Data not found/Error Occurred! Please try again...")
    else:
        print("updating the database...")
        # increase copies count
        q1 = "Select Copies from Books where bookid=%d" % (bookid)
        rows = perform_db_actions(db_name, q1)
        q1 = "Update Books Set Copies =%d where Bookid=%d" % (
            rows[0][0]+1, bookid)
        perform_db_actions(db_name, q1)

        # update transaction
        q1 = '''Update Transactions Set return_date = '%s'
        where tid =%d''' % (str(datetime.now().strftime('%Y-%m-%d')), tid)
        rows = perform_db_actions(
            db_name, q1)
        print("All records updated!")
```

Let us go to our main file **MyLMS.py** and update the code with function and method name. This is how the **MyLMS.py** file will look:

```
import ClassStudents
import ClassBooks
import sql
DB_NAME = "libraryms"


def adminmenu():
    print("\n\nADMIN MENU")
    print("Select the Option from below:")
    print("\n\tAdmin 1. CREATE STUDENT")
    print("\tAdmin 2. DISPLAY ALL STUDENTS")
```

```python
        print("\tAdmin 3. DISPLAY SPECIFIC STUDENT")
        print("\tAdmin 4. MODIFY STUDENT RECORD")
        print("\tAdmin 5. DELETE STUDENT RECORD")
        print("\n\tAdmin 6. CREATE BOOK")
        print("\tAdmin 7. DISPLAY ALL BOOKS")
        print("\tAdmin 8. DISPLAY SPECIFIC BOOK")
        print("\tAdmin 9. MODIFY BOOK RECORD")
        print("\tAdmin 10. DELETE BOOK RECORD")
        print("\tAdmin 11. TAKE BACK TO THE MAIN MENU")
        adminchoice = input("Enter your choice from the above: ")
        if adminchoice == "1":
            s1.create_student()
            return True
        elif adminchoice == "2":

            s1.display_all()
            return True
        elif adminchoice == "3":
            s1.display_specific()
            return True
        elif adminchoice == "4":
            s1.modify_student()
            return True
        elif adminchoice == "5":
            s1.delete_student()
            return True
        elif adminchoice == "6":
            b1.create_book()
            return True
        elif adminchoice == "7":
            b1.display_all()
            return True
        elif adminchoice == "8":
            b1.display_specific()
            return True
        elif adminchoice == "9":
            b1.modify_book()
            return True
        elif adminchoice == "10":
            b1.delete_book()
            return True
        elif adminchoice == "11":
            return False
        else:
            print("Invalid Choice. Try again!")
            return True
```

```python
def menu():
    print("\n\n\n LIBRARY MANAGEMENT SYSTEM")
    print("Select the Option from below:")
    print("\n\tOption 1. BOOK ISSUE")
    print("\tOption 2. BOOK DEPOSIT")
    print("\tOption 3. ADMIN MENU")
    print("\tOption 4. DISPLAY OUT BOOKS")
    print("\tOption 5. EXIT")
    mainchoice = input("Enter your choice from the above: ")
    if mainchoice == "1":
        sql.issue_book(DB_NAME)
        return True
    elif mainchoice == "2":
        sql.return_book(DB_NAME)
        return True
    elif mainchoice == "3":
        adm_cont = True
        while adm_cont:
            adm_cont = adminmenu()
        # Admin menu exited but still in main menu
        menu()
    elif mainchoice == "4":
        sql.check_outbooks(DB_NAME)
        return True
    elif mainchoice == "5":
        return False
    else:
        print("Invalid Option Try Agin!")
        return True


# Creating objects
# creating object of ClassStudents
s1 = ClassStudents.Students(DB_NAME)
# creating object of ClassBooks
b1 = ClassBooks.Books(DB_NAME)

# calling mainmenu
cont = True
while cont:
    cont = menu()
```

We have successfully implemented a mini library application using MYSQL database—another topic under our belt.

Debugging in VS Code

Debugging is an important part of programming, as it helps identify and remove any errors or bugs from the code. This helps ensure that the code runs as expected, without any unexpected behavior or errors. We generally come across three types of errors in programming:

- **Syntax error**: This is easiest of all the errors to identify. This is because Python is designed so well and the error messages are very well commented, which helps us know where and what went wrong in terms of syntax.

- **Runtime errors**: Runtime errors are mistakes that occur during the execution of a program and can cause the program to crash or produce incorrect results. For example, trying to convert text containing alphabets into an integer or dividing a number by zero.

- **Logical errors**: These are the mistakes in a program's source code that result in incorrect or unexpected program behavior. These errors are caused by a programmer's incorrect assumptions or misunderstandings about the program's environment, or by mistakes in the program's logic.

Logical and runtime errors are typically more difficult to detect and fix than syntax errors, since the program may appear syntactically correct despite the incorrect logic. This is where programmers need to use their debugging skills to figure out the piece of code responsible for those errors. VS Code provide us an option to debug the code.

Here is how to perform debugging of Python code in VS Code:

- Open the **Python File** in VS Code.

- On the left side of the VS Code window, click the **Run and Debug** icon available in the activity bar (keyboard shortcut *Ctrl+Shift+D*).

- Select the **Python file** option from the drop-down menu, as shown in Figure 5.5. Selecting **Python file** will open a **launch.json** file in the editor view. If the **launch.json** file has not yet been created, it will prompt you to create one. In case you get a prompt to create, then click on the **create a launch.json** file link, as shown in *Figure 5.5*.

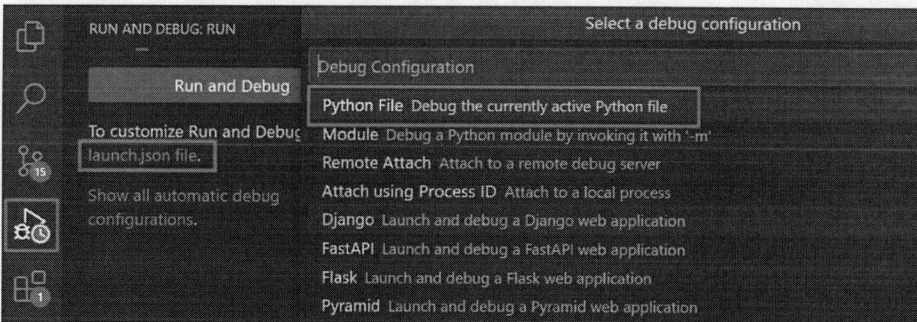

Figure 5.5: *Run and Debug option in the Activity Bar*

Here is the launch configuration generated for Python debugging:

```
{
    // Use IntelliSense to learn about possible attributes.
    // Hover to view descriptions of existing attributes.
    // For more information, visit: https://go.microsoft.com/
fwlink/?linkid=830387
    "version": "0.2.0",
    "configurations": [
        {
            "name": "Python: Current File",
            "type": "python",
            "request": "launch",
            "program": "${file}",
            "console": "integratedTerminal",
            "justMyCode": true
        }
    ]
}
```

Figure 5.6 shows a program in debug mode with breakpoints. In the top-right corner, we have the **Debug** toolbar, which performs the actions listed in *Table 5.2*.

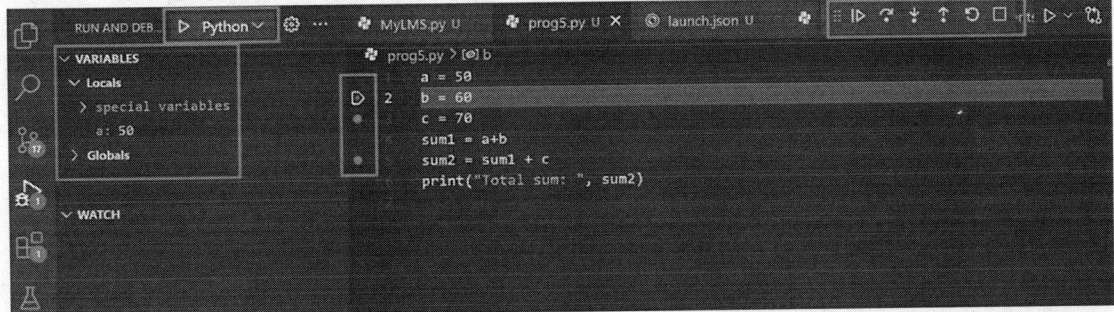

Figure 5.6: Debugging

Action	Description
Continue / Pause (F5)	Continue: Resume normal program/script execution (up to the next breakpoint) Pause: Inspect code executing at the current line and debug line-by-line
Step Over (F10)	Execute the next method as a single command without inspecting or following its component steps
Step Into (F11)	Enter the next method to follow its execution line-by-line
Step Out (Shift+F11)	When inside a method or subroutine, return to the earlier execution context by completing remaining lines of the current method as though it were a single command

Action	Description
Restart (**Ctrl+Shift+F5**)	Terminate the current program execution and start debugging again using the current run configuration
Stop (Shift+F5)	Terminate the current program execution

Table 5.2: Debug toolbar with their description

Follow the given steps to debug a Python program:

1. Add a breakpoint to the code by clicking on the left side of the line of code.

2. Now, click the green **Play** button to start the debugging process.

3. When you reach the breakpoint, the debugger will pause the execution, allowing you to inspect the variables, view the call stack, and step through the code.

4. Press the **Stop** button or *Shift + F5* keys to end the debugging session.

Conclusion

Python applications can create and manage databases that store data for various purposes. Python enables rapid development of database applications due to its comprehensive object-oriented library and ability to interface with many popular database systems. In the example we covered in this chapter, we saw how to create a library management system by connecting to the MYSQL database. Python's support for database development also offers advantages like scalability, portability, and maintainability. Python makes it easy to create database applications that are secure, efficient, and cost-effective. It can also analyze data, allowing businesses to gain valuable insights into their data quickly and easily. Python is an efficient tool for data analysis and processing, so learning to use a database using Python has become important. Our example uses Python to connect to databases, create data structures, perform calculations, and analyze data.

In the last part of the chapter, we learnt to perform debugging in VS Code. Debugging helps improve the code by identifying potential performance issues, making it easier to optimize the code. Furthermore, debugging allows developers to understand the code better and can help them better understand how it works and why a particular bug is occurring.

The next chapter is about advanced algorithm design. We will introduce the process of designing, developing, and implementing algorithms for a given problem. It involves the use of techniques like data structures, problem-solving techniques, and software engineering principles to create efficient and effective algorithms. Algorithm design is an essential part of computer science and is used in many applications, such as web development, artificial intelligence, and data analysis.

## CHAPTER 6

Advanced Algorithm Design

An algorithm is like a recipe.
— *Muhammad Waseem*

Introduction

An algorithm is a set of steps or procedures to solve a problem. Algorithm design refers to developing a step-by-step approach to solve a problem. In computing, algorithms process data, improve search results, optimize web pages, and more. Algorithm design is integral to computer science, allowing us to solve complex problems efficiently. It involves finding the right combination of data structures, programming language constructs, and problem-solving techniques to solve a problem efficiently. It also involves creating algorithms that are easy to understand and implement.

Algorithms are used to solve various problems, from sorting data to finding the shortest route for a delivery truck. Typical problems solved with algorithms include finding the best way for a delivery truck, sorting data, searching for patterns in data, solving mathematical equations, and optimizing resources. They are also used in artificial intelligence, data mining, natural language processing, and robotics.

To learn algorithm design in computing, it is essential to understand the basics of computer science, including data structures and algorithms, programming languages, and problem-solving fundamentals. Additionally, algorithm design and analysis courses can help deepen the understanding of this topic. It is also essential to practice writing and implementing algorithms. This is precisely what we will focus on in this chapter. We will learn the design by practice and cover some of the essential topics under algorithm design learning.

Structure

In this chapter, we will discuss the following topics:

- Introduction to algorithm analysis
- Divide and conquer
- Backtracking
- Binary tree
- Heaps
- Hash table
- Graph algorithm
- Big-O notation: Methodology for analyzing algorithms

Now, let us dive deep into the topics.

Objectives

The objective of learning algorithm design is to develop an understanding of how to design, analyze, and implement algorithms that solve complex problems. This includes understanding the fundamental principles of algorithms, analyzing the complexity of algorithms, and implementing efficient data structures. This is exactly what this chapter is all about. Additionally, readers will understand the different approaches to algorithm design and the different techniques used to implement algorithms. Finally, readers will learn how to apply the knowledge acquired in algorithm design to solve real-world problems.

Introduction to algorithm analysis

Before we dive into algorithm analysis, let us understand the approach one should take to solve a problem:

1. Understand the problem you are trying to solve. Algorithms are used to solve various issues, so understanding the end goal of using an algorithm is essential. Let us say that the problem statement is 'improving the customer experience when interacting with a company'. We want to determine how to make the customer experience more efficient, effective, and enjoyable. We need to find ways to

increase customer satisfaction and loyalty, reduce customer churn, and increase the value of the customer experience. We also need to find ways to improve the customer journey and make it easier for customers to see what they need. Then, we need to develop our algorithms to support the efficient design of the solution.

2. Identify the data structures and algorithms most appropriate for the problem. Some of the popular data structures are as follows:

   a. **Linked lists**: They are data structures that store collections of data elements, called nodes, where each node contains a reference to the next node in the sequence. Linked lists are commonly used in algorithm design because they allow efficient insertion and removal of elements and fast traversal of the list.

   b. **Binary trees**: They are data structures that store data hierarchically, with each node in the tree having up to two children. Binary trees are commonly used in algorithm design because they allow efficient searching and sorting of data.

   c. **Graphs**: They are a type of data structure that store data as nodes connected by edges. They are often used in algorithm design because they allow efficient representation of relationships between data points and can be used to solve complex problems, such as finding the shortest path between two points.

   d. **Hash tables**: Data structures store data using a hash function to generate an index for each data item. They are commonly used in algorithm design because they allow fast access to data and can be used to store large amounts of data efficiently.

3. Analyze the time and space complexity of your algorithm. Its time complexity will depend on what operations it performs and how it is implemented. Time complexity is an analysis technique used in computer science to determine the efficiency of an algorithm. It measures the amount of time an algorithm takes to run as a function of the input size. The time complexity of an algorithm helps understand how the algorithm's performance will scale with larger inputs. It is used to compare different algorithms and determine which one is more efficient in terms of time. Common time complexity notations include $O(1)$ for constant time, $O(n)$ for linear time, $O(n^2)$ for quadratic time, $O(\log n)$ for logarithmic time, and $O(2^n)$ for exponential time.

Space complexity is another analysis technique used in computer science to determine the amount of memory an algorithm requires as a function of the input size. Common space complexity notations include $O(1)$ for constant space, $O(n)$ for linear space, $O(n^2)$ for quadratic space, $O(\log n)$ for logarithmic space, and $O(2^n)$ for exponential space. It is worth noting that space complexity can depend on various factors, such as the data structures used, the recursion depth, and the temporary variables created during the execution of the algorithm. Therefore, it is important to consider the specific implementation details when analyzing the space complexity of an algorithm.

4. Design a step-by-step procedure for solving the problem. There are certain steps to unravel even complex issues:

   a. Identify the problem

   b. Break down the problem into smaller, more manageable pieces

   c. Design an algorithm that solves each piece of the problem

   d. Test the algorithm to make sure it works correctly

   e. Analyze the algorithm for time complexity, memory usage, and other factors

   f. Optimize the algorithm if necessary

5. Implement the algorithm in a programming language. Convert the algorithm into Python code and run it.

6. Test the algorithm to ensure that it produces the expected results. Create test cases with known input and known output and check whether the output generated by the program matches our known output.

7. Document the algorithm and program.

8. Deploy the program and use it to solve the real-time problems.

Let us follow the mentioned steps to solve a problem:

- **Problem statement**: Write a program to find the smallest window in a given string containing all characters of the other string.

- **Understand the problem**: When a user provides two strings, that is, string and pattern, the task is to find the main string's smallest substring containing all the input pattern's characters. We need to read all the characters of the given string and generate all substrings of the string containing the pattern character. And then we need to print the smallest substring containing all characters of the pattern.

Example

> String: `I am on a seafood diet. i see food and i eat it.`
>
> Pattern: `fast`
>
> **Output**: Window: seafood diet
>
> The minimum length of the window is 12

All the correct combinations are shown in *Figure 6.1*. The smallest substring of the given string that has the pattern is seafood diet:

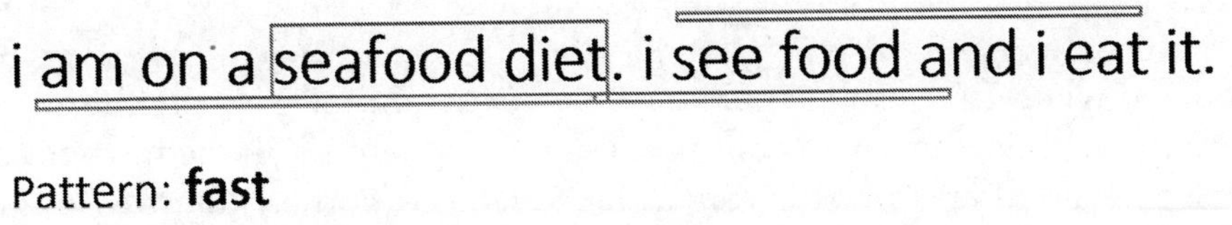

i am on a seafood diet. i see food and i eat it.

Pattern: **fast**

***Figure 6.1**: All the correct combinations, along with the one with the minimum length highlighted*

Data structure required

- We will handle the data using a list that will work like a map representing all possible 256 characters that can be entered in a pattern. The index will be the character, and the value will be the count. *Figure 6.2* shows the map:

```
{0, 0, 0, 0, 0, 0, 0, 0, 0, 0, 0, 0, 0, 0, 0, 0, 0, 0, 0, 0, 0, 0, 0, 0, 0, 0, 0, 0, 0, 0, 0, 0,
0, 0, 0, 0, 0, 0, 0, 0, 0, 0, 0, 0, 0, 0, 0, 0, 0, 0, 0, 0, 0, 0, 0, 0, 1, 0, 0, 0, 0, 0, 0, 0, 0,
0, 0, 0, 0, 0, 0, 0, 0, 0, 0, 0, 0, 0, 0, 0, 0, 0, 0, 0, 0, 0, 0, 0, 0, 0, 0, 0, 0, 0, 0, 0, 0, 0,
0, 0, 0, 0, 0, 0, 0, 0, 0, 0, 0, 0, 0, 0, 0, 0, 0, 0, 0, 0, 0, 0, 0, 0, 0, 0, 0, 0, 0, 0, 0, 0}
```

***Figure 6.2**: Map representing 256 characters*

Algorithm

The problem might look easy. You will think of creating all the possible subarrays (with variable lengths) and then go over each of them, comparing the pattern. Then, among all the matched ways, you will look for the length, and the one with the smallest length will be our answer. However, this would take a lot of time. Regarding time complexity, it will take $O(N*N)$ or $O(N^2)$ to create different subarrays. Then, searching the pattern would take another $O(N)$, resulting in $O(N^3)$. Time complexity is the time required for an algorithm to complete its task. The Big O notation is a way to measure the time complexity of an algorithm. It is expressed as $O(n)$, where n is the number of operations required to complete the algorithm.

In a later section, we will see how *Big O* notation is used to compare the relative performance of two algorithms: first algorithm that we just discussed and the other one is sliding window technique. Sliding window algorithm is the preferred algorithm in this case because its time complexity of $O(N)$ is better than $O(N^2)$.

The sliding window technique is an algorithm design technique used to solve problems involving sequences, such as string matching, by breaking the line down into small chunks and shifting the piece by a certain number of elements at a time. The sliding window algorithm sounds complicated, but it is a window or section formed over parts of your data, and in our case, data is a string. We move this window in increments over our data to perform some computation, which would be finding the minimum window substring. This technique helps find patterns in large datasets and solve problems with time constraints.

Window or section is a variable length group that starts increasing from where the first value is met and rises to the point of the last match. We increase the size of the window by one element at a time. As demonstrated in *Figure 6.3*, we form the window when the first character match is found in the main string and goes up to the last character match. Here, the first match is found when **a** is located at index **2**. A window starts to form and increases up to when *t* is found. This is one subarray and also a possible solution. Next, we begin reducing this window by eliminating it from behind till the next match is found. This time, we get another subarray from index **8**. This is another subarray, and it is a better solution than the first one, as the size of this subarray is the minimum of what we got so far. We continue to build windows and change their size until all the elements have been considered.

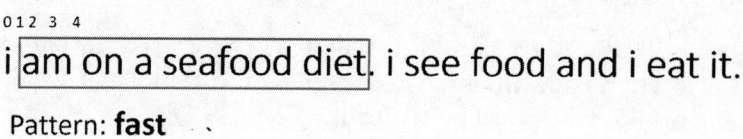

Pattern: **fast**

Figure 6.3: Working of sliding window

Let us do a step-by-step walkthrough of the algorithm using our string and pattern:

1. Let us create a map to generate a count of all the characters in the pattern as we iterate through the main string; we will know how many characters we have seen. We get *F=1, A=1, S=1, T=1*.

2. We need a couple of different variables to be used:

   a. To begin with, we will declare **i** and **j** pointers, pointing at index = 0.

   b. The variable count will be initialized to the number of unique characters in the pattern, which we can get from the map. So, we make count = 4 (for FAST).

   c. Initialize a left and right variable, which will be used to keep track of the minimum substring positions we come across as we iterate through the string.

   d. The `minlength` variable is used to keep track of the difference between the right and left pointer, which will give us the substring from the string. Initially, we will make it one more than the string length, as it would indicate a non-efficient solution. The step is illustrated in *Figure 6.4*:

STRING: i am on a seafood diet. i see food and i eat it.

PATTERN: **fast**

Count = 4

i,j = 0,0

minLength = 14

F	1
A	1
S	1
T	1

MAP

Figure 6.4: Variables all initialized

3. The **j** pointer will start from index **0** of the main string and stop when there is a match with the variable in the map. In our case, when **j** reaches index **2**, there is a match (character **A** is found). We need to decrease the value of the character by 1 in the map. If the case value reaches **zero,** we also decrease **count** by 1, now equal to **3**. We get **A** = 0 and **count**=2. We need to continue looking for **F, S, T** (=1) to find a successful minimum window.

4. We continue to move the **j** pointer ahead looking for other characters from the map. **j** will continue to move until **count**>1. When **j** reaches index 8, there is another match; decrease the count of **A** by 1, so now it is -1. The count value is not affected here because it is only decreased when the value in the map reaches 0, not for any other number (-1 in this case).

5. Now **j** moves to 10, and there is a match again. This time, the value of **S** goes to **zero**, so **count** is decreased by 1 and is now 2.

6. **j** moves to 12 and the map value of A goes to -2.

7. Now, **j** moves to 13 and there is a match again. This time, the value of **F** goes to zero, so **count** is decreased by 1 and now it becomes 1.

8. Now **j** keeps moving until index 21; **T** is made 0 and **count** also becomes **zero**. That means we have found a subarray.

9. Since **i** is less than **j**, it moves till it gets first match (at index 2). Now, **count** of matching character **A** is increased by 1 (to now -1) in the MAP. The **minlength** is calculated as a potential solution. Since **A** is negative, indicating that there is another **A** value that will have a shorter subarray. **i** moves to 10 (A=0, count=0), and now **i** comes to 12, that is, when **A** value in map changes to 1 and **count** is set to 1. This is the first potential solution (when **count** becomes positive). **minlength** is calculated as 21-12 =9 (j=21, i=12), and the subarray is `mainstring[i:i+minlength]`.

10. After this, **j** continues executing, repeating the same steps and finding all possible subarrays and their corresponding lengths. If the next subarray found has a length lower than the previous subarray, then current subarray becomes the potential solution; otherwise, we stick to the previous result. The algorithm ends when **j** reaches the end of the **mainstring**.

This is how the sliding window algorithm can find the solution within a single loop; thus, time complexity is $O(n)$.

Now, let us implement the mentioned login using Python code:

```
total_chars = 256
#total 256 all possible characters

def smallestWindow(mainstr, pattern):
```

```python
n = len(mainstr)
if n < len(pattern):
    return -1
mp = [0]*total_chars

# Starting index of ans
start = 0

# Length of ans
ans = n + 1
cnt = 0

# creating map
for i in pattern:
    mp[ord(i)] += 1
    if mp[ord(i)] == 1:
        cnt += 1

# References of Window: j will move by each character
 #i will be used to remove the duplicate entry
i,j = 0,0

# Traversing the window
while(j < n):

# Calculating
    mp[ord(mainstr[j])] -= 1
    if mp[ord(mainstr[j])] == 0:
        cnt -= 1

        # Condition matching
        while cnt == 0:
            if ans > j - i + 1:

            # calculating answer.
                ans = j - i + 1
                start = i

            # Sliding I:removing from I
            mp[ord(mainstr[i])] += 1
            if mp[ord(mainstr[i])] > 0:
                cnt += 1
            i += 1
    j += 1
if ans > n:
    return "-1"
return mainstr[start:start+ans]
```

Now, we are writing the code to execute the mentioned function:

```
# Driver code
s = 'i am on a seafood diet. i see food and i eat it.'
t = 'fast'
small_window = smallestWindow(s, t)
if small_window =="-1":
    print("No such window possible")
else:
    print(f'Window is "{small_window}" and Minimum length between'
        f'the substring is {len(small_window)}')
```

Output

Window is **seafood diet** and minimum length between the substrings is 12.

Let us summarize the steps to work on while analyzing algorithms:

1. **Describe the algorithm**: The first step in analyzing an algorithm is to describe it in clear and concise terms. This should include the input and output, any variables used, and the steps taken in the algorithm.

2. **Assess the efficiency**: Once the algorithm has been described, it is important to evaluate its efficiency. This should include assessing the time and space complexity.

3. **Identify potential bottlenecks**: After assessing the efficiency of the algorithm, it is important to identify potential bottlenecks or areas of the algorithm that can be improved.

4. **Optimize the algorithm**: Once the potential bottlenecks have been identified, the next step is to optimize the algorithm. This may include changing the data structure, simplifying the code, or changing the order of operations.

5. **Test the algorithm**: Finally, the algorithm should be tested to ensure that it works correctly. This should include testing the algorithm with various input values to ensure that it produces the expected output.

Now that we have understood the process, let us look at some of the approaches to solving problems.

Divide and conquer

Algorithms like the greedy method, dynamic programming, and divide and conquer are fundamental techniques that have various applications. In this section, we will use the divide and conquer technique to solve examples. The general idea behind this technique is to solve a problem by breaking it down into subproblems that are easier to solve.

For example, the merge sort algorithm is a divide and conquer algorithm. It works by taking a list of numbers and breaking the list into two halves until the list only contains one number. It then sorts the two halves and merges them together in the correct order. This process is repeated until the entire list is sorted.

Binary search is another classic example of a divide-and-conquer algorithm. It works by dividing a sorted array in half and then comparing the target value to the value in the middle of the array. If the target is less than the value in the middle, then the algorithm searches the left side of the array. If the target is more than the value in the middle, it searches the array's right side. This process is repeated until the target is found or there are no more elements to search.

Quick sort is another example of a divide and conquer algorithm. It works by choosing a pivot element from the list and then partitioning the list into two halves based on the pivot. The elements less than the pivot are placed on one side of the list, and those more significant than the pivot are placed on the other. This process is repeated on each partition until all elements are sorted.

Problem: Exponential problem solving using divide and conquer

Let us solve: x^n. Traditionally, this is solved using a loop that would perform $x * x * x \ldots * x$ and so on. This algorithm runs in the linear order of n, as shown in the following code:

```
x=12
n=5
exp= 1
for I in range(n):
    exp *=x
print(""{x} to the power of {n} = {exp"")
```

The preceding program runs a for loop to calculate 12 to the power of 5. The time complexity of this algorithm is $O(n)$. We look to improve the running time of the algorithm using divide and conquer. In the divide and conquer approach, the exponential of x^n is achieved by creating subproblems of size $x^{n/2}$. This is demonstrated in *Figure 6.5*:

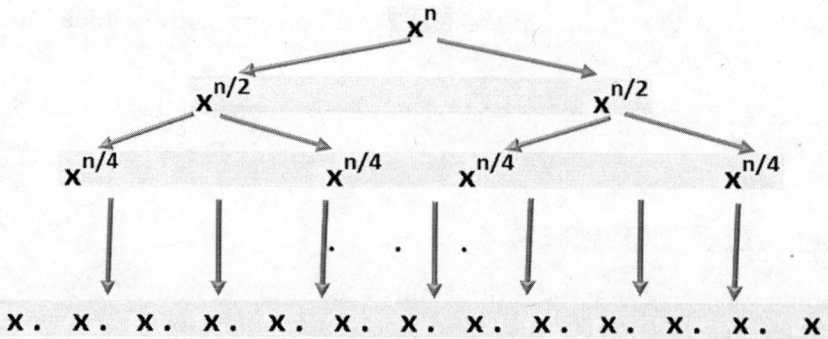

Figure 6.5: Exponential calculation using divide and conquer

The exponential calculation is shown in *Figure 6.6*:

$$x^n = \begin{cases} x^{n/2} \cdot x^{n/2} & \text{if } n \text{ is } \textbf{even} \\ x^{(n-1)/2} \cdot x^{(n-1)/2} \cdot x & \text{if } n \text{ is } \textbf{odd} \end{cases}$$

Figure 6.6: *Exponential calculation representation using divide-and-conquer technique*

Now, let us see the implementation of the preceding logic using Python code:

```python
def calc_pow(x,n):
    '''
    Exponential value calculation using Divide and Conquer technique
    :param x: number
    :param n: power
    :return: multiplication of x and n
    '''
    if(n == 0):
        return 1
    elif n % 2 == 0:
        return calc_pow(x,n/2) * calc_pow(x,n/2)
    else:
        return x * calc_pow(x,n-1)
x,n=12,5
exp_val = calc_pow(x,n)
print(f"{x} to the power of {n} = {exp_val}")
```

Exponential value calculation is done by breaking the logic into smaller, more manageable pieces. It works by dividing the problem into smaller subproblems, solving each subproblem recursively, and then combining the solutions of the subproblems to form the final solution. In this example, divide and conquer can be used to reduce the time complexity of the calculation. The algorithm works by breaking the problem into smaller parts, computing the exponential value of each part, and then combining the results to form the overall answer. The size of each subproblem can be chosen based on the desired accuracy of the result. By breaking the problem down into smaller pieces, the computation time can be significantly reduced to $O(log_2\, n)$.

Backtracking

Backtracking is a type of algorithm that tries different solutions until it finds the right one. It is a systematic, step-by-step approach that incrementally builds candidates to the solutions. It is used to find all possible solutions to a problem by exploring all possible paths. It works by repeatedly making choices, backtracking when a choice leads to a dead end, and tracking the best solution found so far. This process is repeated until a solution is found or all possibilities are exhausted.

These algorithms can be applied to different types of problems. For example, a backtracking algorithm can be used to solve a maze, by trying different paths until the end is reached. It can also be used to solve a Sudoku puzzle, by testing each possible number in each empty cell. Even though it can be a tedious process, it provides an efficient way to solve complex problems.

To illustrate how backtracking works, consider the following example:

We have an array of numbers, and we want to find a subset of the numbers that add up to a given sum. Let us say we have the array [1, 3, 7, 5, 9, 11], and we want to find a subset that adds up to 12.

To solve this problem using a backtracking algorithm, we start by looking at the first number in the array: 1. We add 1 to our running total and move on to the second number: 3. We add 3 to our running total, then move on to the third number: 5. We add 5 to our running total and now have a total of 9. Since 9 is less than 12, we continue to the following number: 7. We add 7 to our running total and now have 16. Since 16 is greater than 12, we backtrack to the previous number, 5, and remove it from our running total. We now have a total of 4. We continue this process until we find a subset of numbers that gives the sum of 12. In this case, the subset of numbers that adds up to 12 is [1, 11], [3, 9], and [7, 5].

Let us look at the Python implementation of the mentioned problem:

```python
class find_subset_sum:
    '''
    Class to implement a method to find
    whether or not there exists any subset
    of array  that sum up to targetSum
    '''
    def __init__(self):
        self.subset_count = 0  #to count the total possibilities
        self.values = []    #to store the valid values for subset
    #BACKTRACKING ALGORITHM
    def subset_sum(self,list_val,sum, st_idx,target):
        if target == sum:
            print("Subset => ",self.values)
            self.subset_count +=1

            if st_idx < len(list_val):
                self.subset_sum(list_val, sum - list_val[st_idx-1], st_idx, target)
        else:
            #generate nodes
            for i in range(st_idx,len(list_val)):
                self.values.append(list_val[i]) #store to find sum
                self.subset_sum(list_val, sum + list_val[i], i + 1, target)
                self.values.pop(-1) #remove as now longer valid

#Driving code
```

```
c1 = find_subset_sum()
c1.subset_sum([1,3,5,2,7] , 0,0,10)
print("Result: ",c1.subset_count)

c2 = find_subset_sum()
c2.subset_sum([1, 3, 7, 5, 9, 11] , 0,0,12)
print("Result: ",c2.subset_count)
```

Output

```
Subset =>  [1, 2, 7]

Subset =>  [3, 5, 2]

Subset =>  [3, 7]

Result:  3

Subset =>  [1, 11]

Subset =>  [3, 9]

Subset =>  [7, 5]

Result:  3
```

Some of the applications of the backtracking algorithm are as follows:

- **Solving problems that require decision-making**: It is widely used to solve problems that require decision-making. Examples include the famous 8 queen problem, the Hamiltonian circuit problem, the knapsack problem, and the Sudoku puzzle.

- **Finding all possible solutions**: The algorithm can be used to find all possible solutions to a problem. For example, it can be used to generate all possible permutations of a string.

- **Optimization problems**: It is used to solve optimization problems, for example, it can be used to find the shortest path between two points in a graph.

- **Parsing**: It is used in many parsing algorithms, such as those used in compilers.

- **Artificial intelligence**: Backtracking is a powerful tool for solving problems in artificial intelligence, such as game playing.

Backtracking algorithms can also be used to solve various real-world problems, such as the following:

- Solving a maze (finding a path from the start to the end point)

- Finding all possible combinations of items in a set (all possible combinations of a list of ingredients)

- Generating all possible permutations of a given string

- Finding the shortest path between two nodes in a graph

- Solving a Sudoku puzzle

- Generating all possible subsets of a given set of elements

We will now solve the queens puzzle. The N-Queen is the problem of placing n queens on a chessboard of dimensions N×N such that no queen can attack another queen in a single move. We need to check if such an arrangement of n queens exists, and if it does, then print the arrangement. Note that a queen in chess can attack in any of the eight directions, that is, left/right, upward/downward, diagonally upward/downward. An example of 4x4 puzzle solution is shown in *Figure 6.7*:

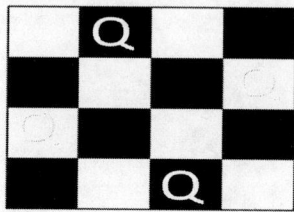

Figure 6.7: Four queens on a 4X4 chessboard

The algorithm starts by placing a queen in the first row and then tries to place the remaining queens in the subsequent rows, one at a time. For each row, the algorithm iterates over all possible positions of the queen in that row and checks if it is safe to place the queen in that position. If it is safe, the queen is set, and the algorithm recursively calls itself to place the remaining queens in subsequent rows. If unsafe, the algorithm backtracks and tries the next possible position. Once all the queens are placed, the algorithm returns true, indicating that a solution has been found. If no resolution is found, the algorithm returns false. *Figure 6.8* depicts the steps we just discussed as algorithmic steps:

Algorithm 1: Backtracking Algorithm for solving the N-Queens Problem

Data: $Q[n]$: an array contains the positions of n queens; k: index of the first empty row

Result: All the possible placement of n non-attacking queens on a chessboard

Procedure NQueen($Q[n]$, k)

  if $k == n + 1$ **then**

    | return Q;

  end

  for $j = 1$ *to* n **do**

    $valid = $ True;

    for $i = 1$ *to* k-1 **do**

      if $(Q[i]=j)$ *or* $(Q[i]=j+k-i)$ *or* $(Q[i]=j-k+i)$ **then**

        | $valid = $ False;

      end

      if $valid = True$ **then**

        | $Q[k] = j$;

        | NQueen($Q[n]$, $k+1$);

      end

    end

  end

end

Figure 6.8: Pseudocode that uses a backtracking technique to solve the n-queens problem

The Python code implementation is shown here:

```python
queenscnt = 0

def IsSafe (board, row, col) :
    # Check if there is a queen 'Q' on the left of col in same row.
    for c in range(col) :
        if (board[row][c] == 'Q') :
            return False

    # Check if there is a queen 'Q' on the upper-left of col in same row.
    for r, c in zip(range(row-1, -1, -1), range(col-1, -1, -1)) :
        if (board[r][c] == 'Q') :
            return False

    # Check if there is a queen 'Q' on the lower left of col in same row.
    for r, c in zip(range(row+1, len(board), 1), range(col-1, -1, -1)) :
        if (board[r][c] == 'Q') :
            return False

    return True

def PlaceAll (board) :
    for row in board :
        for val in row:
            print(val,end="    ")
        print()

def NQueensSolution (chessboard, col) :
    # If all the columns have a queen 'Q', solution has been found.
    global queenscnt

    if (col >= len(chessboard)) :
        queenscnt += 1
        print("\nBoard " + str(queenscnt)+" :")
        print("----"*col)
        PlaceAll(chessboard)
        print("===="*col)

    else :
        #Placing the queen in each row of the column and verify if its safe
        for row in range(len(chessboard)) :
            chessboard[row][col] = 'Q'

            if (IsSafe(chessboard, row, col) == True) :
                # Placing Queen safe hence, trying to place Q in the next column.
                NQueensSolution(chessboard, col + 1)
```

```
            # restore empty space as previously placed queen is not valid
            chessboard[row][col] = '.'

#Driver code
board = []
NSize = int(input("Enter chessboard size : "))
for i in range(NSize) :
    row = ["."] * NSize
    board.append(row)

# place the queen 'Q' from the 0'th column.
NQueensSolution(board, 0)
```

Figure 6.9 displays the output:

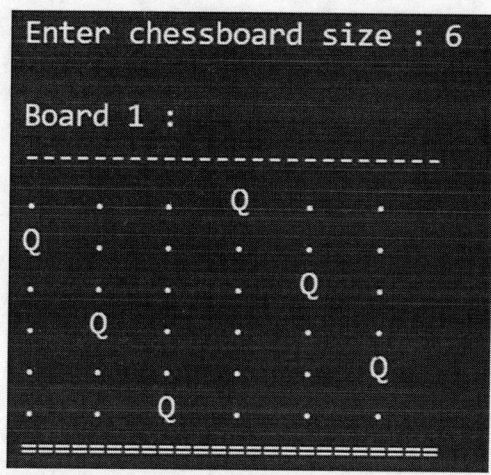

Figure 6.9: *Screenshot of one of the solutions for 6-queens problem*

The first solution can take any position, the second will take among *N-1*, and so on. The time complexity is $O(N) * (N-1) * (N-2) * \ldots *1)$. This results in time complexity of $O(N!)$:

Binary tree

A binary tree is a data structure used in algorithm design to organize data into a tree-like structure, with each node having up to two children. It is commonly used in the design of search algorithms, sorting algorithms, and various other types of algorithms. Binary trees are composed of nodes, each of which contains a value, and each node has up to two children, referred to as the left and right nodes. The root node is the topmost node in the tree, and each node has a unique path from the root. Binary trees have the advantage of being efficient for certain operations, such as inserting, retrieving, and deleting data, because their structure allows quick access to any node in the tree. Some of its applications are as follows:

- **Binary Search Tree (BST)**: It is used to store and search items in a sorted order.

- **Heap**: It is used for implementing priority queues, which are used in scheduling algorithms such as Dijkstra's algorithm.

- **Huffman coding**: It is a form of data compression that uses a binary tree to store and encode data efficiently.

- **Expression trees**: They are used to represent mathematical expressions and are used in compilers and interpreters.

- **B-Trees**: It is a type of self-balancing tree used to store data on disk efficiently.

Before we look at the implementation of the BST, let's understand why BSTs are important and when they are preferred.

Application: A binary search tree can manage database indexes to store and retrieve data from a database efficiently. It is a type of binary tree data structure in which each node has a value greater than or equal to the importance of the nodes in the left subtree and less than or equal to the values of the nodes in the right subtree. The left and right subtrees nodes must also adhere to this property where the nodes on the left have a lower or equal value and nodes on the right have a higher or equal value to the node. A database can quickly traverse an index by utilizing a binary search tree to locate the desired data. This is because a binary search tree stores data so that it can be accessed in a logarithmic time. This means that even if the database has millions of records, a binary search tree can locate the desired records in a fraction of a second. Furthermore, it can be used to store data in a sorted manner, which can be beneficial in managing large databases.

Let us see how we can add members to a BST, and how we can delete and traverse it:

Insertion: To insert a new node into a binary search tree, we first need to find the correct position of the new node. We do this by starting at the root node and then comparing the new node's value to the root node's value. If the new node is smaller than the root node, we move to the left subtree. If it is more extensive, we move to the right subtree. We repeat this process until we find an empty spot where the new node can be inserted.

Deletion: To delete a node from a binary search tree, we first need to find the node. We do this by starting at the root node and then comparing the value of the node to be deleted to it. If the node to be deleted is smaller than the root node, we move to its left subtree. If it is more extensive, we move to its right subtree. We repeat this process until we find the node to be deleted. Once the node is found, we delete it by replacing it with the minor node in its right subtree (if it has one) or the largest node in its left subtree (if it has one).

Search: To search for a node in a binary search tree, we start at the root node and then compare the value of the node to be found to the value of the root node. If the node to be searched for is smaller than the root node, we move to its left subtree. If it is larger, we move to its right subtree. We repeat this process until we find the node or reach an empty subtree.

Let us look at the Python implementation of the code:

```python
COUNT = [5] #spaces away from previous layer

# Binary Search Tree
class BSTree:
    # Function to insert a new node with given data
    def insert(self, root, val):
        # check for empty tree
        if root is None:
            return newNode(val)
        else:
            # If given val is less than root val, then find in left subtree
            if val < root.val:
                root.left = self.insert(root.left, val)
            # If given val is more than root val, then find in right subtree
            else:
                root.right = self.insert(root.right, val)
            return root

    # Search a given val in BST
    def search(self, root, val):
        # Base case
        if root is None or root.val == val:
            return root
        # If given val is less than root's val, then it lies in left
subtree
        if root.val > val:
            return self.search(root.left, val)
        # If given val is more than root's val, then it lies in right
subtree
        return self.search(root.right, val)

    # Delete a node from BST
    def delete(self, root, val):
        # Base case
        if root is None:
            return root
        # If given val is less than root's val, then it lies in left
subtree
        if val < root.val:
            root.left = self.delete(root.left, val)
        # If given val is more than root's val, then it lies in right
subtree
        elif val > root.val:
            root.right = self.delete(root.right, val)
        # If current node is the node to be deleted
        else:
```

```python
        # Node with only one child or no child
        if root.left is None:
            temp = root.right
            root = None
            return temp
        elif root.right is None:
            temp = root.left
            root = None
            return temp
        # Node with two children
        # Get the inorder successor (smallest in the right subtree)
        temp = self.minValueNode(root.right)
        # Copy the inorder successor's content to this node
        root.val = temp.val
        # Delete the inorder successor
        root.right = self.delete(root.right, temp.val)
    return root

    # Helper function to find the smallest node in the given tree
    def minValueNode(self, node):
        current = node
        # loop down to find the leftmost leaf
        while (current.left is not None):
            current = current.left
        return current


# Binary Tree Node: Create a new Node
class newNode:
    # __init__ functions to create a newNode
    def __init__(self, key):
        self.val = key
        self.left = None
        self.right = None


# Function to print binary tree in 2D
# It does reverse inorder traversal
def printTreeUtil(root, space):
    # Base case
    if (root == None):
        return

    # Increase distance between levels
    space += COUNT[0]

    # Process right child first
    printTreeUtil(root.right, space)
```

```
        # Print current node after space
        # count
        print()
        for i in range(COUNT[0], space):
            print(end=" ")
        print(root.val)

        # Process left child
        printTreeUtil(root.left, space)

# Wrapper over print2DUtil()
def printTree(root):
    # Pass initial space count as 0
    printTreeUtil(root, 0)

# Driver Code
if __name__ == '__main__':
    bst = BSTree()
    root = None
    root = bst.insert(root, 10)
    root = bst.insert(root, 8)
    root = bst.insert(root, 15)
    root = bst.insert(root, 6)
    root = bst.insert(root, 9)
    root = bst.insert(root, 12)
    root = bst.insert(root, 17)
    root = bst.insert(root, 14)
    root = bst.delete(root, 8)
    printTree(root)
```

The final structure of the tree is shown in *Figure 6.10*:

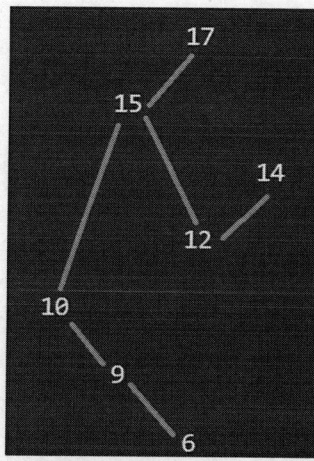

***Figure 6.10**: Reading the output from the BST algorithm*

Heaps

Heaps is a sorting algorithm that uses a data structure called a heap. It is efficient and is used to rearrange elements in an array into a heap. The heap is a special type of binary tree with the property that each node is greater than or equal to each of its children. This allows us to quickly identify the largest element in the array. The algorithm works by repeatedly swapping the root element with the last element in the heap and then adjusting it to maintain the heap property. This process continues until the heap is sorted. It is managed in the form of a complete binary tree, so a new value is always inserted into the leftmost vacant position at the last level.

The Heaps algorithm can be used to create a graph of the shortest possible path between two points, taking into consideration factors like terrain, traffic, and weather. The algorithm will examine all the possible paths and determine the shortest one that meets the criteria. This could be used to help plan a route for a delivery driver or for a traveller who is looking for the quickest route to their destination. The algorithm can be used to implement a priority queue, for example, a hospital may use a priority queue to manage the order in which patients are seen by a doctor. Patients with the most urgent medical conditions would be given the highest priority and placed at the front of the queue. The heap algorithm could be used to ensure that the highest-priority patient is always at the top of the queue.

Let us implement an example to insert and delete from a heap. The root node always has to be higher than its left and right child. For every insert and delete, the tree has to readjust to maintain the properties discussed earlier. Let's see the implementation of Heap algorithm below:

```python
class Heap:
    def __init__(self):
        # initialize Heap array
        self.heap_array = []

    def display_heap(self):
        #Display the content in 1-D array format
        print(self.heap_array)

    def parent(self, i):
        #formula to get access to the parent
        return (i - 1) // 2

    def insert(self, k):
        self.heap_array.append(k)
        i = len(self.heap_array) - 1
        self.fix_up(i) #move up if required
        #display
        self.display_heap()
```

```python
    def fix_up(self, i):
        p = self.parent(i)
        #if parent is lower than the child's value then swap
        while p >= 0 and self.heap_array[p] < self.heap_array[i]:
            self.heap_array[p], self.heap_array[i] = self.heap_array[i],
self.heap_array[p]
            i = p
            p = self.parent(i)

    def fix_down(self, i):
        '''
        heapify the subtree to manage delete
        :param i: root with node i
        :return:
        '''
        left = 2 * i + 1 #access to left child
        right = 2 * i + 2 #access to right child
        largest = i
        # If left child is larger than root
        if left < len(self.heap_array) and self.heap_array[left] > self.
heap_array[i]:
            largest = left
        # If right child is larger than largest so far
        if right < len(self.heap_array) and self.heap_array[right] > self.
heap_array[largest]:
            largest = right
        # If largest is not root
        if largest != i:
            self.heap_array[i], self.heap_array[largest] = self.heap_
array[largest], self.heap_array[i]
            self.fix_down(largest)

    def delete(self, i):
        #deleting element at ith position
        n = len(self.heap_array)
        if n == 0:
            return None
        self.heap_array[i], self.heap_array[n - 1] = self.heap_array[n -
1], self.heap_array[i]
        del self.heap_array[n - 1]
        self.fix_down(i)
        self.fix_up(i)
        # display
        self.display_heap()
#Testing the above code
h1=Heap()
h1.insert(50)  #Run 1: [50]
```

```
h1.insert(10)   #Run 2: [50, 10]
h1.insert(30)   #Run 3: [50, 10, 30]
h1.delete(1)    #Run 4: [50, 30]
h1.insert(20)   #Run 5: [50, 30, 20]
h1.insert(80)   #Run 6: [80, 50, 20, 30]
h1.delete(2)    #Run 7: [80, 50, 30]
h1.insert(70)   #Run 8: [80, 70, 30, 50]
```

The value changed in the tree is shown in *Figure 6.11*:

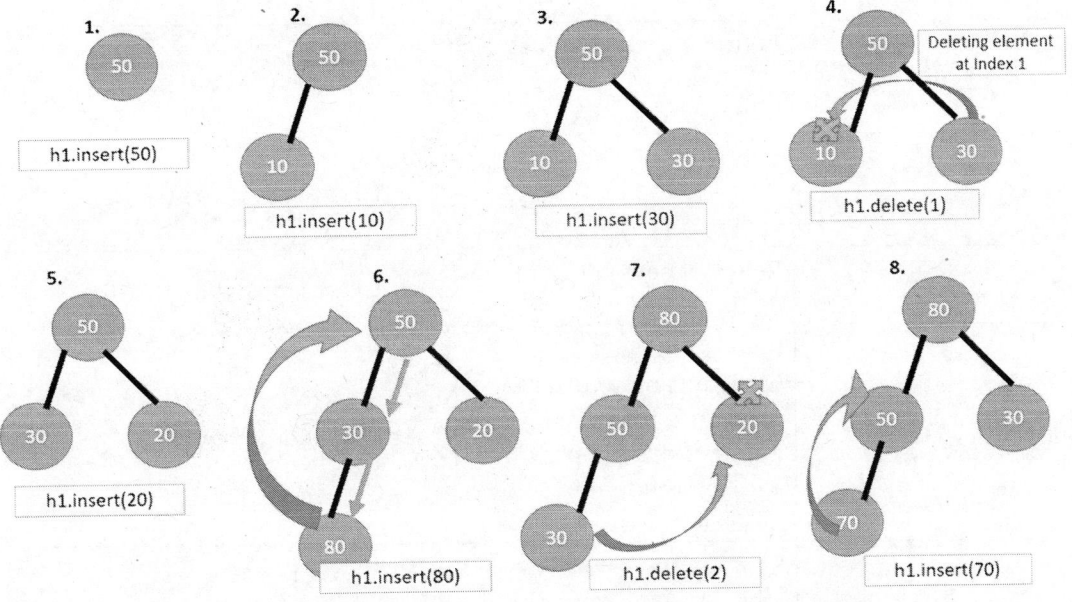

Figure 6.11: Heap tree changing with insert and delete operations

Time complexity: *O(log(n))* (where n is no of elements in the heap)

Hash table

Hash table is a data structure used to store key-value pairs and are commonly used as part of an algorithm design to optimize the performance of an algorithm by reducing the time complexity of searches, insertions, and deletions. Hash tables use a hashing function to map the keys to an index in an array, which allows quick lookups and insertions. The key-value pairs can be stored in any data structure, like an array, linked list, or tree, depending on the algorithm design. The dictionary, which is a familiar data structure in Python, is a hash table implementation. Dictionaries are used to store data in the form of key-value pairs. Each element is accessed using a key. These keys must be unique, immutable objects, and usually strings or numbers. Values can be any type of object. Some of the methods available in the dictionary are listed in *Table 6.1*:

Method	Description	Example
`clear()`	Remove all items form the dictionary	`thisdict.clear()`
`copy()`	Return a shallow copy of the dictionary	`dict2 = thisdict.copy()`
`fromkeys(seq[, v])`	Return a new dictionary with keys from seq and value equal to v(defaults to None)	`thisdict = dict.fromkeys(x, y)`
`get(key[,d])`	Return the value of key. If key doesn't exit, return d (defaults to None)	`x = car.get("model")`
`items()`	Return a new view of the dictionary's items (key, value)	`x = thisdict.items()`
`keys()`	Return a new view of the dictionary's keys	`x = thisdict.keys()`
`pop(key[,d])`	Remove the item with key and return its value or d if key is not found; if d is not provided and key is not found, raises KeyError	`thisdict.pop("model")`
`popitem()`	Remove and return an arbitary item (key, value); raises KeyError if the dictionary is empty	`thisdict.popitem()`
`setdefault(key[,d])`	If key is in the dictionary, return its value; if not, insert key with a value of d and return d (defaults to None)	`x = thisdict.` `setdefault("model", "Brand")`
`update([other])`	Update the dictionary with the key/value pairs from other, overwriting existing keys	`thisdict.` `update({"color": "White"})`
`values()`	Return a new view of the dictionary's values	`x = thisdict.values()`

Table 6.1: Inbuilt methods provided by the dictionary class

Let us look at a simple program that implements dictionary:

```python
my_dict = {
    "name": "Snehil Saurav",
    "age": 27,
    "country": "UK"
    }
# Accessing the dictionary items
print(my_dict["name"])
print(my_dict["age"])
print(my_dict["country"])

# Adding an item
my_dict["gender"] = "Male"

# Removing an item
del my_dict["age"]

# Looping through a dictionary
for key, value in my_dict.items():
    print(key + ": " + value)
```

We will write another program to generate a random password that is 8 characters long, consisting of a combination of lower case letters, upper case letters, numbers and special characters using dictionary:

```python
import string
import random

#Create a dictionary of all possible characters
possible_characters = {
    'lowercase_letters': string.ascii_lowercase,
    'uppercase_letters': string.ascii_uppercase,
    'numbers': string.digits,
    'special_characters': string.punctuation
}

#Create an empty list to store the password
password = []

#Loop 8 times and randomly pick one character from each dictionary
for i in range(8):
    #Randomly select one of the 4 character types
    character_type = random.choice(list(possible_characters.keys()))
    #Randomly select one character from the selected character type
    character = random.choice(possible_characters[character_type])
    #Add the character to the password list
    password.append(character)
```

```
#Join the characters in the password list together
password = ''.join(password)

#Print the password
print("Your new random password is:", password)
```

There exists different types of **dictionary** that have been created to perform certain tasks:

- **Counter**: It is a special type of dictionary that keeps track of the number of occurrences of a particular item. It is an unordered collection of objects that can store any type of data, and it is often used to count the number of times an item appears in a list or other collection of data.

- **OrderedDict:** It is a dictionary subclass that remembers the order in which its contents are added. It can be particularly useful when you want to have a consistent output order for a dictionary or when you want to make sure a dictionary is processed in a particular order.

- **Defaultdict**: It is a dictionary-like object in Python that provides a way to handle missing keys. It is a subclass of the built-in **dict** class. The only difference is that when a key is not found, instead of a **KeyError** being raised, a new entry is created. The type of this new entry is given by the argument of the **defaultdict** constructor.

- **ChainMap**: It is a type of data structure in Python that is used to store multiple dictionaries in a single mapping. It allows you to create a single, unified view of multiple mappings, which makes it easier to look up and manipulate values stored in multiple dictionaries at once.

Graph algorithm

It is a method for solving problems in graph theory. It solves problems by exploring the graph and looking for a path that leads from one node to another. The algorithm is based on the assumption that the graph is undirected and has no cycles. A graph algorithm takes a graph data structure as input and provides a solution to a specific problem. It is used to solve various problems, including finding the shortest path between two nodes, determining whether a graph is bipartite, finding the lowest cost path between two nodes, and finding the maximum flow between two nodes.

The most common graph algorithm finds the shortest path between two nodes. This algorithm uses a breadth-first search algorithm to traverse the graph. It starts at one node and explores its neighbors before moving on to the next node. This process is repeated until the destination node is reached. The number of edges from the starting node to the destination node determines the shortest path between the two nodes.

Another standard graph algorithm is the minimum spanning tree algorithm. It uses Kruskal's algorithm to find the minimum spanning tree of a graph. The algorithm starts with the set of all edges and then selects the border with the lowest weight. This process is repeated until all edges are included in the minimum spanning tree.

The maximum flow algorithm is another common graph algorithm. It finds the maximum flow between two nodes and uses the Ford-Fulkerson algorithm to find the maximum flow between two nodes. It starts by assigning a flow value to each edge and then it iteratively updates the flow values until the maximum flow is found.

Finally, the graph coloring algorithm is used to color a graph. It uses the Welsh-Powell algorithm and assigns a color to each vertex, and then it iteratively updates the colors until no two adjacent vertices have the same color. The algorithm is complete when there are no two adjacent vertices with the same color.

Let us look at the Python implementation of Dijkstra's algorithm, finding the shortest path from the source to all nodes.

Algorithm

Step 1: Set all distances from the source node to infinity, except for the source node itself, which is set to 0.

Step 2: Set the unvisited node with the shortest distance as the current node.

Step 3: Calculate the distance of each unvisited node from the current node.

Step 4: Set the unvisited node with the shortest distance as the new current node and mark it as visited.

Step 5: Repeat steps 3 and 4 until all nodes have been visited.

Step 6: Return the shortest distance from the source node to all other nodes.

Figure 6.12 shows the source (O) and the distance to other vertices:

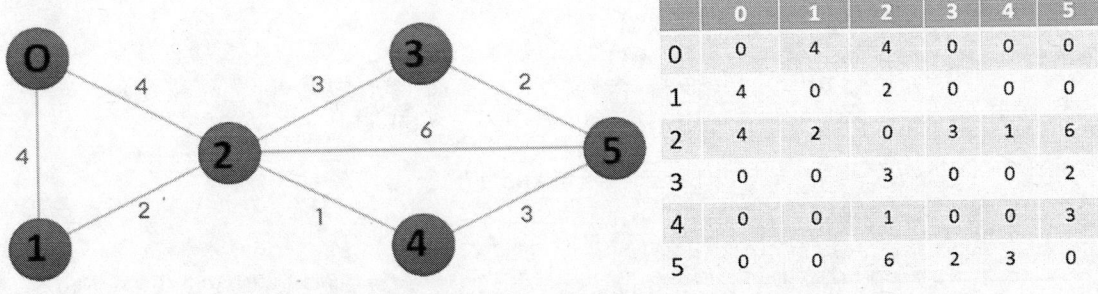

	0	1	2	3	4	5
0	0	4	4	0	0	0
1	4	0	2	0	0	0
2	4	2	0	3	1	6
3	0	0	3	0	0	2
4	0	0	1	0	0	3
5	0	0	6	2	3	0

Figure 6.12: Problem statement with distance from O to other vertices

Here is the Python code:

```python
import numpy as np

class GenGraph():
    def __init__(self, vertx):
        self.V = vertx
        self.plot_graph = [[0 for col in range(vertx)]
                           for row in range(vertx)]

    def Display_Solution(self, dist):
        print("Vertex \t: \tDistance from Source")
        for node in range(self.V):
            print("\t", node, "\t:\t", dist[node])
    # Find the vertex with minimum distance value
    # from the set of vertices not yet in shortest path
    def calc_min_distance(self, dist, spSet):
        min = np.inf   # default max distance
        min_idx = 1
        # Look for not nearest vertex not in shortest path
        for v in range(self.V):
            if dist[v] < min and not spSet[v]:
                min = dist[v]
                min_idx = v
        return min_idx


    # Implementing Dijkstra's shortest path algorithm
    # using graph using adjacency matrix representation
    def dijkstra_algo(self, source):
        dist = [np.inf] * self.V
        dist[source] = 0
        spSet = [False] * self.V
        for cout in range(self.V):
            # Pick the minimum distance vertex
            # x is always equal to src in first iteration
            x = self.calc_min_distance(dist, spSet)

            # Put the min distance in the shortest path
            spSet[x] = True

            # Update dist value if distance is greater than new distance
            # and the vertex in not in the shortest path tree
            for y in range(self.V):
                if self.plot_graph[x][y] > 0 and spSet[y] == False and \
                        dist[y] > dist[x] + self.plot_graph[x][y]:
                    dist[y] = dist[x] + self.plot_graph[x][y]

        self.Display_Solution(dist)
```

```
if __name__ == "__main__":
    prb1 = GenGraph(6)
    prb1.plot_graph =[[0,4,4,0,0,0],
                      [4,0,2,0,0,0],
                      [4,2,0,3,1,6],
                      [0,0,3,0,0,2],
                      [0,0,1,0,0,3],
                      [0,0,6,2,3,0]]

    prb1.dijkstra_algo(0)
```

The final solution is shared in *Figure 6.13*:

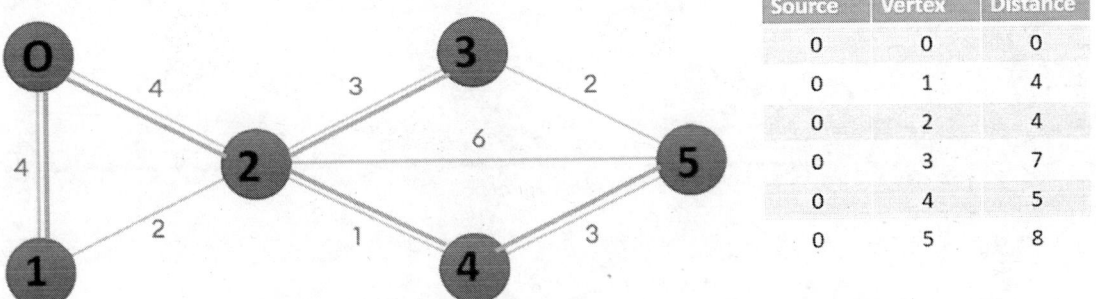

Source	Vertex	Distance
0	0	0
0	1	4
0	2	4
0	3	7
0	4	5
0	5	8

Figure 6.13: *Final solution of finding distances from O to other vertices*

BigO notation: Methodology for analyzing algorithms

Big O notation is a way of measuring the complexity of an algorithm. It is often used to express the worst-case scenario of an algorithm, which is the amount of time or memory it will take to complete its task. Big O notation is a mathematical expression that describes the upper bound of an algorithm's running time or space complexity. It is expressed as $O(f(n))$, where $f(n)$ is the complexity of the algorithm in terms of the size of the input, usually expressed as n. This means the algorithm will take no more than $f(n)$ time or memory to complete its task. It is used to represent the upper bound of an algorithm's complexity.

For example, if an algorithm has a complexity of $O(n^2)$, then it will take no more than n*n steps to complete its task. This type of notation is useful because it allows us to quickly compare the relative complexity of different algorithms without having to actually measure the exact time or memory it takes for each one.

Big O notation is useful for analysing algorithms in terms of their performance and scalability. It is often used to compare different algorithms and determine the most efficient one. *Figure 6.14* shows a complexity chart of different Big O values:

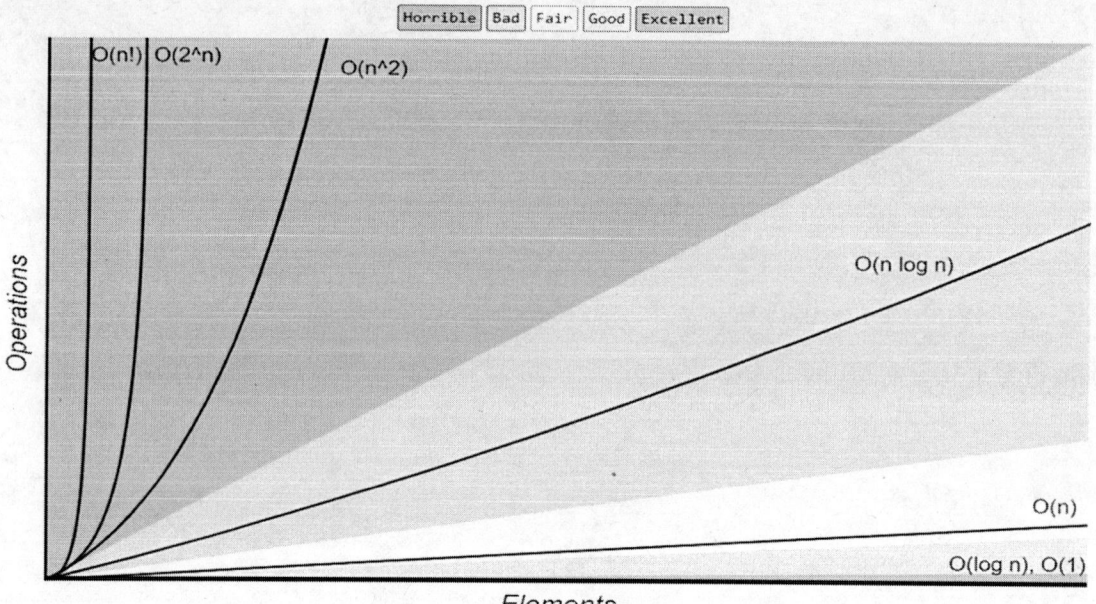

Figure 6.14: *Big O complexity chart*
(**Image source**: *bigocheatsheet.com*)

Let us look at some of the widely used algorithms and their time and space complexities in *Figure 6.15*:

Data Structure	Time Complexity								Space Complexity
	Average				Worst				Worst
	Access	Search	Insertion	Deletion	Access	Search	Insertion	Deletion	
Array	Θ(1)	Θ(n)	Θ(n)	Θ(n)	O(1)	O(n)	O(n)	O(n)	O(n)
Stack	Θ(n)	Θ(n)	Θ(1)	Θ(1)	O(n)	O(n)	O(1)	O(1)	O(n)
Queue	Θ(n)	Θ(n)	Θ(1)	Θ(1)	O(n)	O(n)	O(1)	O(1)	O(n)
Singly-Linked List	Θ(n)	Θ(n)	Θ(1)	Θ(1)	O(n)	O(n)	O(1)	O(1)	O(n)
Doubly-Linked List	Θ(n)	Θ(n)	Θ(1)	Θ(1)	O(n)	O(n)	O(1)	O(1)	O(n)
Skip List	Θ(log(n))	Θ(log(n))	Θ(log(n))	Θ(log(n))	O(n)	O(n)	O(n)	O(n)	O(n log(n))
Hash Table	N/A	Θ(1)	Θ(1)	Θ(1)	N/A	O(n)	O(n)	O(n)	O(n)
Binary Search Tree	Θ(log(n))	Θ(log(n))	Θ(log(n))	Θ(log(n))	O(n)	O(n)	O(n)	O(n)	O(n)
Cartesian Tree	N/A	Θ(log(n))	Θ(log(n))	Θ(log(n))	N/A	O(n)	O(n)	O(n)	O(n)
B-Tree	Θ(log(n))	Θ(log(n))	Θ(log(n))	Θ(log(n))	O(log(n))	O(log(n))	O(log(n))	O(log(n))	O(n)
Red-Black Tree	Θ(log(n))	Θ(log(n))	Θ(log(n))	Θ(log(n))	O(log(n))	O(log(n))	O(log(n))	O(log(n))	O(n)
Splay Tree	N/A	Θ(log(n))	Θ(log(n))	Θ(log(n))	N/A	O(log(n))	O(log(n))	O(log(n))	O(n)
AVL Tree	Θ(log(n))	Θ(log(n))	Θ(log(n))	Θ(log(n))	O(log(n))	O(log(n))	O(log(n))	O(log(n))	O(n)
KD Tree	Θ(log(n))	Θ(log(n))	Θ(log(n))	Θ(log(n))	O(n)	O(n)	O(n)	O(n)	O(n)

Figure 6.15: *Time and space complexities for some common data structure operations*
(**Image source**: *bigocheatsheet.com*)

Conclusion

Algorithms are like tools; they help us accomplish tasks more efficiently and effectively, and they also help increase our productivity. They can help us perform tasks that would otherwise be difficult or impossible to do by manual effort. You can use specialized or general-purpose tools to do your work. They are designed to perform one specific task or a set of related tasks. They tend to be designed for efficiency so that they can do the job quickly and accurately. However, they tend to be expensive or not at all versatile when used for tasks for which they are not intended. General-purpose tools are designed to perform a wide range of tasks. They are usually more affordable than specialized tools and are often more versatile because they can be used for a variety of tasks. However, they may not be as efficient as specialized tools. We discussed both types of algorithms in this chapter. We looked at specialized algorithms like sliding window and general-purpose fundamental algorithms like divide and conquer. We also looked at tree-type data structures and graph-type data structures. There is only one way to master these concepts, and that is by practice. Practice these concepts as much as you can.

In the next chapter, we will learn to build multi-threading applications. Multi-threading is a process that allows a single process to have multiple threads of execution running concurrently. This means that multiple pieces of code can be running at the same time within a single process, enabling more efficient utilization of resources and faster completion of tasks. Multi-threading also allows better responsiveness and scalability, as multiple threads can be used to handle more concurrent requests. In addition, it can provide better fault tolerance, as one thread can take over the work of another if it fails.

Join our book's Discord space

Join the book's Discord Workspace for Latest updates, Offers, Tech happenings around the world, New Release and Sessions with the Authors:

https://discord.bpbonline.com

CHAPTER 7

Building Multithreading Application

Everybody who learns concurrency thinks they understand it, ends up finding mysterious races they thought weren't possible, and discovers that they didn't actually understand it yet after all.

— Herb Sutter, chair of the ISO C++ standards committee, Microsoft

Introduction

Multithreading is a programming technique that allows a program to execute multiple threads (or tasks) concurrently. Each thread runs independently and can work on its task while sharing resources with other threads in the same program. It is used in many applications and different ways. It can be used to improve performance and scalability, to provide a better user experience, or to make programming easier. For example, a web server can use multiple threads to handle multiple requests at once. This improves the web server's performance since it can process multiple requests at once.

This chapter will look at the concept of multithreading and its implementation in Python. We will cover topics like the differences between multithreading and multi-processing, the use of the threading module, synchronization techniques, and strategies for utilizing multiple cores of a processor. It will also explain techniques like thread pooling and parallel processing, and it will provide examples of their use. Parallel processing is a technique in which multiple threads are executed concurrently to increase the speed and performance of a program. These threads can run independently, in parallel, and share resources like memory and processors. Finally, it will discuss best practices for programming with threads in Python, such as handling thread errors in a safe and effective manner.

Multithreading in Python can be used to improve the performance of a program. For example, it can be used to process multiple streams of data simultaneously, run multiple tasks simultaneously, or execute multiple pieces of code concurrently. This can be achieved using the threading module, which provides the basic functions for creating and running threads.

Python threads can also communicate with each other using shared memory. This communication is called inter-thread communication, allowing threads to exchange data and synchronize their execution. This can be used to coordinate tasks and achieve greater efficiency.

It can also make programs more responsive, as threads can handle user input while other threads run in the background. This can help reduce latency and improve the user experience.

Overall, multithreading in Python can achieve greater performance and responsiveness in programs.

Structure

In this chapter, we will discuss the following topics:

- Introduction to the multithreading concepts
- Synchronizing threads
- Inter-thread communication in Python
- Thread pooling with Python
- Multithreaded priority queue
- Optimizing Python threads for performance
- Snake Game: Using multithreading and turtle

Now, let us dive deep into the topics.

Objectives

The main objective of learning multi-threading in this chapter is to enable developers to write code that will increase performance, reduce latency by spreading out tasks across multiple threads, improve reliability, and ensure easier program maintenance. The topics covered here are in accordance with this objective.

Introduction to multithreading concepts

Multithreading is the process of running multiple threads at once. It is a way to improve the performance of an application by running multiple tasks simultaneously. Threads are lightweight processes that share the same memory space and can therefore, communicate with each other easily.

Multithreading is achieved by allowing multiple threads to run concurrently. This is done by dividing the program code into multiple small tasks or processes. Each process is given its thread, and each thread can execute its own instructions. By doing this, the program can use multiple processors or cores in a single computer. Let us look at an example.

Starting a new Thread

By default, every program will have one main thread running. If you want to spawn a second thread, you can do by calling the **Thread()** method available in the **threading** module:

```
threading.Thread(target=function).start()
```

The **start()** method will begin executing the thread. Then there is another method, **join()**, which waits for a thread/process to terminate. This will make the main thread wait until it completes the execution. To see the difference, run the following program and then run it again after uncommenting the **join()** method:

```
import threading

def thread_action():
    for x in range(5):
        print("Run by Child Thread...")

thread1 = threading.Thread(target=thread_action)
thread1.start()
#thread1.join()
print("Main Program Thread Here!")
```

Note: If you are using a powerful computer with high RAM then you may not see the difference.

In the preceding program, we see that the child and main thread run almost simultaneously in the first run, but when we call **join()**, the main thread waits until the child thread completes execution.

Multithreading can help improve the efficiency of the program by allowing it to take advantage of the extra computing power available. This is because each thread can be assigned to a different processor or core, allowing more tasks to be done simultaneously. It also allows the program to use resources more efficiently, as there is no need to wait for a single process to finish before starting another. Let us look at another Python program, as follows:

```python
import time
import threading as th

def cal_square(list_num):
    print("CALCULATING SQUARE OF NUMBERS: ")
    for i in list_num:
        time.sleep(1) #wait for a second
        print('square: ', i**2)

def cal_cube(list_num):
    print("CALCULATING CUBE OF NUMBERS: ")
    for i in list_num:
        time.sleep(1) #wait for a second
        print('cube: ',i**3)

#Main calling
num = [0,5,10,15,20,25,30]
thread1 = th.Thread(target = cal_square,args=(num,))
thread2 = th.Thread(target = cal_cube,args=(num,))
# creating two threads here t1 & t2
thread1.start()
thread2.start()
# starting threads at the same time
thread1.join()  #making main thread to wait
thread2.join()  #making main thread to wait
print("I am from Main, expecting both the threads to have terminated by now")
```

In the preceding example, we can see that both functions run in parallel, making the best use of CPU time.

Multithreading can be implemented at both the hardware and software levels. The program code is divided into multiple threads on the software side, and each thread is assigned to a different processor or core. On the hardware side, the processor is designed to run multiple threads simultaneously.

Synchronizing threads

It refers to the process of ensuring that multiple threads of execution are performing operations in a coordinated manner. This is typically used to ensure that critical sections of code cannot be accessed by more than one thread at a time, preventing race conditions and ensuring data integrity. A critical section is part of a multithreaded application that accesses a shared resource and must be executed in a thread-safe way. A synchronization object such as a mutex, semaphore, or spinlock usually protects the critical section. The critical section allows only one thread to enter at a time, ensuring that the shared resource is not corrupted by simultaneous access from multiple threads. *Figure 7.1* is an illustration of the critical region being accessed by threads A, B, and C:

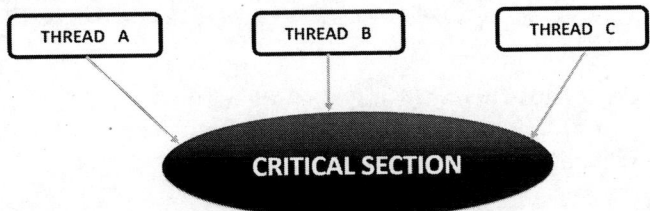

Figure 7.1: *Three critical sections: Threads accessing shared resources at the same time*

A race condition occurs when two or more threads or processes compete for a shared resource (such as a critical section of code, a data item, a hardware device, or a network connection) and the behavior of the program or system depends on the timing of events that occur while the threads or processes are executing. In other words, the outcome of the program may vary depending on the order in which the threads or processes access the shared resource. Race conditions can cause unexpected or incorrect results in programs, such as deadlocks or data corruption. Reading data does not cause any harm but writing/ editing can give unexpected result. The readers-writers problem is a classic example of a multithreading synchronization problem. It describes a situation wherein multiple threads try to access a shared resource. The problem is that either readers or writers can access the resource, but not both at the same time. This generally leads to a condition in which writers need to wait for readers to finish before they can write, or readers have to wait for writers to finish before they can read. This results in one type of thread accessing a resource while it is locked or blocked by another type. Let us take a simple implementation of the readers-writers problem here. Consider the following Python program that lets both readers and writers perform their tasks. When we run the following code multiple times, we get different outputs:

```python
import threading as thread
import time

global val #Shared value
val = 0

def Reader():
    global val
    time.sleep(0.2)
    print('Reader is Reading Shared Value: val=', val)

def Writer():
    global val
    print('Writer is increasing value of val by 1!')
```

```
    time.sleep(0.2)
    val += 1                    #Write on the shared value
    print('Writing done: val =',val)
    print()

#Driver code
if __name__ == '__main__':
    for i in range(0, 10):
        ThreadA = thread.Thread(target = Reader)
        ThreadA.start()
        ThreadB = thread.Thread(target = Writer)
        ThreadB.start()

ThreadA.join()
ThreadB.join()
```

Now, we will rewrite the same code, treating the reading and writing portions of the code as critical sections. The next program is a simple example where we are not using inter-thread communication. **Writer** tasks are competing for *writing*, and **readers** compete for the *reading* sections. The data will not be written by another writer process until the previous process completes it. The same logic goes for the readers block.

```
import threading as thread
import time

global val #Shared value
val = 0
lock = thread.Lock()     #Lock for synchronising access

def Reader():
    global val
    lock.acquire()  # Acquire lock before Reading
    time.sleep(0.2)
    print('Reader is Reading Shared Value: val=', val)
    lock.release()  # Release the lock before Reading

def Writer():
    global val
    lock.acquire()  # Acquire the lock before Writing
    print('Writer is increasing value of val by 1!')
    time.sleep(0.2)
    val += 1                    #Write on the shared value
    print('Writing done: val =',val)
    lock.release()  # Release the lock after Writing
    print()
```

```
#Driver code
if __name__ == '__main__':
    for i in range(0, 10):
        ThreadA = thread.Thread(target = Reader)
        ThreadA.start()
        ThreadB = thread.Thread(target = Writer)
        ThreadB.start()
```

```
ThreadA.join()
ThreadB.join()
```

Thread synchronization in Python is achieved using locks, semaphores, events, and conditions. A lock is a synchronization primitive, which ensures that only one thread is executing a piece of code at one time. Semaphores are also used to control access to shared resources, while events and conditions are used to synchronize threads. Locks, semaphores, and events are provided by Python's threading module, while conditions are provided by the **threading.Condition** class. Let us understand the components of thread synchronization:

- **Locks**: They are the basic form of thread synchronization. At any given time, a lock will allow only one thread to enter a protected section of code. The other threads are blocked until the lock is released. A lock is acquired by calling the **lock.acquire()** method, and it is released by calling the **lock.release()** method.

- **Semaphores**: It is used to control access to the critical or shared resource. A semaphore maintains a counter that represents the number of available resources. The semaphore has an internal counter that is initialized to a given value. When a thread wants to access the shared resource, it acquires the semaphore. When the semaphore's counter goes above 0, the thread can access the resource, and the counter is decremented. If the counter is 0, the thread is blocked until the semaphore is released by another thread. The semaphore is released by calling the **release()** method.

- **Events**: These are another form of synchronization used to signal changes in the state of a thread. An event is created by calling the **threading.Event()** function. The event can then be set or cleared using the **set()** and **clear()** methods. The **wait()** method blocks the thread until the event is set.

- **Conditions**: It is a synchronization primitive that is similar to an event, but with the added ability to wait for multiple conditions. We will discuss this in detail in the next section.

Inter-thread communication in Python

Inter-thread communication is a method of communication between two or more threads in a process. It is a way to synchronize the execution of multiple threads, allowing them to exchange information, share resources, and coordinate their actions. This communication in Python can be achieved using queues, events, semaphores, or conditions.

Queues are a type of thread-safe data structure for storing data that can be accessed by multiple threads. They allow these threads to put data into the queue and take data from the queue, ensuring that no data is lost and that no thread is blocked from accessing the queue.

Conditions: It is a synchronization primitive that is similar to an event, but with the added ability to wait for multiple conditions. A condition is created by calling the **threading. Condition()** function. The condition can then be set or cleared using the **acquire()** and **release()** methods. A thread can wait for a condition to be set by calling the **wait()** method. The **wait()** method blocks the thread until the condition is set.

Using the **condition()** method of threading is better than using the event object for inter-thread communication. **Condition** represents some type of state change between threads, like send notification or got notification. The methods used here are as follows:

- **release()**: This method frees the condition object from their tasks and releases the internal lock obtained by the threads.

- **acquire()**: The compulsory **acquire()** is used to obtain the internal lock system.

- **notify()**: **notify()** is used to send notifications to exactly one thread that is in waiting; **notifyAll()** is used to send notifications to all waiting threads.

- **wait(time)**: This can be used to make a thread wait till the notification is received; in other words, this thread is to wait until the execution of the **notify()** method is done.

Let us look at an example where we will implement communication between two threads:

```python
from threading import Condition, Thread
import random
patients = ['Sachin','Virat','Rohit']
doctors = ['Kapil','Sunil','Ravi']
class BookAppointment:
    def PatientRequest(self):
        condition_obj.acquire()
        print(f'Patient {random.choice(patients)} is waiting for the
appointment')
        condition_obj.wait()  # Thread enters wait state
        print('Appointment Successfully Booked')
        condition_obj.release()

    def DoctorConfirm(self):
        condition_obj.acquire()
        print(f'Dr {random.choice(doctors)} is checking time for
appointment!')
```

```
    time = random.randint(1, 9)
    print('Time Confirmed')
    print('Appointed Booked for {} PM'.format(time))
    condition_obj.notify() #communication made
    condition_obj.release()

condition_obj = Condition()
class_obj = BookAppointment()

TP = Thread(target=class_obj.PatientRequest)
TD = Thread(target=class_obj.DoctorConfirm)
TP.start()
TD.start()
```

Thread TP or TD can start first, but TP has to wait till TD fires notify. In a way, notify tells TP to continue as the appointment condition has been met. The **acquire()** and **release()** methods are used to obtain or acquire the condition object and release the condition object, respectively.

Thread pooling with Python

Thread pooling is a way of executing multiple threads simultaneously in a single application. It involves creating a pool of threads that can be reused to execute a variety of tasks. This is useful for applications that need to handle a large number of tasks concurrently, such as web servers. The main advantage of thread pooling is that it allows efficient utilization of system resources, such as CPU and memory, by avoiding the overhead associated with creating and managing a large number of threads.

The pool manages a fixed number of threads and controls when the threads are created, such as just-in-time, when they are needed. The pool also decides what a thread does when not in use, for example, making them wait without letting them consume computational resources.

Threads in the pool are called worker threads. Each worker thread is agnostic to the type of tasks that are executed. They are designed for reuse once the task is completed. It provides protection against the unexpected failure of the task, like raising an exception, with no impact on the worker thread itself. It is much more efficient to use a thread pool over the manual process of starting, managing, and closing threads, more so when there are a large number of tasks.

Python provides a thread pool via the **ThreadPool** and **ThreadPoolExecutor** classes. The main difference between the two is that **ThreadPool** is a module from the Python standard library, while **ThreadPoolExecutor** is a class from the **concurrent.futures** module, which is part of the Python 3.2+ standard library. **ThreadPool** is a high-level interface that abstracts away the process of creating and managing threads, making it easier to use. It provides a pool of threads that can be used for executing tasks. The number of threads are created at the time of class instantiation.

ThreadPoolExecutor is a more low-level interface. It provides an executor that can be used to manage threads. It allows more control over the thread pool, such as setting the maximum number of threads, the minimum number of threads, and the maximum number of tasks that can be queued up. It also provides methods for submitting tasks and retrieving the results.

ThreadPoolExecutor class has three methods:

- **submit()**: It takes a task to execute.

- **map()**: It executes a task by element (iterable).

- **shutdown()**: It shuts down the execution.

ThreadPool has many methods. Essentially, they work in four stages: create, submit, wait, and shutdown.

Let us implement a simple task to check whether the given Wikipedia page exists. First, we will check without using thread, and then we will run both **ThreadPool** and **ThreadPoolExecutor**. We will also record the time taken to execute the program.

Here are the libraries that we need:

```python
from multiprocessing.pool import ThreadPool
from concurrent.futures import ThreadPoolExecutor, as_completed
import time
import requests
```

Let us write the function (task) first, which looks something like the one that follows. Python **List url_list** has the list of **Uniform Resource Locator (URL)** for which we will verify whether pages for them exist or not.

```python
url_list = ['india', 'python', 'programmers', 'swapnil', 'hyderabad',
'tiger',
          'peacock', 'guido%20van%20rossum']

def is_wiki_page_exist(url, time=10):
    response = requests.get(url=url, timeout=time)
    page_status = "unknown"
    if response.status_code == 200:
        page_status = "Exists"
    elif response.status_code == 404:
        page_status = "Can not find"

    return url + " - " + page_status
```

Now, we will execute the program without creating a thread:

```
print("Method 1: Running without threads")
method1_start = time.time()
for url in url_list:
    print(is_wiki_page_exist(
        url="https://en.wikipedia.org/wiki/" + url))
method1_end = time.time()
print("Time taken without threads:", method1_end - method1_start)
```

Let us see how we can manage the thread pool using **ThreadPoolExecutor**:

```
print("Method 2: Using ThreadPoolExecutor")
method2_start = time.time()
with ThreadPoolExecutor() as executor:
    futures = []
    for url in url_list:
        urls = "https://en.wikipedia.org/wiki/"+url
        futures.append(executor.submit(is_wiki_page_exist, url=urls))
    for future in as_completed(futures):
        print(future.result())
method2_end = time.time()
print("Time taken with ThreadPoolExecutor:", method2_end - method2_start)
```

Let us see how we can manage the thread pool using **ThreadPool**:

```
print("Method 3: Using ThreadPool")
method3_start = time.time()
# create the thread pool: count exists
with ThreadPool(len(url_list)) as pool:
    # creating the arguments
    urls = []
    for url in url_list:
        urls.append("https://en.wikipedia.org/wiki/"+url)
    args = [(url, 10) for url in urls]
    # dispatch all tasks
    results = pool.starmap(is_wiki_page_exist, args)
    # report results in order
    for result in results:
        print(result)

method3_end = time.time()
print("Time taken with ThreadPool:", method3_end - method3_start)
```

Using thread made the program dramatically faster. Even for a small program where we are checking eight pages, we can see so much improvement. Output from the code will be in the format shown in *Figure 7.2*:

```
Time taken without threads: 2.8822784423828125
Time taken with ThreadPoolExecutor: 0.6651451587677002
Time taken with ThreadPool: 0.7278456687927246
```

Figure 7.2: Time taken by the program to execute with no thread management and with ThreadPool

Multithreaded priority queue

It is a thread-safe implementation of a priority queue in Python, which allows multiple threads to access and manipulate the queue without any interference or race conditions. Priority queues in threading are used to ensure that items with higher priority are processed first. For example, in a web server, requests with higher priority can be processed first, and requests with lower priority can wait until the higher priority requests have been serviced. Priority queues in threading also provide an efficient way to store and retrieve data in a multi-threaded application.

A multithreaded priority queue in Python can be implemented using the queue class from the Python standard library. We will look at an example, where we create a random value and random priority in **producer()** function. In this example, **consumer()** function will consume the value with the highest priority first (which is the one with the lowest priority number). Let us implement this with an example; the explanation is given along with the code. As with any Python program, step 1 is to import the required libraries.

Step 1: Import the required libraries

```python
from queue import PriorityQueue
from random import random, randint
from threading import Thread
from time import sleep
```

Step 2: Create the producer() to generate random values and priority

The task here is to iterate 10 times in a for loop, where each iteration will generate a new random value (using **random.random()**) and priority, which is a random integer (created using **random.randint()**). The value and priority are paired into a tuple and passed to the priority queue. Once the task is complete, the **join()** function blocks on the queue until all items have been processed and marked as done by the consumer. This is called a sentinel value and is a common way for threads to communicate via queues to signal an important event, like a shutdown. It is important that we send this signal after all items have been processed, as it will not be comparable with our tuples, resulting in an exception. Now, let us look at the implementation:

```python
# generates random numbers
def producer(pqueue):
    print('Producer method is running now')
    # generate value
    for i in range(10):
```

```
    # creating work: generating a random number
    value = random()
    # generating a priority
    priority = randint(1, 100)
    print(f"Value = {value} : Priority = {priority}")
    # create tuple with priority and value
    item = (priority, value)
    # adding to the priority queue
    pqueue.put(item)
# wait for all items to be processed
pqueue.join()
# send sentinel value
pqueue.put(None)
print('Producer is completed')
```

Step 3: Create the `consumer()` to use up the values based on the priority

The **consumer()** function takes the queue instance as an argument. In each iteration, it finds an item from the queue and blocks it if there is no item available. The task will break the loop when the item retrieved from the queue has the value none, and will terminate the thread. The implementation is as follows:

```
# consume the work generated by producer
def consumer(pqueue):
    print('Consumer is now Running')
    # consuming the work
    while True:
        # get a unit of work
        item = pqueue.get()
        # check for stop
        if item is None:
            break
        # block
        sleep(item[1])
        # report

        print(f'\n ==> Consuming : {item}')
        # mark it as processed
        pqueue.task_done()
    # all done
    print('Consumer is completed')
```

Step 4: Execute the program

We have now configured the start of the producer thread to generate tasks. They are added to the priority queue and available for the consumer to access. The main thread waits (blocked) until the producer and consumer threads terminate; then, the main thread terminates itself. Let us look at the code for this:

```
# create the shared queue
pq = PriorityQueue()
# start the producer
producer = Thread(target=producer, args=(pq,))
producer.start()
# start the consumer
consumer = Thread(target=consumer, args=(pq,))
consumer.start()
producer.join()
consumer.join()
```

When you run the preceding program, you can see that a lower priority number is always consumed before its higher number counterpart. This is how a multithreaded priority queue can be implemented.

Optimizing Python threads for performance

Programs using threads are supposed to perform better than loops, but if you try on your computer, you may not see the difference; in fact, you might see loops performing better than multi-threading programs. This is because threads in Python are subject to the **Global Interpreter Lock (GIL)**.

GIL is a mechanism used in Python to ensure that only one thread can execute at any given time. This lock is necessary because the Python interpreter is not thread-safe, so if multiple threads were to execute Python code simultaneously, it could lead to unexpected behavior. The GIL is implemented by acquiring a lock before executing any Python bytecode and releasing the lock when the execution is finished. This ensures that only one thread can execute at any given time, preventing any concurrency issues. GIL are only allowed to run some X Python instructions before releasing the GIL to another thread. That is why for simple operations, the cost of creating a thread, locking, and context switching is much bigger than the cost of simple computation. However, it works well if you have large number of computations in a program.

Snake game: Using multithreading and turtle

In the section, we will learn to build the classic snake game. This game was first released on Nokia phones in 1997. It was pre-installed on many Nokia phones and is still available to be downloaded on some Nokia phones. The game itself is a simple one. Control a snake-like creature around the screen, eating the little dots, and avoiding running into the walls or itself. Let us build it. The opening screen of the game would look something like *Figure 7.3*:

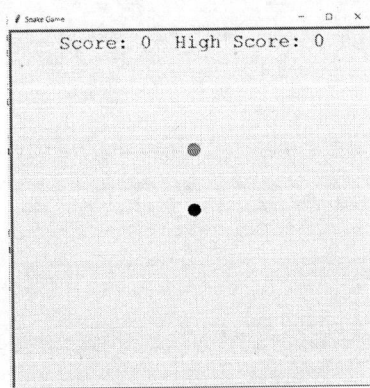

Figure 7.3: *Starting screen*

Let us program to see how this game is implemented. We will briefly describe our approach here:

Step 1: Import the libraries

```
#### Developing Snake game in python
import turtle
import time
import random
import threading
```

Step 2: Set the initial values

```
delay = 0.1
final = 0
# Score
flag = 0
score = 0
high_score = 0
a,b,n,m = 1000,1000,1000,1000
z,i,t,eat = 0,0,0,0
```

Step 3: Set up the screen

```
ts = turtle.Screen()
ts.title("Snake Game")
ts.bgcolor("light green")
wid,hgt = 600,600
ts.setup(width=wid, height=hgt)
ts.tracer(0)  # Turns off the screen updates
```

Step 4: Create snake head

```
head = turtle.Turtle()
head.speed(0)
head.shape("circle")
```

```python
head.color("black")
head.penup()
head.goto(0, 0)
head.direction = "stop"
st = 1
```

Step 5: Create snake food (round ball)

```python
food_1 = turtle.Turtle()
food_1.speed(0)
food_1.shape("circle")
food_1.color("red")
food_1.penup()
food_1.goto(0, 100)
a1 = food_1.xcor()
b1 = food_1.ycor()


ff = 0
food_2 = turtle.Turtle()
food_2.speed(0)
food_2.shape("circle")
food_2.shapesize(2, 2, 1)
food_2.color("brown")
food_2.penup()
food_2.goto(1000, 1000)
segments = []
```

Step 6: Create welcome screen

```python
# Pen
load = turtle.Turtle()
load.speed(0)
load.shape("circle")
load.shapesize(0.2, 0.2, 1)
load.color("black")
load.penup()
load.goto(0, -25)


draw = turtle.Turtle()
draw.speed(0)
draw.shape("square")
draw.color("black")
draw.penup()
draw.hideturtle()
draw.goto(0, 0)
draw.write("welcome to my world!! \n                          -Python", align="center",
font=("Times New Roman", 24, "normal"))

time.sleep(1.5)
```

```
draw.clear()
load.goto(1000,1000)
draw.goto(0, 260)
draw.write("Score: 0  High Score: 0", align="center", font=("Times New
Roman", 24, "normal"))
```

Step 7: Write the functions to control the directions

```
def go_up():
    if head.direction != "down":
        head.direction = "up"
def go_down():
    if head.direction != "up":
        head.direction = "down"

def go_left():
    if head.direction != "right":
        head.direction = "left"

def go_right():
    if head.direction != "left":
        head.direction = "right"

def move():
    if head.direction == "up":
        y = head.ycor()
        head.sety(y + 20)
    if head.direction == "down":
        y = head.ycor()
        head.sety(y - 20)
    if head.direction == "left":
        x = head.xcor()
        head.setx(x - 20)
    if head.direction == "right":
        x = head.xcor()
        head.setx(x + 20)

def coll_border():
    global score, delay, head, z, final
    if head.xcor() > 280 or head.xcor() < -290 or head.ycor() > 260 or
head.ycor() < -290:
        z = 1
        final = score
        score = 0

        # Reset the delay
        delay = 0.1
```

```python
def coll_food():
    global delay, score, high_score, food_1, head, a, b, flag, i, m, n, t,
eat, a1, b1

    for j in segments:
        if j.distance(a1, b1) < 5:
            j.shapesize(1.5, 1.5, 1)
            # j.color("black")
        else:
            j.shapesize(1, 1, 1)

    if head.distance(food_1) < 50 or head.distance(food_2) < 30:
        head.shapesize(1.5, 1.5, 1)
    else:
        head.shapesize(1, 1, 1)

    if head.distance(food_1) < 15:
        # Move the food to a random spot
        head.shapesize(1, 1, 1)
        a1 = food_1.xcor()
        b1 = food_1.ycor()
        a = random.randint(-280, 280)
        b = random.randint(-280, 220)

        # Shorten the delay
        delay -= 0.001

        # Increase the score
        score += 10

        if score > high_score:
            high_score = score
    if flag != 1:
        ran = random.randint(1, 10)

        if i % ran == 0 and i % 70 == 0 and i != 0 and head.xcor() != 0:
            while True:
                m = random.randint(-280, 280)
                n = random.randint(-280, 220)
                if m != food_1.xcor() and n != food_1.ycor():
                    t = 1
                    flag = 1
                    break

    if flag == 1:
        if head.distance(food_2) < 25:
            # Move the food to a random spot
```

```python
        flag = 0
        t = 0
        eat = 1
        # Shorten the delay
        delay -= 0.001

        # Increase the score
        score += 20

        if score > high_score:
            high_score = score

def coll_body():
    global z, score, delay, segments, final
    for segment in segments:
        if segment.distance(head) < 20:
            z = 1
            # Reset the score
            final = score
            score = 0
            # Reset the delay
            delay = 0.1

def do1():
    global z
    head.goto(0, 0)
    head.direction = "stop"
    # time.sleep(1)

    for i in segments:
        i.goto(1000, 1000)

    segments.clear()

    draw.clear()
    head.color("light blue")
    food_1.color("light blue")
    food_2.color("light blue")

    draw.goto(0, 0)
    ts.update()

    draw.write("Game Over!! \n Score:{}".format(final), align="center",
            font=("Times New Roman", 24, "normal"))
    time.sleep(1.5)
    food_1.goto(0, 100)
```

```python
    head.color("black")
    food_1.color("red")
    food_2.color("brown")

    draw.goto(0, 260)
    # score = 0
    draw.clear()

    draw.write("Score: {}  High Score: {}".format(score, high_score),
align="center",
            font=("Times New Roman", 24, "normal"))
    z = 0


def do2():
    global a, b, a1, b1

    # last.goto(a1, b1)
    food_1.goto(a, b + 1)

    # Add a segment
    new_segment = turtle.Turtle()
    new_segment.speed(0)
    new_segment.shape("circle")
    new_segment.color("green")
    new_segment.penup()
    segments.append(new_segment)
    draw.clear()
    draw.write("Score: {}  High Score: {}".format(score, high_score),
align="center",
            font=("Times New Roman", 24, "normal"))
    a,b = 1000,1000

# Keyboard bindings
ts.listen()
ts.onkeypress(go_up, "Up")
ts.onkeypress(go_down, "Down")
ts.onkeypress(go_left, "Left")
ts.onkeypress(go_right, "Right")

if __name__ == "__main__":
    while True:
        ts.update()

        t1 = threading.Thread(target=coll_border)
        t2 = threading.Thread(target=coll_food)
        t3 = threading.Thread(target=coll_body)
```

```
        t1.start()
        t2.start()
        t3.start()
        t1.join()
        t2.join()
        t3.join()
        if z == 1:
            do1()

        if a < wid:
            do2()

        if flag == 1:
            if m < hgt:
                food_2.goto(m, n)
                m = 1000
                n = 1000
            else:
                t = t + 1

            if t > 40:
                food_2.goto(1000, 1000)
                flag = 0
                t = 0
                draw.clear()
                draw.write("Score: {} High Score: {}".format(score, high_
score), align="center",
                        font=("Times New Roman", 24, "normal"))
        if eat == 1:
            draw.clear()
            draw.write("Score: {} High Score: {}".format(score, high_
score), align="center",
                    font=("Times New Roman", 24, "normal"))
            eat = 0
            food_2.goto(1000, 1000)

        if t != 0:
            draw.clear()
            if t:
                if ff == 0:
                    if st == 1:
                        food_2.shapesize(1.75, 1.75, 1)
                        st = 2
                    elif st == 2:
                        food_2.shapesize(1.5, 1.5, 1)
                        st = 3
                    else:
```

```
                        food_2.shapesize(1, 1, 1)
                        ff = 1
                else:
                    if st == 3:
                        food_2.shapesize(1.5, 1.5, 1)
                        st = 2
                    elif st == 2:
                        food_2.shapesize(1.75, 1.75, 1)
                        st = 1
                    else:
                        food_2.shapesize(2, 2, 2)
                        ff = 0


        draw.write("Score:{} HighScore:{} time:{}".format(score, high_
score, 40 - t), align="center",
                    font=("Times New Roman", 24, "normal"))

    for index in range(len(segments) - 1, 0, -1):
        x = segments[index - 1].xcor()
        y = segments[index - 1].ycor()

        segments[index].goto(x, y)
        # Move segment 0 to where the head is
    if len(segments) > 0:
        x = head.xcor()
        y = head.ycor()
        segments[0].goto(x, y)
        if segments[0].distance(a1, b1) < 5:
            segments[0].shapesize(1.5, 1.5, 1)
        else:
            segments[0].shapesize(1, 1, 1)

    move()
    i = i + 1
    time.sleep(delay)

ts.mainloop()
```

This ends our program. It was fun developing this simple yet powerful game implementing thread concepts, wasn't it?

Conclusion

Threading in Python is used to run multiple threads (tasks, function calls) at the same time. This does not mean that they are executed on different CPUs. Python threads will not make your program faster if it already uses 100% CPU time. In that case, you probably want to look into parallel programming.

Python threads are used in cases where the execution of a task involves some waiting. One example would be interaction with a service hosted on another computer, such as a web server. Threading allows Python to execute other code while waiting; this is easily simulated with the **sleep** function.

Running several threads is similar to running several different programs concurrently, but with the following benefits:

- Multiple threads within a process share the same data space with the main thread and can therefore, share information or communicate with each other more easily than if they were separate processes.

- Threads are sometimes called light-weight processes, and do not require much memory overhead; they come cheaper than processes.

- A thread has a beginning, an execution sequence, and a conclusion. It has an instruction pointer that keeps track of where within its context it is currently running.

- It can be pre-empted (interrupted).

- It can temporarily be put on hold (also known as sleeping) while other threads are running; this is called yielding.

In conclusion, multi-threading is a useful way to improve the performance of an application by running multiple tasks simultaneously. It can be implemented at both the hardware and software levels and can help improve the efficiency of the program.

Now, it is time to add some color to our work. In the next chapter, we will cover the building of an interactive dashboard. An interactive dashboard is important because it allows users to gain insights into their data quickly and efficiently. With dashboards, users can quickly visualize their data in simple, easy-to-read graphics. This allows them to quickly spot trends, outliers, or any other patterns that might not be apparent from simply looking at tables or lists of raw data.

Join our book's Discord space

Join the book's Discord Workspace for Latest updates, Offers, Tech happenings around the world, New Release and Sessions with the Authors:

https://discord.bpbonline.com

## Chapter 8

Building an Interactive Dashboard using Jupyter Notebook

Data-driven dashboards are the key to unlocking the powerful insights that can drive success.
— *Satya Nadella, CEO of Microsoft*

Introduction

Dashboards are the best way to analyze business data because they provide a comprehensive overview in an easy-to-understand, visual format. Dashboards present data in a way that is easy to digest and can provide insights that may not be obvious when looking at raw data. Dashboards also provide an interactive platform, allowing users to drill down into the data and view more detailed information or create reports. Dashboards can be customized to display the data that is most relevant to a business, allowing users to quickly identify issues and make informed decisions. They also provide a way to track performance over time, allowing businesses to quickly identify changes in trends or performance gaps.

Jupyter Notebook with VS Code is a powerful combination for creating interactive dashboards. With Jupyter Notebook, you can easily create and share documents that contain live code, equations, visualizations, and explanatory text.

Structure

In this chapter, we will discuss the following topics:

- Introduction to Jupyter Notebook

- Setting up a Jupyter Notebook environment on VS code

- Working with widgets and visualizations in Jupyter Notebook

- Developing sample program using widgets and visualization

- Project: Covid-19 Interactive dashboard

Objectives

The objective of this chapter is to introduce you to Jupyter Notebook on VS Code and create interactive dashboards using widgets. In this chapter, we will learn to create a COVID-19 dashboard that can help us access, understand, and share information about the coronavirus pandemic quickly and easily. In the process, we learn about libraries like Matplotlib, Seaborn and dashboarding frameworks like Panel and Voila. We will also learn to connect to the data sources, clean the data before using, and perform exploratory data analysis to understand more about the data.

Introduction to Jupyter Notebook

Jupyter Notebook is a web-based, open-source tool that allows you to create and share documents containing live code, equations, visualizations, and narrative text. It supports various programming languages, including Python, R, Julia, and Scala, and is widely used in data science, scientific computing, and machine learning. It is used by some of the world's leading companies to power their data science and machine learning workflows. Jupyter Notebook provides an interactive environment with various features, including the following:

- **Code execution:** You can execute code directly in your browser and see the results in real time.

- **Visualizations:** Rich graphical outputs are supported, including interactive plots and maps.

- **Collaboration:** Jupyter Notebook supports collaboration, allowing multiple users to work on the same notebook.

- **Notebook sharing**: You can share your notebooks with others via the web or email.

- **Documentation:** You can write narrative text, equations, and other information directly in your notebook, making it easier to document and share your work.

Overall, Jupyter Notebook is a powerful tool for data science, scientific computing, and machine learning. It is easy to use, allows collaboration, and enables rapid prototyping and testing of ideas.

Setting up a Jupyter Notebook environment on VS code

You can use Jupyter Notebook in Visual Studio Code. Visual Studio Code has an extension for Jupyter Notebooks that allows you to easily create and edit Jupyter Notebooks. This extension allows you to easily access the Jupyter Notebook environment directly from Visual Studio Code, making it easier to work with large notebooks and complex code.

The following are the steps to install Jupyter Notebook in a VS code:

1. Open Visual Studio Code.
2. Navigate to the **Extensions** tab in the left sidebar (or press *Ctrl + Shift + X*).
3. Search for **Jupyter** in the search bar.
4. Select the Jupyter extension from the list of results and click **Install**.
5. After the installation is complete, click **Reload** to activate the extension.
6. Open the **Command Palette** by pressing *Ctrl + Shift + P*.
7. In the Command Palette, type **Jupyter** and select the **Jupyter: Launch Notebook** option.
8. Select a directory to save the notebook, give it a name, and click **Create**.
9. A new tab will open with the Jupyter Notebook, as shown in *Figure 8.1*:

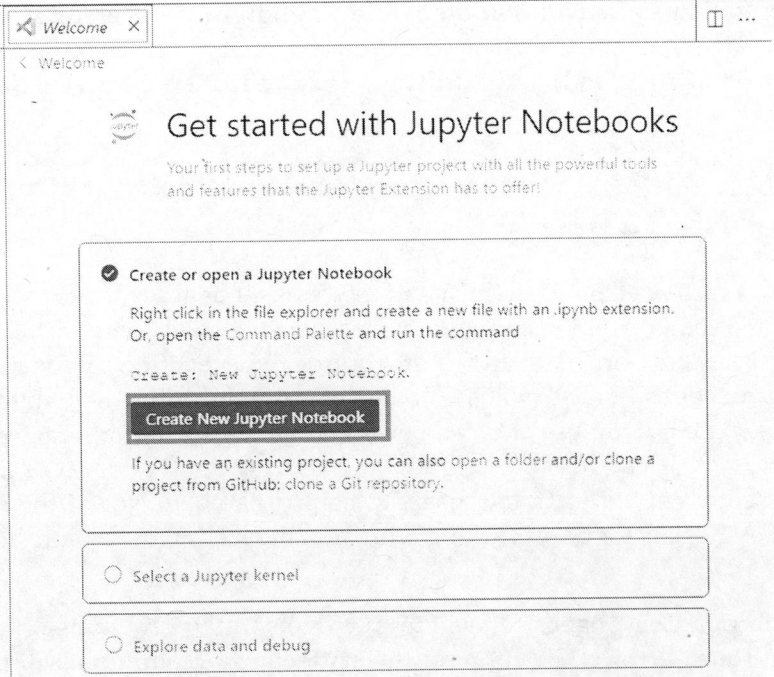

Figure 8.1: Launching Jupyter notebook on VS Code

10. You will see an option to create a new Jupyter notebook as shown in *Figure 8.1*. Click on **Create New Jupyter Notebook**. Create a new file and save it as a **.ipynb** file.

11. Then, write the code for your program in the cell of the newly created Jupyter Notebook.

12. To execute the program, press the **Run** button at the top of the Notebook.

13. The program will be executed, and you will be able to see the output in the output cell. A sample program and the output is shown in *Figure 8.2*.

14. Save the Notebook.

The running program will look as shown in the following figure:

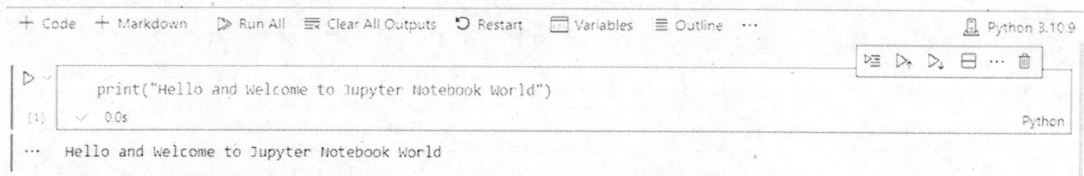

Figure 8.2: An example program running in Jupyter notebook on VS Code

Now we are ready to work with Jupyter Notebook in VS Code.

Note: The mentioned installation steps may be slightly different if you are using macOS. On macOS, create a virtual environment (venv) and then install the Jupyter package. Once it is installed successfully, you can execute the Jupyter Notebook.

Working with widgets and visualizations in Jupyter Notebook

Widgets are interactive elements in Jupyter Notebooks that allow users to manipulate and visualize data in real time. By using widgets, users can interact with visualizations, plots, and images; filter and sort data; and even control the execution of code. Widgets are a part of the **ipywidgets** library, which is installed automatically when you install Jupyter Notebook. They are easy to use and can be used to quickly build interactive applications with very little code. In addition, widgets can be used with other libraries like matplotlib, pandas, and scikit-learn. They allow users to control the behavior of their code and the visualization of the data they are working with, making it easier to explore and understand the data.

You need to import **ipywidgets** to use these widgets in the programs. In case you get a **module not found** error while running the **widgets** program, you will have to install **ipywidgets** library. Follow these steps to install the library:

1. **Install `ipywidgets`**: Open the integrated terminal (**View | Terminal** or **Ctrl +**) in VS Code and run the following command:

```
pip install ipywidgets
```

2. Enable the **`ipywidgets nbextension`:** In the terminal, run this command:

```
jupyter nbextension enable --py --sys-prefix widgetsnbextension
```

3. **Restart the kernel:** Finally, you will need to restart the kernel to ensure that the extension is properly loaded. In the notebook, open the Kernel menu and select **Restart Kernel**.

Now, you can use **`ipywidgets`** in Jupyter Notebook in VS Code.

Note: The mentioned installation may not be required if you are using macOS. You can proceed with the following steps.

Run the following sample code to see if widgets are appearing correctly:

```
import ipywidgets as widgets


# Create a sample text widget
txt_wid = widgets.Text(value='Welcome to VS Code World!')
# Display the widget
display(txt_wid)


# Create a sample button widget
btn_wid = widgets.Button(description='Submit the Data!')
# Display the widget
display(btn_wid)
```

The output for the code is shown in *Figure 8.3*:

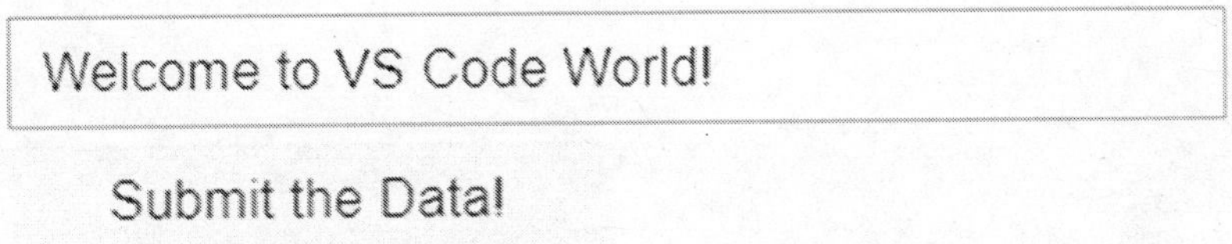

Figure 8.3: Output of the sample widget code

Visualization is the process of creating plots, charts, maps, and other visual representations of data to gain insights and make more informed decisions. Visualization helps to quickly identify patterns, trends, and correlations between multiple variables, which can help identify areas that require further investigation. Popular visualization libraries used in

Jupyter Notebook Python include matplotlib, seaborn, bokeh, and plotly. Matplotlib is the basic plotting library for the Python programming language and its numerical mathematics extension **NumPy**. It provides an object-oriented **Application Programming Interface (API)** for embedding plots into applications using general-purpose **Graphical User Interface (GUI)** toolkits like Tkinter, wxPython, Qt, or GTK+.

Install matplotlib at the terminal using this command:

```
pip install matplotlib
```

Run the following sample code to see if the plots are appearing correctly:

```
import matplotlib.pyplot as plt
plt.plot([1, 2, 3, 4], [1, 16, 81, 256])
plt.title("Sample line graph")
plt.show()
```

The output will be as shown in *Figure 8.4*:

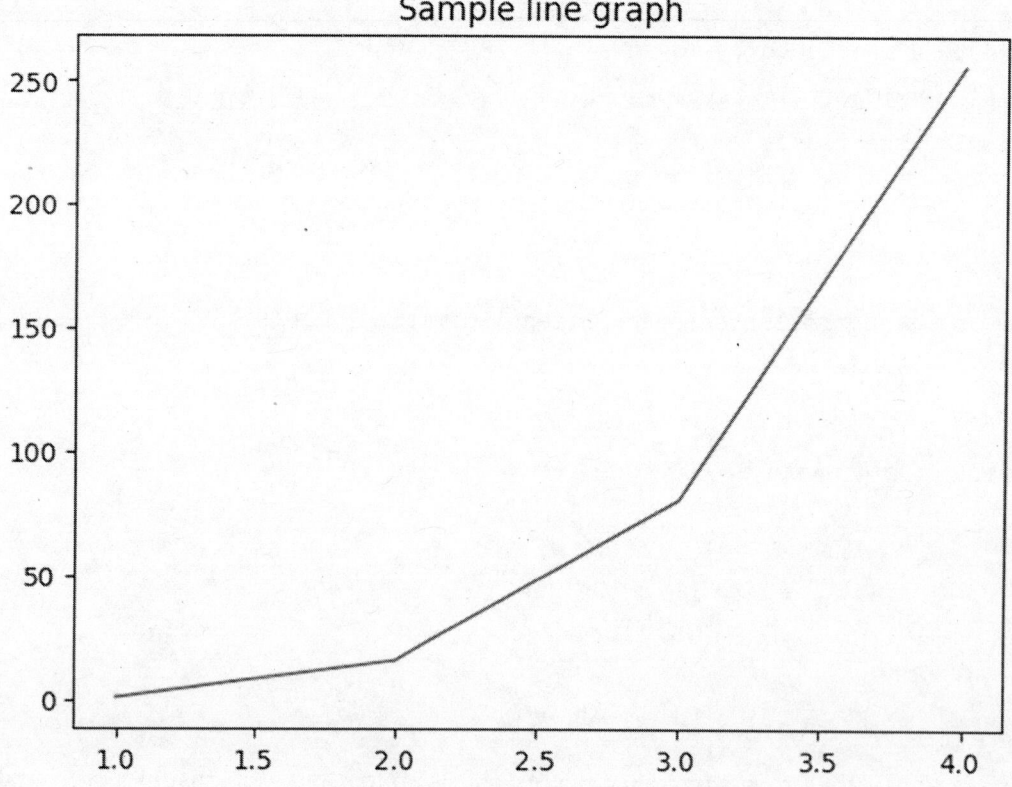

Figure 8.4: *Output of the preceding sample matplotlib code*

Developing a sample program using widgets and visualization

In this section, we will develop a sample program connecting widgets and visualization.

Problem statement

We need to display the total municipal tax collected by five major cities of the country. The taxes collected are in the ratio of **2:3:2.5:1:3.25**. To the bar graph, we will add a slider so that the graph is updated based on the multiple values selected on the slider. Let us look at the code:

```python
import ipywidgets as widgets

import matplotlib.pyplot as plt

# Define data

x_data = ['City A', 'City B', 'City C','City D','City E']

y_data = [2, 3, 2.5,1,3.25] #initial value


# Define a slider widget

slider_wid = widgets.IntSlider(min=0, max=10, step=1, value=0,
description='Slider:',

                                disabled=False, continuous_update=False,

                                orientation='horizontal', readout=True,

                                readout_format='d')


# Define a function to update the graph when slider value changes

def update_graph(x):

    # x is of type: <class 'traitlets.utils.bunch.Bunch'>

    val = x['new']

    plt.clf()

    plt.bar(x_data , [element * val for element in y_data])

    plt.xlabel('Cities name')

    plt.ylabel('Rupees (Crores)')

    plt.title('Municipal Tax Collection (Rs Crores)')

    plt.show()
```

```
# Call the function when the slider value changes
slider_wid.observe(update_graph, 'value')

# Display the slider
display(slider_wid)
```

Explanation

The preceding code creates a bar graph with five data points and links it with a slider **ipywidget** to control the bar graph. Firstly, the necessary libraries, such as matplotlib, and ipywidgets are imported. Secondly, the x-axis and y-axis data sets are created. The third step is to create the slider widget using the **IntSlider** function. This function takes in the min and max values, step size, readout format, and other parameters of the slider. In the fourth step, we have the **update_graph()** function that plots the bar graph. Finally, the graph is linked to the slider using the **observe()** method of the widget. The **observe()** method takes in the **update_graph** function name and value from the slider as arguments and calls the **update_graph** function to plot the bar graph taking in the value of the slider. *Figure 8.5* illustrates the explanation through a bar graph:

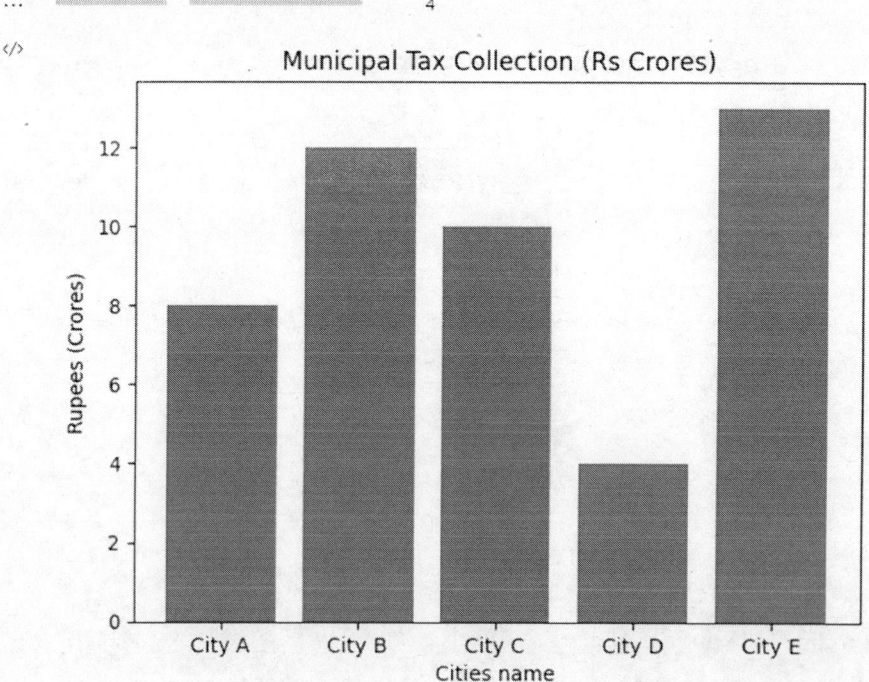

Figure 8.5: Data visualization linked with ipywidget example

Matplotlib Library

Matplotlib is a comprehensive library for creating static, animated, and interactive visualizations in Python. It provides a large number of different plotting capabilities, such as line plots, bar charts, histograms, and scatter plots. It is also capable of creating 3D plots and pseudo-color plots. Matplotlib is designed to be a flexible and powerful tool for creating all kinds of visualizations. It is highly customizable and provides many options for controlling the look and feel of the plots. For example, it allows the user to choose the colors, line widths, font properties, and even the layout of the plot.

In addition to the basic plotting capabilities, Matplotlib provides a number of other features. These include the ability to customize the plot with annotations and labels, and the ability to export the plot in various formats, such as PDF, SVG, and EPS. It also supports logarithmic and semi-logarithmic plots and provides several options for creating contour plots. Matplotlib also provides various functions for creating statistical plots, such as box plots, violin plots, and kernel density estimation plots. It is also capable of creating animations and interactive plots and can be used to generate interactive web applications.

In the next section, we will take public data and create a dashboard for tracking Covid-19 cases.

Project: Covid-19 interactive dashboard

In this section, we will build the Covid-19 dashboard to provide a comprehensive overview of the Covid-19 pandemic. This dashboard will provide a visual representation of the latest data taken from **CSV** files on the pandemic, making it easy for users to quickly analyze and track the spread of the virus. The dashboard will display a range of metrics, including the number of confirmed cases, active cases, recoveries, and deaths related to the virus around the world. The dashboard will be designed to be both easy to use and informative, giving users a detailed overview of the current situation in the fight against the virus. This dashboard can become an invaluable resource for anyone looking to stay informed about the global pandemic.

Let us build the dashboard step by step.

Interactive dashboard with Panel

Panel is an open-source Python library that allows you to create interactive dashboards and data visualizations within Jupyter Notebooks. It is a powerful tool for data exploration and analysis. Jupyter notebook provides a simple yet powerful way to create interactive dashboards along with other data-driven applications. While Panel is relatively new, it has already been used to create some impressive dashboards and applications. It is an excellent tool for creating interactive, data-driven dashboards in Jupyter notebooks. Follow these steps to create a dashboard with Panel:

1. **Import the required libraries**

   If you have not installed them already, it is time to do so. We need to use the **pip** command to install the following libraries before importing the following libraries: **pandas**, **matplotlib**, **panel**, **seaborn**, **plotly**, **geopandas**, **numerize**, and **hvplot**. For example, to install **matplotlib**, you can use the following:

   ```
   pip install matplotlib
   ```

   Now, you can start importing them as shown here:

   ```python
   import pandas as pd

   import numpy as np

   import panel as pn

   import matplotlib.pyplot as plt

   import seaborn as sns

   import plotly.graph_objs as go

   import plotly.express as px

   from numerize import numerize

   pn.extension('tabulator')

   import hvplot.pandas

   import geopandas as gpd
   ```

2. **Read the datasets (Covid and Vaccines)**

   ```python
   # cache data to improve dashboard performance

   if 'data' not in pn.state.cache.keys():

       df = pd.read_csv('WHO-COVID-19-global-table-data.csv')

       pn.state.cache['data'] = df.copy()

   else:

       df = pn.state.cache['data']

   df_vaccination = pd.read_csv('vaccination-data.csv')
   df_vaccination.shape
   # Make DataFrame Pipeline Interactive
   idf = df.interactive()
   ```

3. **Understand the data and the content**

   WHO-Covid 19 data:

   ```python
   df.head(2)
   df.describe()
   ```

Vaccines data:

```
df_vaccination.head(3)
df_vaccination.shape
df_vaccination.describe()
```

4. **Perform data cleaning**

WHO-Covid 19 data:

```
# Check null values in each column in percentage
(df.isnull().sum() / len(df.index)) * 100

# This heatmap shows us the null columns for WHO Covid 19 data
sns.heatmap(df.isnull(), yticklabels=False, cmap='viridis',
cbar=False)
```

The output from the preceding code is shown in *Figure 8.6*:

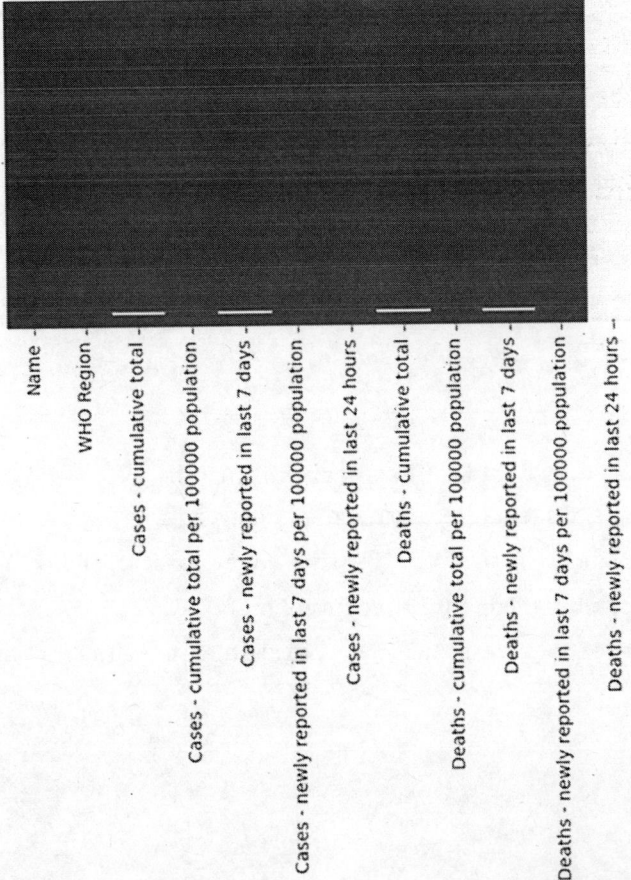

Figure 8.6: *Heatmap showing missing columns in WHO Covid 19 dataset*

Drop columns that have almost blank values:

```
df.drop(columns='Deaths - newly reported in last 24 hours', inplace = True)
```

Now, let us drop the rows that have null values:

```
df.dropna(inplace=True)
# Check null values in each column in percentage
(df.isnull().sum() / len(df.index)) * 100
```

Now all columns have got rid of null values, and you get the output shown in *Figure 8.7*:

```
Name                                                          0.0
WHO Region                                                    0.0
Cases - cumulative total                                      0.0
Cases - cumulative total per 100000 population                0.0
Cases - newly reported in last 7 days                         0.0
Cases - newly reported in last 7 days per 100000 population   0.0
Cases - newly reported in last 24 hours                       0.0
Deaths - cumulative total                                     0.0
Deaths - cumulative total per 100000 population               0.0
Deaths - newly reported in last 7 days                        0.0
Deaths - newly reported in last 7 days per 100000 population  0.0
dtype: float64
```

Figure 8.7: Null values in each column after cleaning the WHO Covid 19 dataset

Get the unique list of region names:

```
country_list = list(set(df.Name))
country_list
```

Now columns:

```
df.columns
```

Data cleaning of Vaccines data that has been imported:

```
# Check null values in each column in percentage
(df_vaccination.isnull().sum() / len(df_vaccination.index)) * 100
# This heatmap shows us the null columns
sns.heatmap(df_vaccination.isnull(), yticklabels=False, cmap='viridis', cbar=False)
```

Figure 8.8 shows the heatmap output:

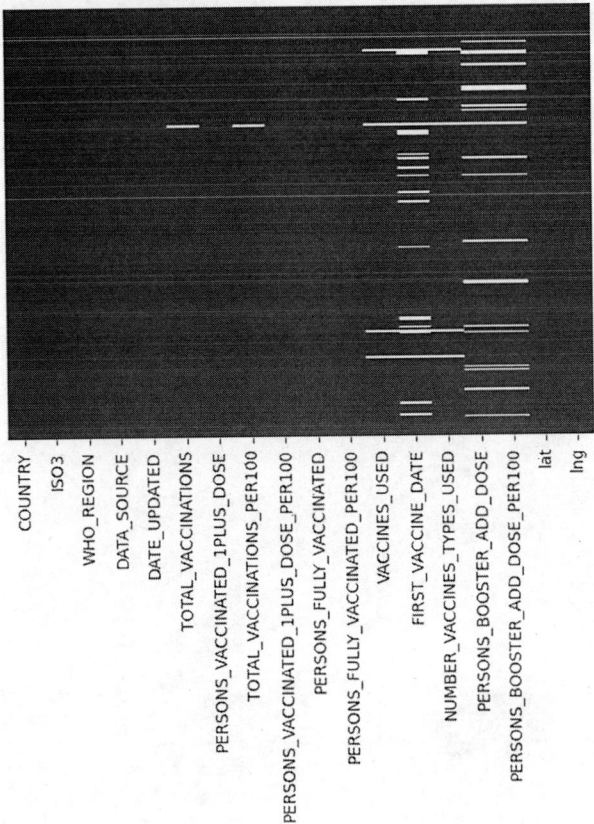

Figure 8.8: Heatmap showing the missing columns in the Vaccines dataset

Drop all the rows with null values:

```
df_vaccination.dropna(inplace = True)
vacinated_country_list = list(set(df_vaccination.COUNTRY))
df_vaccination.columns
```

5. **Perform data visualization**

   First Visual:

```
# Creating Bar Graph in Hvplot
colors = {
    'Americas': '#1f77b4',
    'Europe': '#ff7f0e',
    'Africa': '#2ca02c',
    'Western Pacific': '#324d67',
```

```
   'Eastern Mediterranean': '#ffca3a',
   'South-East Asia': '#ff595e'
}
def plot_bars_1():
   return df.hvplot.bar('Name', 'Cases - cumulative total', c='Name',
   cmap=colors, height=300, width=750, legend=False, rot = 45,
   yformatter='%.0f').aggregate(function=np.sum).
opts(xlabel="Regions",
   ylabel="Cumulative Cases",
   title="Covid Cases across Regions")

plot_bars_1()
```

Figure 8.9 shows the first visual we get:

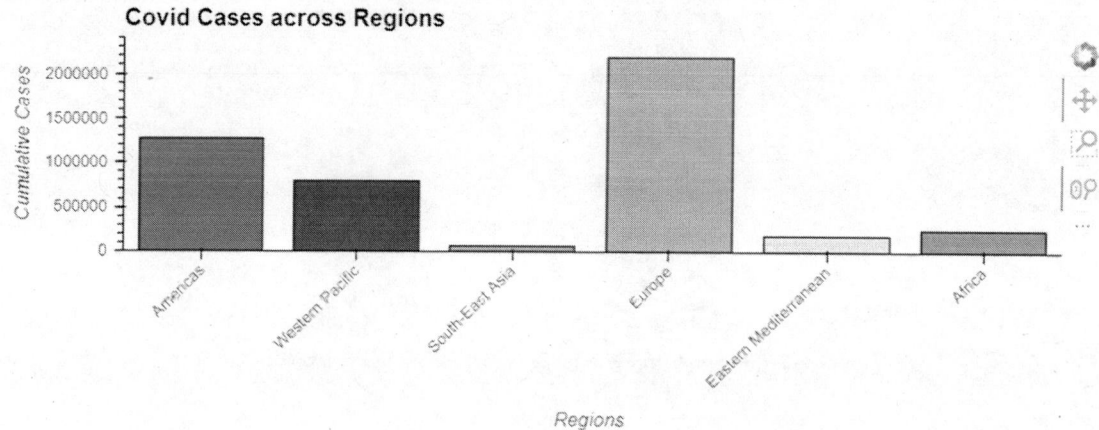

Figure 8.9: *First visual, i.e., a bar graph showing cumulative cases across regions*

Second Visual:

```
# Creating Bar Graph in Hvplot
colors = {
   'Americas': '#1f77b4',
   'Europe': '#ff7f0e',
   'Africa': '#2ca02c',
   'Western Pacific': '#324d67',
   'Eastern Mediterranean': '#ffca3a',
   'South-East Asia': '#ff595e'
```

```
}
def plot_bars_2():
  return df.hvplot.bar('Name', 'Deaths - cumulative total',
c='Name',
  cmap=colors, height=300, width=750, legend=False, rot = 45,
  yformatter='%.0f').aggregate(function=np.sum).
opts(xlabel="Regions",
  ylabel="Cumulative Death Cases",
  title="Covid Death Cases across Regions")

plot_bars_2()
```

The figure given below will be the second visual we get:

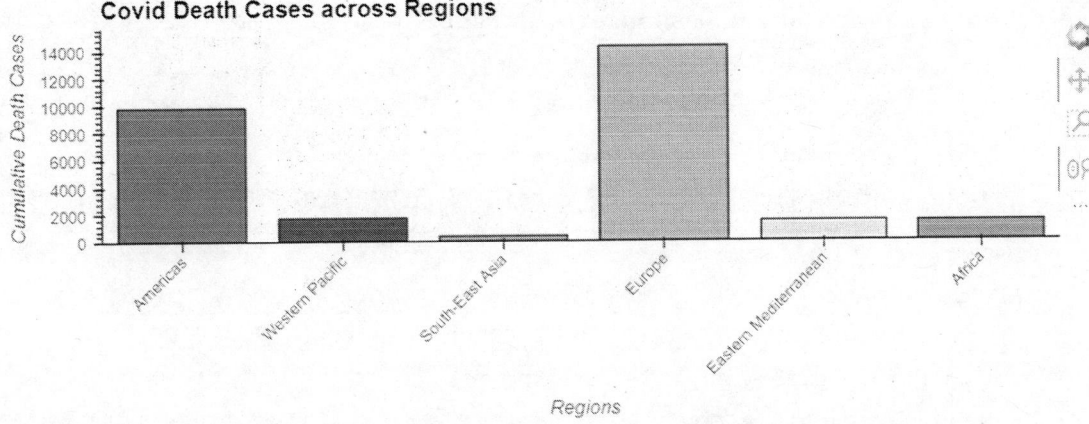

Figure 8.10: Second visual, i.e., a bar graph showing cumulative death cases across regions

Third Visual:
```
columns = list(df.columns[1:-1])

x = pn.widgets.Select(value='Cases - cumulative total', options=columns,
name='x')

y = pn.widgets.Select(value='Deaths - cumulative total', options=columns,
name='y')

scatter_plot = pn.Row(pn.Column('## Covid Scatter Plot', x, y), pn.bind(df.
hvplot.scatter, x, y, by='Name', width = 1190, height = 500))

scatter_plot.show()
```

The third visual is created using Panel widgets, which are displayed in a web browser; so, the preceding code will open a web browser, as shown here:

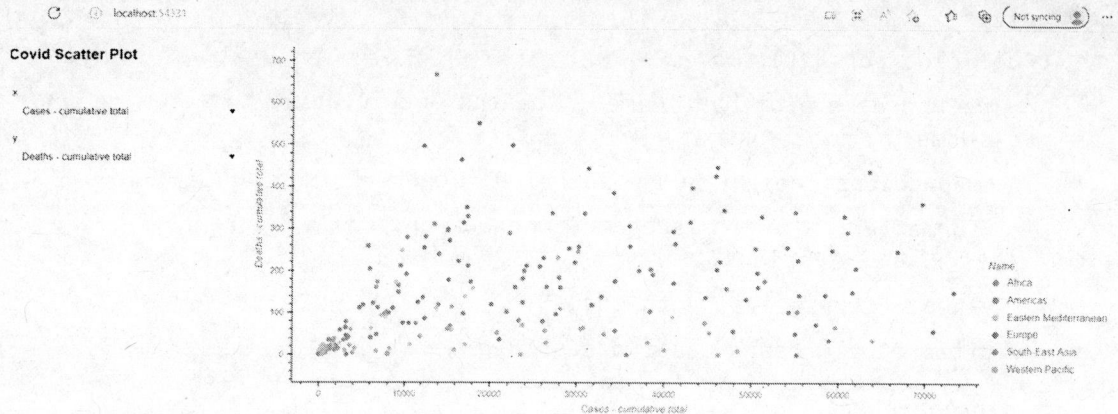

Figure 8.11: *Third visual, i.e., scatter plots showing Cases versus Deaths across regions*

6. **Prepare for creating a dashboard with Panel**

```python
# Card 1 - Total Vaccinated person

TOTAL_VACCINATION = df_vaccination.TOTAL_VACCINATIONS.sum()

# Card 2 - Total Vaccinated person

FULLY_VACCINATED_PEOPLE = df_vaccination.PERSONS_FULLY_VACCINATED.
sum()

# Card 3 - Total Vaccinated person

TOTAL_BOOSTER_DOSE = df_vaccination.PERSONS_BOOSTER_ADD_DOSE.sum()

# Card 4 - Total Vaccinated person

df['TOTAL_PEOPLE_RECOVERED'] = df['Cases - cumulative total'] -
df['Deaths - cumulative total']

TOTAL_PEOPLE_RECOVERED = df.TOTAL_PEOPLE_RECOVERED.sum()

TOTAL_VACCINATION = numerize.numerize(TOTAL_VACCINATION)

FULLY_VACCINATED_PEOPLE = numerize.numerize(float(FULLY_VACCINATED_
PEOPLE))

TOTAL_BOOSTER_DOSE = numerize.numerize(TOTAL_BOOSTER_DOSE)

TOTAL_PEOPLE_RECOVERED = numerize.numerize(TOTAL_PEOPLE_RECOVERED)

table = df_vaccination.groupby(['COUNTRY'])['NUMBER_VACCINES_TYPES_
USED'].mean().sort_values()

vaccination_vs_country_bar = df_vaccination.hvplot.bar('COUNTRY',
'NUMBER_VACCINES_TYPES_USED', stacked=False, legend='bottom_right',
height = 600, width=1510, rot = 90)
```

7. **Create a dashboard using Panel**

```
#Layout using Template

from panel.template import DarkTheme

template = pn.template.MaterialTemplate(title = 'Covid-19
Dashboard', theme = DarkTheme,
    sidebar=[pn.pane.PNG('Corona_1.png'),
    pn.pane.Markdown("# Total Vaccination Completed : " + f"{TOTAL_
VACCINATION}"),
    pn.pane.Markdown("# Fully Vaccinated People : " + f"{FULLY_
VACCINATED_PEOPLE}"),
    pn.pane.Markdown("# Total Booster Dose Completed : " + f"{TOTAL_
BOOSTER_DOSE}"),
    pn.pane.Markdown("# Total Recovered Population : " + f"{TOTAL_
PEOPLE_RECOVERED}")
            ],
    main = [
      pn.Row(plot_bars_1(), plot_bars_2()),
      pn.Row(vaccination_vs_country_bar),
      pn.Row(scatter_plot),
        ] )
template.show();
```

This will launch the server, and you will get a message, which is something like the following:

Launching server at http://localhost:65185

Clicking on the URL will launch a dashboard shown in *Figure 8.12*:

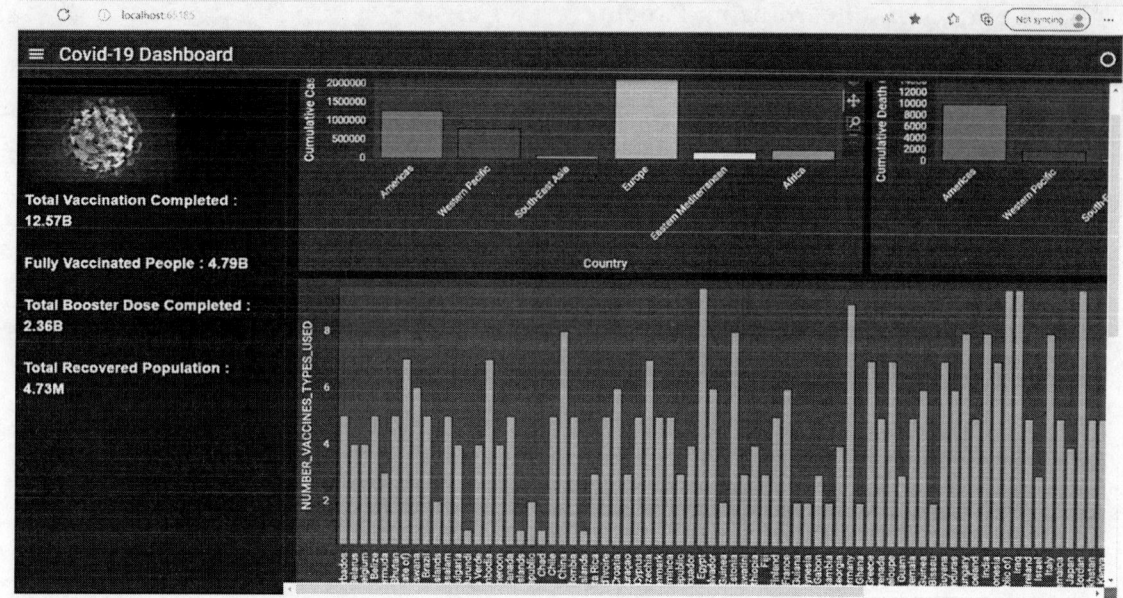

Figure 8.12: Dashboard view

Interactive dashboard with Voila

Voila is preferred when it comes to creating dashboards in Jupyter Notebook because it provides an interactive environment for building and sharing interactive dashboards in Jupyter Notebook. Voila allows users to combine their data, code, and narrative into a single, interactive experience by leveraging the power of the Jupyter Notebook. It also provides extensive support for interactive widgets, which makes it easy to create interactive dashboards without having to write any code. Finally, Voila is highly extensible, which allows users to customize the look and feel of their dashboards.

In this section, we will build another dashboard with widgets and maps and display using Voila. First, folium library needs to be installed before proceeding with the following code:

1. **Import libraries**

```
import folium

from ipywidgets import Layout

import ipywidgets as widgets

import matplotlib.pyplot as plt

from folium import plugins

from ipywidgets import Layout

import pandas as pd
```

```
import seaborn as sns
import numpy as np
```

Folium library will give access to folium maps, which we will draw using **Latitude** and **Longitude** values given in the **Vaccines data**.

2. **Check the dataset**

```
df_vaccination = pd.read_csv('vaccination-data.csv')
df_vaccination.shape

df_vaccination.head(3)

df_vaccination.describe()
```

Perform the same set of analysis as done in the previous section.

3. **Perform data cleaning**

Check and drop the null values from the dataset:

```
# Check null values in each column in percentage
(df_vaccination.isnull().sum() / len(df_vaccination.index)) * 100

# This heatmap shows us the null columns
sns.heatmap(df_vaccination.isnull(), yticklabels=False,
cmap='viridis', cbar=False)

df_vaccination.dropna(inplace = True)
```

4. **Add ipywidgets**

Now, we will add three widgets: one for slider and two multiple selectors to select the country and region:

```
style = {'description_width': 'initial'}

limit_case = widgets.IntSlider(
    value=10,
    min=1,
    max=100,
    step=1,
    description='FULLY VACCINATED/100',
    disabled=False,
    style=style)

unique_country = df_vaccination.COUNTRY.unique()
```

```python
unique_region = df_vaccination.WHO_REGION.unique()

country = widgets.SelectMultiple(
  options = unique_country.tolist(),
  value = ['India', 'China','France'],
  #rows=10,
  description='Country',
  disabled=False,
  layout = Layout(width='50%', height='80px')
)

category = widgets.SelectMultiple(
  options = unique_region.tolist(),
  value = ['EURO', 'AFRO', 'SEARO'],
  #rows=10,
  description='Region',
  disabled=False,
  style=style,
  layout = Layout(width='50%', height='80px')
)
```

5. **Create the `Update()` function**

   Add the **update** function to read the changes in the **widgets** and update the dashboard:

```python
def update_map(country, category, limit):
  #df_vaccination
    latitude = 60
  longitude = -2.2

  df_country = df_vaccination.loc[df_vaccination['COUNTRY'].isin(np.
array(country))]

  df_category = df_country.loc[df_country['WHO_REGION'].isin(np.
array(category))]

  cat_unique = df_category.groupby('WHO_REGION')['PERSONS_FULLY_
VACCINATED_PER100'].mean()

  country_unique = df_country.groupby('COUNTRY')['PERSONS_FULLY_
VACCINATED_PER100'].mean()
```

```
fig, (ax1, ax2) = plt.subplots(1, 2, figsize=(20,10))
# create map and display it
country_map = folium.Map(location=[latitude, longitude], zoom_
start=2)

country_count = plugins.MarkerCluster().add_to(country_map)

# loop through the dataframe and add each data point to the mark
cluster
for lat, lng, label, in zip(df_category.lat, df_category.lng, df_
category.WHO_REGION):
    folium.Marker(
    location=[lat, lng],
    icon=None,
    popup=label,
    ).add_to(country_count)
# show map
    display(country_map)

#Bar graph to show Fully Vaccinated Person per 100
    ax1.bar(df_category['WHO_REGION'],cat_unique)
ax1.set_title('Fully Vaccinated Person per 100')
    ax2.bar(df_country['COUNTRY'], country_unique)
    ax2.set_title('Fully Vaccinated Person per 100')
    plt.show()
```

6. **Execute the dashboard**

Display the dashboard using the **interactive()** function of **widget**:

```
widgets.interactive(update_map, country = country, category =
category,limit=limit_case)
```

The dashboard will look like the following figures. *Figure 8.13* shows the selection widgets. *Figure 8.14* shows the world folium map, and *Figure 8.15* shows the bar graph connected to the selection widget:

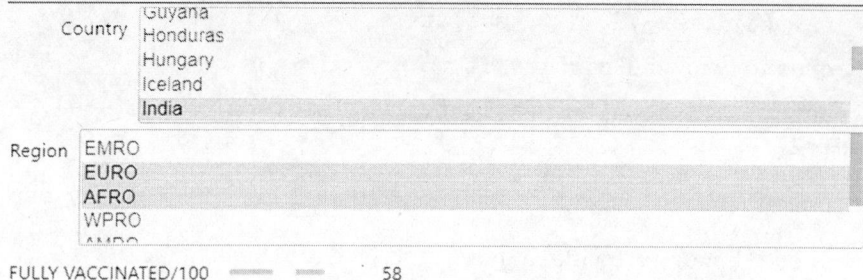

Figure 8.13: *Widgets created for the dashboard*

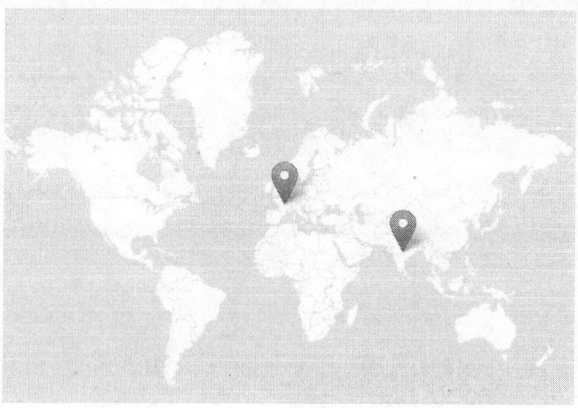

Figure 8.14: *Countries presented on the map using folium*

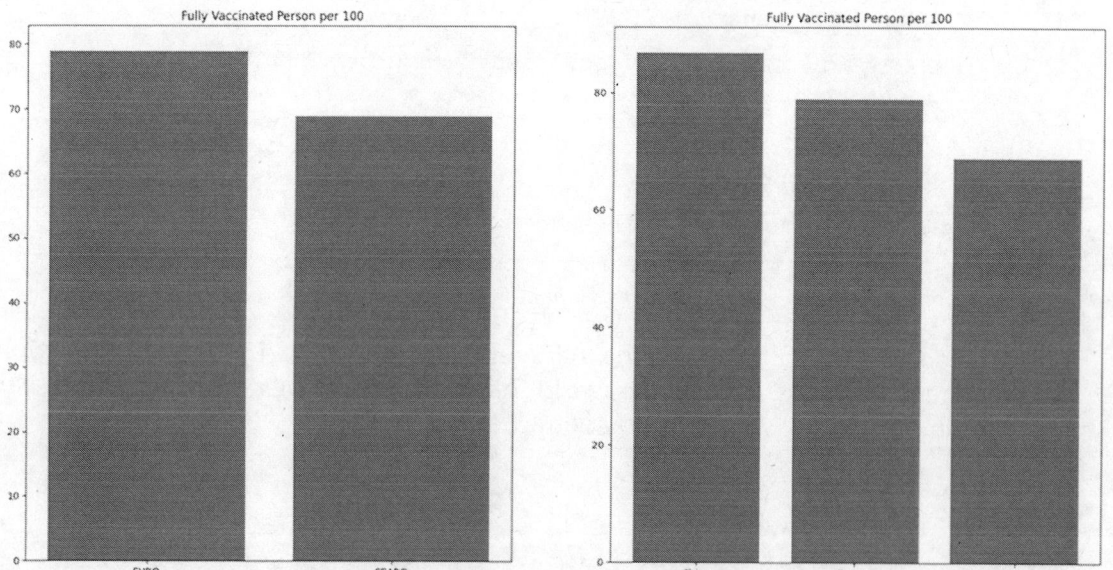

Figure 8.15: *Bar graph connected to multiple select widget*

7. **Use Voila to present the dashboard**

   If you have not installed the **voila** library yet, you must install it before exporting the dashboard.

   To install the **library:** at the terminal, type the following:

   ```
   pip install voila
   ```

   Then, run the following command at the terminal to launch the dashboard in a web browser:

   ```
   voila path/to/your/notebookfilename.ipynb
   ```

   Apart from Panel and Voila, which we have used earlier, there are two popular dashboarding frameworks available in Python: Streamlit and Plotly Dash. Readers are encouraged to practice two other frameworks as well. Here is a brief description to just understand these frameworks:

   - **Streamlit:** It turns Python scripts into interactive dashboard applications, which are shareable as well.

   - **Dash:** Dash is built on top of **Plotly.js**, a JavaScript library for creating interactive, web-based data visualizations. With Dash, users can create interactive, data-driven dashboards and data visualizations that are responsive and look great on any device. Dash also provides a wide range of user-friendly features, such as a drag-and-drop GUI, built-in user authentication, and a range of powerful data manipulation and plotting tools.

   - **Voilà:** It converts Jupyter Notebooks into standalone interactive web-based dashboard applications, along with the exploratory data analysis phase.

   - **Panel:** It is a flexible dashboard framework that works the same in Python script files and Jupyter Notebook.

Conclusion

In this chapter, we learnt to work with Jupyter Notebook and to create interactive and shareable dashboard. Dashboards allow us to quickly identify areas with high concentrations of cases, compare countries, and track the impact of interventions. Creating a COVID-19 dashboard is not a simple task; it requires careful planning, data collection, and analysis. It is important to ensure that the data and information included in the dashboard is accurate and up to date. Furthermore, it is important to ensure that the dashboard is user friendly and easily understandable, as it should be accessible to a wide range of audience.

Overall, this dashboard provides users with an interactive and detailed view of the global spread of COVID 19. It is a useful tool for understanding the current situation and for tracking the progress of the virus.

In the next chapter, you will learn how to use VS Code interface to edit, and debug in Jupyter Notebook. This will include setting up breakpoints, inspecting variables, and creating and managing launch configurations.

Join our book's Discord space

Join the book's Discord Workspace for Latest updates, Offers, Tech happenings around the world, New Release and Sessions with the Authors:

https://discord.bpbonline.com

## CHAPTER 9

Editing and Debugging Jupyter Notebook

Program testing can be used to show the presence of bugs, but never to show their absence.
— Edsger W. Dijkstra, Computer Scientist

Introduction

Editing and debugging are two important tasks that need to be done when writing computer code. Editing is correcting errors in the code and making it more readable, while debugging is the process of finding and fixing errors in the code. In *Chapter 8, Jupyter Covid-19 Interactive Dashboard*, we built an application using Jupyter Notebook, and now we will learn how to debug a Jupyter Notebook program in **Visual Studio Code (VS Code)**.

This chapter introduces the process of debugging a Jupyter Notebook file in VS Code. Debugging is an essential skill for any software professional, and Jupyter Notebook is a popular open-source tool for interactive computing, data analysis, and scientific computing. VS Code is a popular source code editor with a wide array of features and extensions, making it a great choice for debugging Jupyter Notebook files.

This chapter covers the basics of debugging Jupyter Notebook files in VS Code. First, we will discuss the basics of configuring VS Code for debugging. This includes setting up breakpoints, inspecting variables, and creating and managing launch configurations. Then, we will discuss how to debug a Jupyter Notebook file in VS Code. We will also cover the roles of the Python Interactive Window and the Debug Console, and we will look at debugging tips and best practices. Finally, we will discuss how to debug Jupyter Notebook files without using VS Code.

Structure

In this chapter, we will discuss the following topics:

- Introduction to debugging in Jupyter Notebook
- Types of errors
- Checking your code syntax
- Verifying the output

Objectives

Continuing with the interactive dashboard application from the previous chapter, in this chapter, you will learn how to use VS Code interface to edit and debug in Jupyter Notebook. You will learn how to edit and arrange cells. In the Notebook environment, you will learn about editing features like code completion, definition, declaration, and formatting. By the end of this chapter, you should have a solid understanding of how to debug a Jupyter Notebook file in VS Code.

Introduction to debugging in Jupyter Notebook

A good program to practice debugging is the classic **FizzBuzz program**. It prints out numbers from 1 to 100, replacing any number divisible by 3 with the word **Fizz** and any number divisible by 5 with the word **Buzz**. Any number divisible by both 3 and 5 should be replaced with **FizzBuzz**.

This program is simple enough to understand and complex enough to require debugging. Writing the code out and debugging should give you the practice you need to become a better programmer.

The program goes like this:

```python
class MyFizzBuzz:
    def __init__(self, start, end):
        self.start = start
        self.end = end

    def run(self):
```

```
        for value in range(self.start, self.end+1):
            if value % 3 == 0 and value % 5 == 0:
                print("FizzBuzz")
            elif value % 3 == 0:
                print("Fizz")
            elif value % 5 == 0:
                print("Buzz")
            else:
                print(value)
fb = MyFizzBuzz(1, 100)
fb.run()
```

The expected output is as follows:

```
                            1
                            2
                            Fizz
                            4
                            Buzz
                            Fizz
```

Figure 9.1: Output from the program

There are two ways to debug a Jupyter Notebook:

- Run by line - a simpler mode
- Full debugging mode

To debug in any of these modes, make sure you have the following:

- Need to have installed: **ipykernel 6+** in the environment
- Need to have kernel based on **Python 3.7+**
- VS Code version should be **v1.60+**
- Jupyter extension version should be **v2021.9+**

Follow these steps to install ipykernel:

1. Open the terminal and activate the Notebook environment.

2. Run: **pip install -U ipykernel**

3. Close and reopen VS Code. Now, when you open a Jupyter notebook file, you should be able to select the kernel you just installed from the kernel dropdown menu (top-right corner of the notebook interface). In case of any problem, go to `The Developer:` **`Reload Window command`** and reload it.

Note: This installation may look different if you are using macOS.

Debug the program line by line

Run by line allows you to execute a cell one line at a time without being distracted by other VS Code debug features.

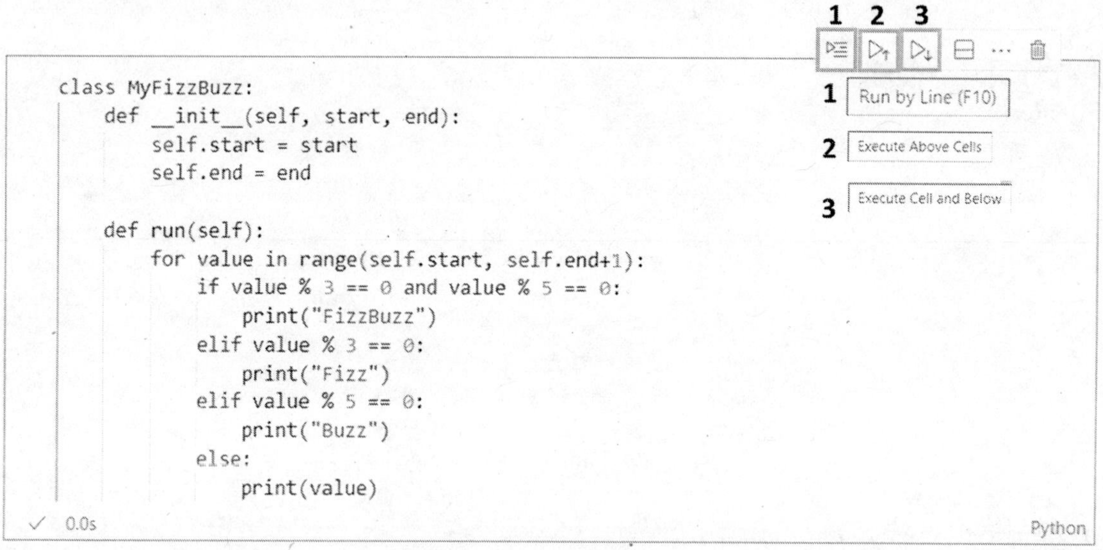

```python
class MyFizzBuzz:
    def __init__(self, start, end):
        self.start = start
        self.end = end

    def run(self):
        for value in range(self.start, self.end+1):
            if value % 3 == 0 and value % 5 == 0:
                print("FizzBuzz")
            elif value % 3 == 0:
                print("Fizz")
            elif value % 5 == 0:
                print("Buzz")
            else:
                print(value)
```

1 Run by Line (F10)

2 Execute Above Cells

3 Execute Cell and Below

Figure 9.2: Line-by-line options

Follow these steps to debug the program line by line in Jupyter notebook:

1. To begin, click the **Run by Line** button in the cell toolbar. This will open the **debug control panel**, which will let you step through the code line-by-line.

2. You can also set breakpoints, examine variables, and more without leaving the cell. You can use the same **Run by Line** button to advance to the next statement in your code. To stop before the end of the cell, click the **Stop** button. To continue running to the end of the cell, click the **Continue** button in the toolbar.

3. Launch the debugger by clicking on the **Run by Line** option or hitting *F10*.

4. When the debugger is running, you will notice another option available, which is to **Continue Execution** or use the shortcut option *Ctrl+Enter*.

The original options are shown in *Figure 9.2,* and the in-progress option is shown in *Figure 9.3*:

```python
class MyFizzBuzz:
    def __init__(self, start, end):
        self.start = start
        self.end = end

    def run(self):
        for value in range(self.start, self.end+1):
            if value % 3 == 0 and value % 5 == 0:
                print("FizzBuzz")
            elif value % 3 == 0:
                print("Fizz")
            elif value % 5 == 0:
                print("Buzz")
            else:
                print(value)
```

Continue Execution (Ctrl+Enter)

Python

Figure 9.3: Line by line debugging in-progress

Follow these simple steps to debug:

1. Run the program by pressing the **Run Cell** button.

2. If the program does not produce the expected output, go back and check the logic of each line of the program.

3. If you find any mistakes in the logic, correct them and then run the program again.

4. If the program produces the expected output, go back and check the input values to ensure that they are correct.

5. If the input values are incorrect, correct them and then run the program again.

6. If the program still does not produce the expected output, use the **print()** statement to print out the intermediate results of each step of the program. This will help you identify the bug.

7. Once you have identified the bug, correct it and then run the program again.

8. If the program produces the expected output, you can be sure that the FizzBuzz program has been successfully debugged.

Full debugging option

The full set of debugging features supported in VS Code can be used. Some of the features available here are breakpoints, the ability to step into other cells, and the ability to step into imported modules.

Follow these steps to debug the program thoroughly:

- Open **VSCode** and the **Python file** containing the code you want to debug.

- Click on the **Debug** tab at the top of the window, as shown in *Figure 9.4*:

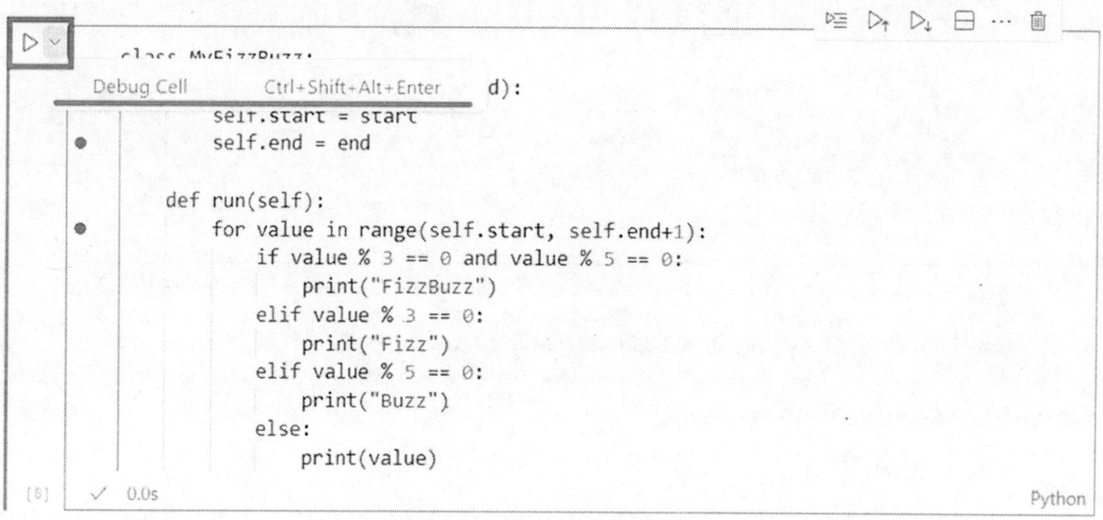

```
class MyFizzBuzz:

    Debug Cell        Ctrl+Shift+Alt+Enter     d):
            self.start = start
            self.end = end

    def run(self):
        for value in range(self.start, self.end+1):
            if value % 3 == 0 and value % 5 == 0:
                print("FizzBuzz")
            elif value % 3 == 0:
                print("Fizz")
            elif value % 5 == 0:
                print("Buzz")
            else:
                print(value)
```

Figure 9.4: Option to start full debugging

- On the **Debug** tab, select **Python: Attach to Jupyter Kernel** from the drop-down list.

- Click the green play button to start the debugger.

- Set breakpoints in the code by clicking in the left gutter of the code editor.

- Run the code in Jupyter, and the debugger will hit the breakpoints when encountered.

If you are new to VS Code, you will see many new things here, as shown in *Figure 9.5*:

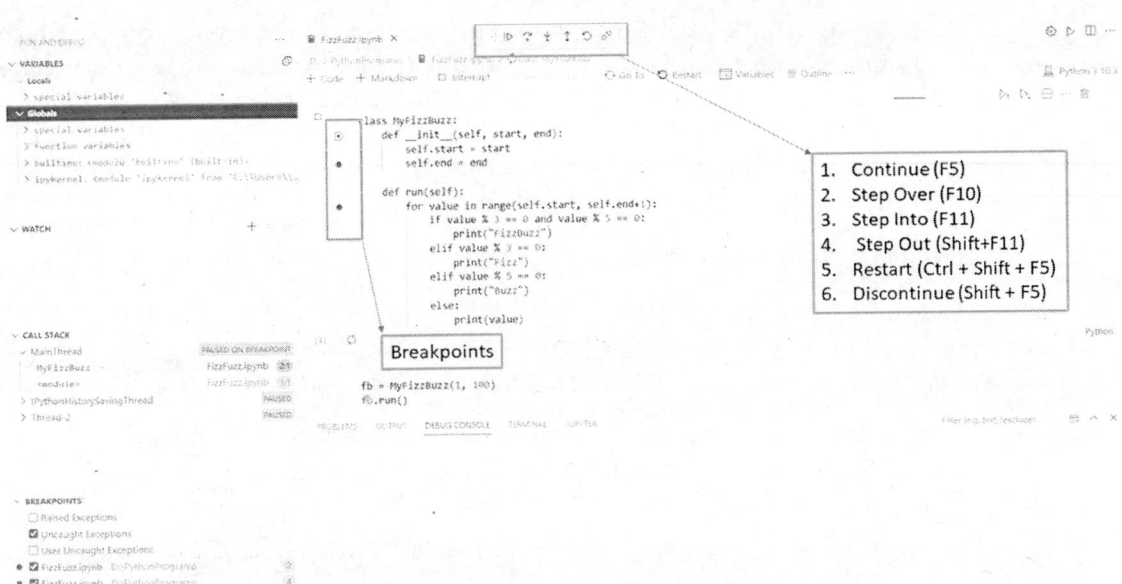

Figure 9.5: Full debugging option in action

Let us understand them to get some clarity on their purpose.

- **Variables pane:** You can easily inspect the variables that are created while debugging is in progress. You can see the entire list of variables with their current values stored. You can also see the difference between global and local variables. The local variables are the ones that have limited scope, for example, variables in the function.

- **Watch pane:** This pane is like a subset of the variables pane, which shows only the variables you are interested in and not the entire list. You can add the variables you are interested in to the watch pane by clicking on the + icon when we hover over the pane. The watch pane is a great way to watch and monitor only the variables that seem not to work.

- **Call stack pane:** Consider a situation where you have multiple inner methods to debug to precisely reach the line of code that is throwing the error or not working as expected. The call stack pane helps in such cases to navigate deep inside a stack data structure where the output of the functions is stored and helps by precisely identifying the area from which the error came.

- **Breakpoints:** We discussed earlier as well that breakpoints are a very important concept while debugging. In normal execution, you do not define or specify any breakpoints as you want the program to run without any stoppage and give us the desired outcome. But when there is an error, the execution stops at the line that caused the error. However, while debugging you might want to control the execution of a program earlier and monitor the state of the variables at a particular point to understand what could have caused the error. So, you can place a breakpoint by simply clicking to the left of the line number in the editor. The created breakpoint will be indicated by a red dot, similar to what we see in *Figure 9.4*. The advantage of running the script with breakpoints is that it will stop at the breakpoint and watch what has happened to the program.

- Use the debugger controls to step through the code line by line, inspect variables and evaluate expressions. Other options available here are as listed here:

    o **Continue**: It executes the next line of code in the current function. If there is no next line of code, the execution jumps to the next statement outside the current function.

    o **Step Into**: It executes the next line of code in the current function. If it encounters a function or method call, the debugger will enter the code of that function or method.

    o **Step Over**: It executes the next line of code in the current function. If it encounters a function or method call, the debugger will execute that line of code without entering the code of that function or method.

    o **Step Out**: It exits the current function and executes the next line of code outside the function.

    o **Set Breakpoint:** It sets a breakpoint at the specified line of code. The debugger will pause the execution of the program when it reaches the breakpoint.

    o **Clear Breakpoint:** It removes breakpoint from the specified line of code. The debugger will no longer pause the execution of the program when it reaches the breakpoint.

- When finished, click the red stop button to end the debugging session.

- You can use the **Debug view**, **Debug Console**, and other options as well from the **Debug Toolbar** as you normally would in VS Code.

We learned about adding breakpoints and using them to check the program's status. It is important to know that VS Code has three different types of breakpoints, each one for a different purpose. To select one of these, first you need to create a normal breakpoint, and then right-click on it and select **Edit Breakpoint…**, as shown in *Figure 9.6*:

```
class MyFizzBuzz:
    def __init__(self, start, end):
        self.start = start
        self.end = end
```

Remove Breakpoint   Delete

Edit Breakpoint...   .start, self.end+1):

Disable Breakpoint   nd value % 5 == 0:

```
            print("FizzBuzz")
        elif value % 3 == 0:
            print("Fizz")
        elif value % 5 == 0:
            print("Buzz")
        else:
            print(value)
```

Figure 9.6: Breakpoint options available after creating one

Now, let us understand the purpose and characteristics of the different types of breakpoints:

- **Expression:** This is the normal breakpoint, which triggers and stops the code's execution when the condition is met. The condition can be seen in the watch pane or the variable pane. You can set the code to stop executing when the given condition is met. Also, this type of breakpoint is characterized by having "=" in the breakpoint red dot. Expression breakpoints allow you to set a breakpoint based on an expression. This expression can be a variable, an object, or a function. When the expression evaluates to be accurate, the breakpoint will be triggered. **Expression** breakpoints can be set in the debugger and used in conjunction with other types of breakpoints. *Figure 9.7* shows how to add **Expression** breakpoint:

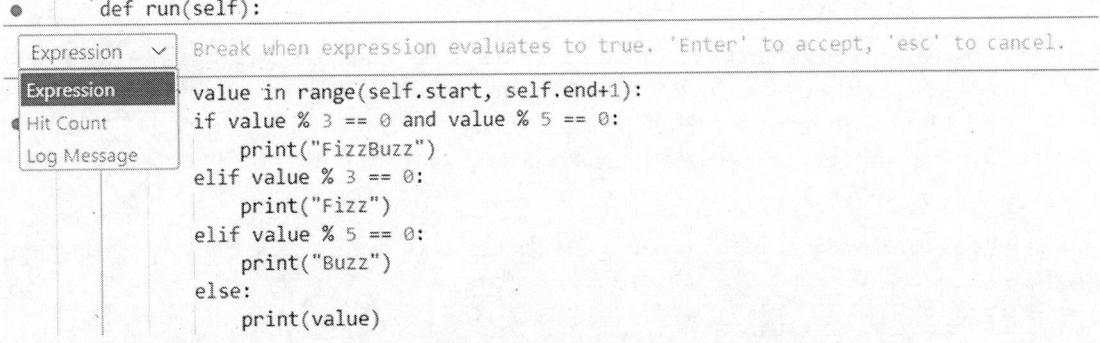

```
    def run(self):
```

| Expression ∨ | Break when expression evaluates to true. 'Enter' to accept, 'esc' to cancel.

| **Expression** | value in range(self.start, self.end+1):
| Hit Count | if value % 3 == 0 and value % 5 == 0:
| Log Message | print("FizzBuzz")
                     elif value % 3 == 0:
                         print("Fizz")
                     elif value % 5 == 0:
                         print("Buzz")
                     else:
                         print(value)

Figure 9.7: Types of Breakpoint options to choose

- **Hit Count:** A hit count breakpoint allow you to set a breakpoint that will be triggered after a line of code has been executed a certain number of times. This breakpoint is helpful for debugging code that has a loop or is executed a set number of times.

- **Log Message:** Log message breakpoints allow you to set a breakpoint that will be triggered when a certain message is logged in the console. This type of breakpoint is helpful in monitoring a program's progress or debugging an issue related to a particular message. A log message breakpoint can be set in the debugger and used in conjunction with other types of breakpoints. This breakpoint does not stop the execution; instead, it is used for printing out some message to the log in the debug console.

- A breakpoint can be disabled by right-clicking it and selecting **Disable Breakpoint**.

These are the different options available to debug a Python program for Jupyter in VS Code.

Types of errors

Errors in Python programs occur when the program encounters an unexpected situation that is beyond its capacity to handle. These errors can stem from syntax issues, runtime problems, or logical flaws. Programmers and developers tend to make three types of errors:

- **Syntax errors**: Syntax errors are the basic type of error and occur when the programmer fails to follow the proper syntax for the language. This type of error will produce a Syntax error exception when the code is run. Examples of syntax errors include missing parentheses, incorrect indentation, and misspelled keywords.

- **Runtime errors**: Runtime errors occur when the code is syntactically correct but fails to execute properly. These errors usually occur when the code tries to perform an action that it cannot, such as dividing by zero. These errors will produce a runtime error exception when the code is run.

- **Logical errors:** Logical errors occur when the code is syntactically correct and executes without producing any runtime errors, but the result is not what was intended. These errors are usually caused by incorrect logic in the code or incorrect assumptions about the data. These types of errors are often difficult to track down and fix.

Now, that we understand the types of errors that can occur, let us look at how to debug in Python.

Checking your code syntax

When debugging a Python program, there are a few basic steps you can take to check your code syntax and identify any errors.

- **Check your indentation:** Python relies on indentation to denote the scope of code blocks and functions. Therefore, it is important to make sure all indentation is correct. If there are any errors in the indentation, your program may not run as expected.

- **Check your variable names:** It is important to make sure that all your variable names are correct and match up with the correct objects. This can help avoid errors such as trying to assign a value to a variable that does not exist.

- **Check your syntax:** Make sure all the syntax in your program is correct. This includes ensuring that all punctuation, brackets, and quotes are in the right places.

- **Check your logic:** Make sure the logic of your program is sound. This includes ensuring that loops are running correctly and conditions are checked correctly.

- **Check your functions:** Make sure all your functions are being called correctly and returning the expected results.

Jupyter helps fix most of these things by highlighting the error in the code.

Verifying the output

Always test your program's output by giving known values and verify that it works fine. While testing, make sure the following techniques are kept in mind:

- **Functional tests:** Functional tests are usually done by manually executing the application and verifying that the expected results are produced. Functional tests often involve a combination of manual and automated tests, such as test scripts, to ensure that all aspects of the system are tested.

- **Algorithmic tests:** Algorithmic tests are tests used to assess a person's ability to think logically and solve complex problems. Check if the logic has been correctly and efficiently implemented.

- **Positive tests:** Positive testing is a form of software testing that aims to verifies that the functionality of a system or application confirms to its predetermined specifications. It involves testing the system with valid input to see if the expected output is produced. Positive testing, also known as confirmation testing, is used to ensure that a system works as expected.

- **Negative tests:** Negative testing is a type of software testing that involves testing the system by providing invalid or unexpected inputs to ensure that the system handles the input correctly. This type of testing helps ensure that the system can detect invalid inputs and respond accordingly. Negative testing is often used to identify boundary conditions, errors in input validation, and unexpected system behaviour.

- **Boundary tests:** Boundary tests (or edge case tests) verify the behaviour of a program or system when the inputs are at the boundaries of the range of valid inputs. These tests are designed to check how the system behaves when given values that are slightly beyond the normal range of inputs.

Debugging can be a complicated process, but it will get easier with practice. We are suggesting some easy tips to follow to debug your program easily:

- **Use print statements: Print statements** are one of the most helpful tools when debugging in Python. By adding print statements to your code, you can see what is happening and determine where the error is occurring.

- **Use a debugger: Debugger** is a tool that allows you to step through your code line by line, which helps you to identify exactly where the error is occurring.

- **Check for typos:** Typos can often be the cause of errors. Make sure you double-check your code for any typos before running it.

- **Simplify the code:** If you are having trouble finding the error, try simplifying the code. This means removing any unnecessary code and making the code as simple as possible.

With these tips, you can debug your code quickly and efficiently!

Conclusion

In this chapter, we have seen the basics of debugging in Jupyter Notebook running in VS Code. Debugging is the process of finding and fixing errors in a program. The purpose of editing and debugging in programming is to ensure that the code is error-free and follows the language's syntax. Editing also makes the code more readable, allowing others to understand it better. Debugging a Jupyter Notebook file using VS Code is a great way to find and fix errors in your code. VS Code provides an interactive debugging environment where you can set breakpoints, inspect variables, view the stack trace, and step through code. It also integrates with the Jupyter Notebook, allowing you to debug code within Jupyter Notebooks as well.

By using VS Code for debugging, you can quickly and easily find and fix errors in your Jupyter Notebook files.

In the next chapter, we will build **graphical user interface (GUI)** applications using Tkinter. Tkinter is a Python library used for building GUI. It provides a set of tools and widgets for creating windows, buttons, menus, dialog boxes, and more. Tkinter is included with the standard Python distribution and is easy to learn and use, making it a popular choice for GUI development in Python.

CHAPTER 10

Mastering Tkinter GUI Capabilities using VS Code

The graphical user interface is the point of contact between people and computers, and it should be designed to let people get the most out of their machines.

— *John Maeda, a popular contemporary American graphic designer and also a renowned author and computer scientist.*

Introduction

Tkinter is a Python library that allows Python applications to create **Graphical User Interfaces (GUIs)**. It is a thin object-oriented layer on top of Tcl/Tk. Tcl/Tk is an open-source, cross-platform GUI toolkit that provides powerful GUI elements, such as buttons, labels, frames, and menus. It is commonly used for creating graphical user interfaces, rapid prototyping, and scripting. Tkinter provides various controls, such as buttons, labels, and text boxes used in a graphical user interface to interact with a user. It is the most popular and easy-to-use GUI library for Python, making it a great choice for developing desktop applications.

Tkinter provides various widgets, such as labels, buttons, frames, checkboxes, radio buttons, list boxes, and scroll bars. These widgets are used as building blocks for creating a graphical user interface. They can be used to create interactive applications with a graphical interface. Widgets can be arranged in a window using various layout managers, such as pack, grid, and place. Tkinter also provides a mechanism for binding events to user interface elements, such as mouse clicks, keypresses, and other events.

Tkinter is a popular choice for developing GUI applications in Python due to its simplicity and ease of use. It is also available as part of the standard Python distribution, making it easy to create a graphical user interface in Python. It is also well supported by a wide range of third-party libraries and resources.

Structure

In this chapter, we will discuss the following topics:

- Introduction to Tkinter
- Understanding Tkinter widgets
- Working with Tkinter events
- Creating menus and toolbars with Tkinter
- Developing an application: A quiz game

Objectives

The objective of learning Tkinter in Python is to gain an understanding of how to develop GUIs and widgets using the Tkinter package. By learning Tkinter, you will be able to create more interactive and user-friendly programs to suit your needs. Additionally, you will understand the basic principles of object-oriented programming, which is essential for creating GUIs.

Introduction to Tkinter

The window is the foundation element of **Tkinter GUI**. Some features of Tkinter window are listed here:

- A window in Tkinter is an object that contains a graphical window.
- It is the main window object and provides access to all other window objects and widgets.
- It provides methods for creating and manipulating all types of widgets, such as buttons, labels, menus, and frames.
- It allows the creation of complex graphical user interfaces.

Widgets are the components that are used to create a graphical user interface, such as buttons, labels, and text boxes. Widgets are used to interact with a user, display information, and manage the layout of the GUI.

Let us build our first GUI program with a window and a couple of widgets. But before that, we need to import the **Tkinter module**.

Step 1: Import the Tkinter Module

You can import the Tkinter module in **Visual Studio Code (VS Code)** by going to your project directory in the terminal and typing:

```
pip install tkinter
```

This will install the Tkinter module in your project directory. Then, you can import the module by typing the following at the top of your Python file:

```
import tkinter
```

Step 2: Creating First GUI Program

Create your Python file; the first line in the code should be as follows:

```
import tkinter as tk
```

Next, you need to create a window that is an instance of Tkinter's **Tk** class. Using the following code, you can create a new window and assign it to the variable **my_window** and add labels and button widgets:

```python
import tkinter

#Create the main window
my_window = tkinter.Tk()

#set window size
my_window.geometry("300x300") #widthxheight

#Set window title
my_window.title("Mastering TKinter GUI capabilities using VS Code!")

#Create a Label
label = tkinter.Label(my_window, text="This is a sample label!")
label.pack()

#Create a button
button = tkinter.Button(my_window, text="Click Here to Quit", command=my_window.quit)
button.pack()

#Start the mainLoop
my_window.mainloop()
```

In the preceding code, you can see that we have set the window size to **300 x 300** pixels using the **geometry()** method. The **title()** method has been used to set the title of the window that appears on the top. This is seen in the output, as shown in *Figure 10.1*. The last line of the program, **window.mainloop()**, is added to run the Tkinter event loop. This method runs infinitely and listens for any events that could be fired, like a button click.

The window that you see in *Figure 10.1* appears on a Windows machine. The appearance will change based on the operating system.

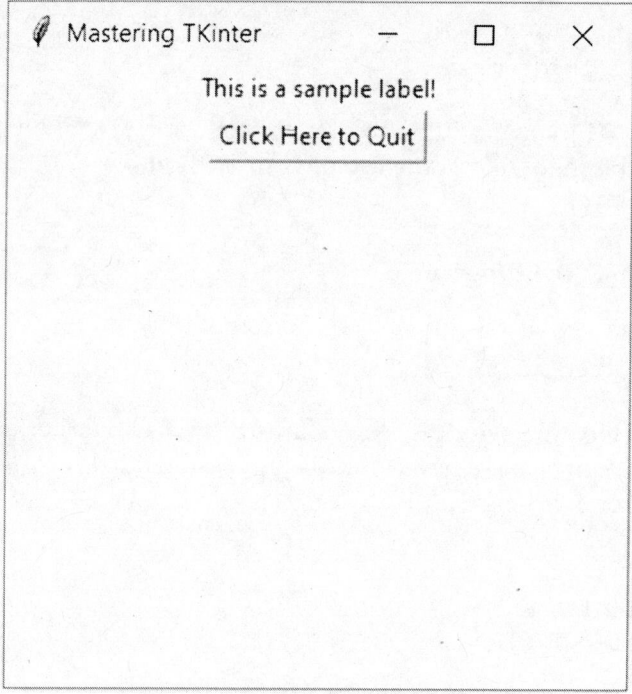

Figure 10.1: Tkinter window (on Windows)

We have added basic widgets in this example. In the next section, we will learn more about widgets.

Understanding Tkinter widgets

Tkinter provides a wide variety of widgets that can be used to build GUIs. These widgets are used to create interactive applications in Python. To create a widget, you must first create a window using the `Tk()` function and then create the widget using its constructor function. Finally, you can add the widget to the window and bind it to a function. Some of the commonly used Tkinter widgets are as follows:

- **Button**: A widget used to create a button that can be used to execute a command or perform an action

- **Label**: A widget used to display static text or an image

- **Check button**: A widget used to create a checkbox that can be used to select or deselect an option

- **Entry**: A widget used to create a single-line text entry field

- **List box**: A widget used to create a list of items from which the user can select one or more given options

- **Menu**: A widget used to create a menu bar with pull-down menus

- **Message**: A widget used to display a multi-line text message

- **Radio button**: A widget used to create a radio button that can be used to select one option from a group of options

- **Scale**: A widget used to create a slider that can be used to set a value on a scale

- **Scrollbar**: A widget used to create a scrollbar that can be used to scroll through a list of items

- **Text**: A widget used to create a multi-line text entry field

Once the window has been created, you can create a Tkinter widget using the widget's constructor function. For example, to create a button widget, you would use the following code:

```
button = tkinter.Button(root, text="Click Me!")
```

The first parameter of the constructor function is the parent window (in this case, the root window), and the second parameter is a dictionary of options that configure the widget. Once the widget has been created, you can add it to the window using the **grid()** or **pack()** method. Take a look at this example:

```
button.grid(row=0, column=0)
```

This will add the button to the window at the specified row and column. The next step is to add functionality. We will discuss this in the next section: *Working with Tkinter Events*.

Let us build a mini example where we will add different widgets. In the next section, where we talk about events, we will add events to this example, and similarly, we will add a menu bar when we discuss **Menus** and **Toolbars**.

We will first import the required packages:

```
import tkinter
import tkinter.messagebox as msgbox
```

Now, we will add the driving code which will have widgets:

```
if __name__ =="__main__":
    root = tkinter.Tk()
    root.geometry('700x550')
    root.title("Reporting and Analysis Application")
    createmenu(root) #we will add the tool bar in this function later

    root_label0 = tkinter.Label(root, text="Enter Database Alpha Details")
    root_label0.place(x=60, y=10)
```

```python
    root_label1 = tkinter.Label(root, text="Your Username: ")
    root_label1.place(x=30, y=30)
    root_e1 = tkinter.Entry(root, show=None, font=('Arial', 8), bg='pink',
fg="green")  # Display in text form
    root_e1.place(x=150, y=30)

    root_label2 = tkinter.Label(root, text="Your Password: ")
    root_label2.place(x=30, y=55)
    root_e2 = tkinter.Entry(root, show='*', font=('Arial', 8), bg='pink',
fg="green")  # Display in ciphertext form
    root_e2.place(x=150, y=55)

    root_label3 = tkinter.Label(root, text="8 Digit Access Key: ")
    root_label3.place(x=30, y=80)
    root_e3 = tkinter.Entry(root, width= 22, show=None, font=('Arial', 8),
bg='pink', fg="green")  # Display in text form
    root_e3.place(x=150, y=80)

    root_label02 = tkinter.Label(root, text="Enter Database Beta Details")
    root_label02.place(x=60, y=140)

    root_label12 = tkinter.Label(root, text="Your Username: ")
    root_label12.place(x=30, y=165)
    root_e12 = tkinter.Entry(root, show=None, font=('Arial', 8), bg='pink',
fg="green")  # Display in text form
    root_e12.place(x=150, y=165)

    root_label22 = tkinter.Label(root, text="Your Password: ")
    root_label22.place(x=30, y=190)
    root_e22 = tkinter.Entry(root, show='*', font=('Arial', 8), bg='pink',
fg="green")  # Display in ciphertext form
    root_e22.place(x=150, y=190)

    #Check button
    chkbutton_Var1 = tkinter.IntVar()
    chkbutton_Var2 = tkinter.IntVar()

    ChkBttn = tkinter.Checkbutton(root,text = "Select Option1", width=15,
variable=chkbutton_Var1)
    ChkBttn.place(x=130, y=210)

    ChkBttn2 = tkinter.Checkbutton(root, text = "Select Option2",width=15,
variable=chkbutton_Var2)
    ChkBttn2.place(x=130, y=230)

    #Radio button
    radiobutton_Var1 = tkinter.StringVar()
```

```
    RBttn = tkinter.Radiobutton(root, text="Goto Step 3",
variable=radiobutton_Var1,value=1)
    RBttn.place(x=30, y=260)
    RBttn2 = tkinter.Radiobutton(root, text="Goto Step 7",
variable=radiobutton_Var1,value=2)
    RBttn2.place(x=170, y=260)

    #Scale implementation
    scale_label1 = tkinter.Label(root, text="Give your rating (1-10): ")
    scale_label1.place(x=30, y=290)
    scale_var1 = tkinter.DoubleVar()
    scale = tkinter.Scale(root, variable=scale_var1, from_=1, to=10,
orient=tkinter.HORIZONTAL)
    scale.place(x=170, y=290)
    #Scrollbar linked to a Listbox
    scrollbar = tkinter.Scrollbar(root)
    scrollbar.place(x=200, y=340)

    mylist = tkinter.Listbox(root, yscrollcommand=scrollbar.set)
    for line in range(100):
        mylist.insert(tkinter.END, "This is line number " + str(line))

    mylist.place(x=310, y=320)
    scrollbar.config(command=mylist.yview)

    #Save info
    root_button1 = tkinter.Button(root, text="Save my info for this
session", command=save_all_info)
    root_button1.place(x=30,y=425)

    root.mainloop()
```

The preceding code will display a window with all the widgets added to itself, as shown in *Figure 10.2*:

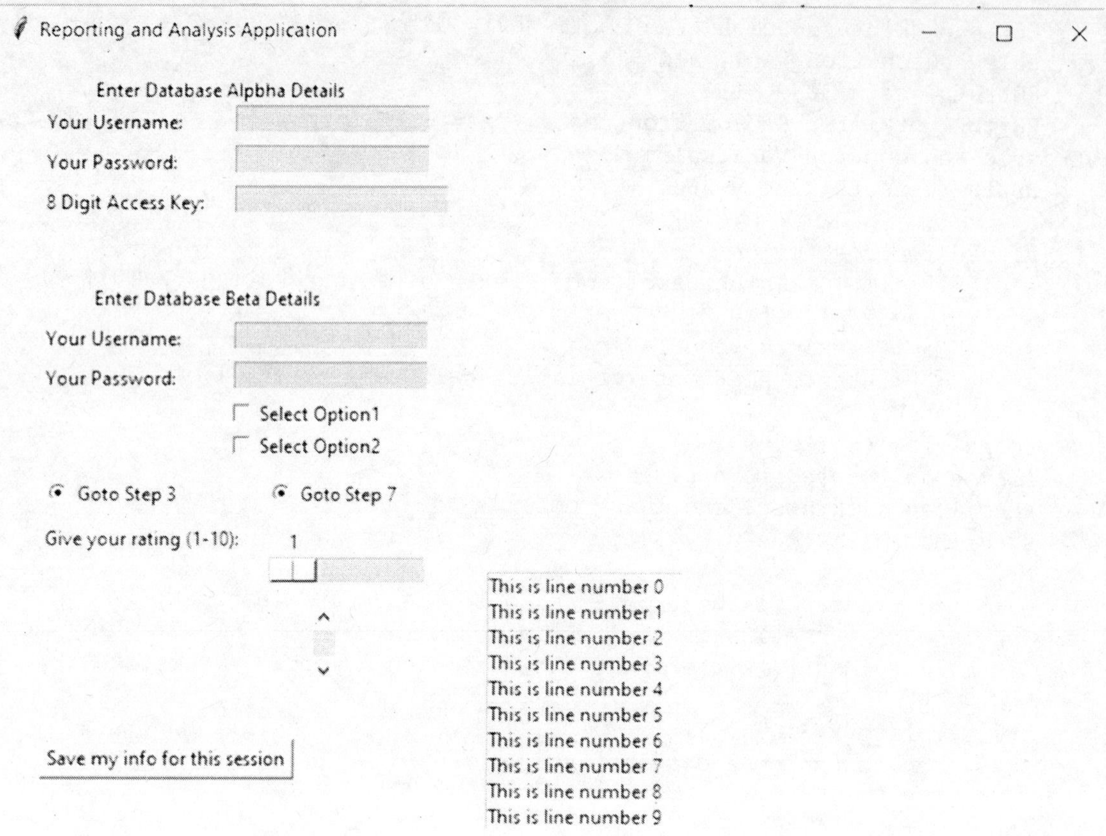

Figure 10.2: *Multiple Tkinter widgets added to a Window*

In the preceding example, we added labels, text boxes, buttons, check boxes, radio buttons, list box, scale, and scrollbar. In the last line, you will see that the button calls a function **save_all_info()**, which we will implement in the *Working with Tkinter Events* section.

Note: This application may look different if you are using macOS.

Working with Tkinter events

Events are an important part of any GUI application, as they allow the user to interact with the application. In this section, we will learn how to use Tkinter events to create interactive applications. Events are user actions that can be generated by the user or by the system. Examples of user events include mouse clicks, mouse movements, and keyboard presses. System events, such as timer events or window size changes, are generated by the system. Events can trigger changes in an application, such as updating the display or changing the state of the application.

Tkinter provides several methods for handling events. The **bind()** method is used to bind an event to a function or method to be executed when the event occurs. The **bind_all()** method is used to bind an event to all widgets in the application. The **event_generate()** method is used to generate an event programmatically.

The bind() method

The **bind()** method is used to bind an event to a specific widget. The syntax is as follows:

```
widget.bind(event, handler)
```

In the preceding example, the *widget* is to bind the event, the event variable takes the event name, and the handler is the function or method to be executed when the event occurs. The event name is a string representing the event type, such as **<Button-1>** for a mouse click or **<Return>** for the return key.

Let us look at the example to capture any keypress on your keyboard. In this example, we created a button widget and then used **bind(<KeyPress>,button_function)** to detect any key pressed on the keyboard:

```
import tkinter
import random

#Create the main window
my_window = tkinter.Tk()
#set window size
my_window.geometry("300x300")
#Create button
button = tkinter.Button(my_window, text="Hit Any Key on YourKeybord!")
def button_function(e):
    print("Your score is: ",random.randint(1,100))

button.grid(row=0, column=0)
my_window.bind("<KeyPress>", button_function)

#Start the mainloop
my_window.mainloop()
```

The bind_all() method

The **bind_all()** method is used to bind an event to all widgets in the application. The syntax is as follows:

```
root.bind_all(event, handler)
```

Here, root is the application's root window, the event is the event name, and the handler is the function or method to be executed when the event occurs.

The event_generate() method

The **event_generate()** method is used to generate an event programmatically. The syntax is as follows:

```
widget.event_generate(event, **options)
```

In the preceding example, the given widget is to generate the event, the event variable takes the event name, and options are optional keyword arguments.

Let us look at an example of how to use Tkinter events. We will create a simple application that prints the co-ordinates of the mouse when the user clicks on the window:

```python
import tkinter as tk
#First, let's create the window and set the title:
root = tk.Tk()
root.title("Event Example")

#Next, we will define a function to handle the mouse click event:
def on_click(event):
    # Get the coordinates of the mouse click
    x = event.x
    y = event.y
    print("Clicked at ", x, y)

#Finally, we will bind the mouse click event to the window and start the
main loop:
root.bind("<Button-1>", on_click)
root.mainloop()
```

Output:

```
Clicked at   138 53

Clicked at   125 69

Clicked at   54 105

Clicked at   58 50
```

When the user clicks the window, the coordinates of the mouse click will be printed in the console.

Now, let us return to the mini project we started building in the previous section. First, add a dummy event that we will link to all the widgets to indicate that we are still adding the code. As we move ahead, we will replace the dummy event code with the respective event's code.

```python
def run_sample():
```

```
    msgbox.showwarning("Not Implemented","Just a sample function to handle
all the events")
```

Let us now complete **save_all_info()**, which is called by the main program:

```python
def save_all_info():
    alphausername = root_e1.get()
    alphapassword = root_e2.get()
    alphakey = root_e3.get()
    betausername = root_e12.get()
    betapassword = root_e22.get()
    text_disp = ""
    if len(betausername) > 0:
        text_disp += "Beta Username: "+betausername
    if len(betapassword) > 0:
        text_disp += ", Beta Password: "+betapassword

    if len(alphausername) > 0:
        text_disp += ", Alpha Username: "+alphausername
    if len(alphapassword) > 0:
        text_disp += ", Alpha Password: "+alphapassword
    if len(alphakey) > 0:
        text_disp += " and Alpha Key: "+alphakey

    if chkbutton_Var1.get() == 1:
        text_disp += ", \n Option 1 selected"
    if chkbutton_Var2.get() == 1:
        text_disp += ", \n Option 2 selected"

    if radiobutton_Var1.get()=="1":
        text_disp += ", Goto step 3 selected"
    if radiobutton_Var1.get()=="2":
        text_disp += ", Goto step 7 selected"

    if scale_var1.get()>0:
        text_disp += ", Rating given: "+str(int(scale_var1.get()))
    #get list of selected items:
    for i in mylist.curselection():
        text_disp += ", "+mylist.get(i)

    if len(text_disp) < 1:
        text_disp = "NONE"

    tkinter.messagebox.showinfo("Information Saved",
                        "Following information have been saved for
the current session only: \n" + text_disp)
```

The preceding code will be called when the **Save All Info** button is clicked. This function demonstrates how we can read the values from different widgets. This will open a message box with information that looks like *Figure 10.3*:

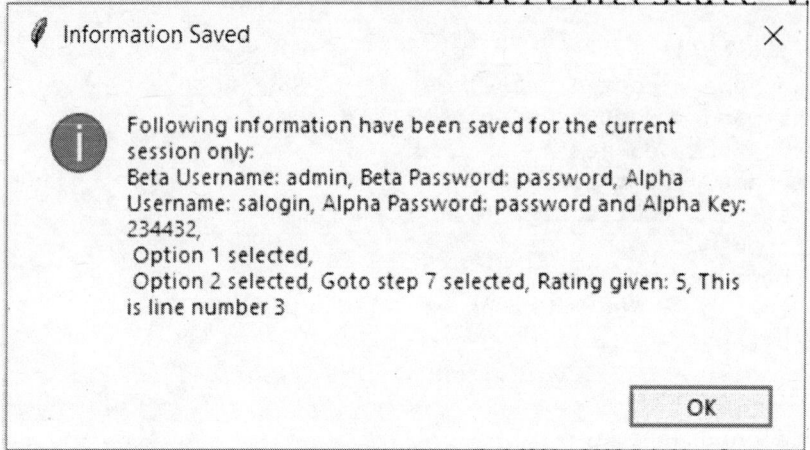

Figure 10.3: *Capturing the values from the widgets using an event*

Let us now move on to the next section to add the toolbar.

Creating menus and toolbars with Tkinter

Menus and toolbars are essential components of any GUI. They provide users with a way to navigate a program, access important features, and carry out tasks. This section will teach us to create menus and toolbars with Tkinter, the standard Python GUI toolkit. We will go through the basics of how to create menus and toolbars, and we will also learn how to add items and customize the look and feel. By the end of this tutorial, you should have a better understanding of how to create and customize menus and toolbars with Tkinter.

Once we have created a **window** object using the **Tk()** function, we will use this **window** object to create our menu. To create a menu, we must first create a **Menu** object. This can be done using the following line of code:

```
menu = Menu(window)
```

The **Menu** object takes one argument, which is the **window** object we created earlier. Once the **Menu** object is created, we can add items using the **add_command**() method. This method takes two arguments: a label, which is a string that will be displayed on the menu; and a command, which is a function that will be called when the item is selected. For example, to create an item with the **Open** label and the **open_file()** command, we would use the following line of code:

```
menu.add_command(label="Open", command=open_file)
```

We can also add separators to our menu using the **add_separator()** method. This method takes no arguments. Once all the items have been added to the menu, we can display it using the window object's **configure**() method. This method takes one argument, which is the menu object we created earlier.

For example, to display the menu on the window, we would use the following line of code:

```
window.configure(menu=menu)
```

Creating toolbars with Tkinter

Creating toolbars with Tkinter is just like creating menus. To create a toolbar, we must first create a **Toolbar** object. This can be done using the following line of code:

```
toolbar = Toolbar(window)
```

The **Toolbar** object takes one argument, which is the **window** object we created earlier. Once the **Toolbar** object has been created, we can add buttons using the **add_button**() method. This method takes three arguments: an **image**, which is a bitmap image to be used as the button's icon; a *command*, which is a function that will be called when the button is clicked; and a *tooltip*, which is a string that will be displayed when the user hovers over the button.

For example, to create a button with the image **icon.gif**, the command **open_file()**, and the tooltip **Open File**, we would use the following line of code:

```
toolbar.add_button(image="icon.gif", command=open_file, tooltip="Open File")
```

Once all the buttons have been added to the toolbar, we can display all of these buttons using the window object's **configure()** method. This method takes one argument, which is the toolbar object we created earlier. For example, to display the toolbar on the window, we would use the following line of code:

```
window.configure(toolbar=toolbar)
```

Customizing menus and toolbars

Once menus and toolbars have been created, they can be customized to suit the user's needs using the **configure()** method. This method takes two arguments: an option, which is a string specifying the option to be configured; and a value, which is the value to be set for the option. For example, to select the font size of a menu to 12, we would use the following line of code:

```
menu.configure(fontsize=12)
```

Let us now turn our focus to the mini project we have been building over the last two sections and add the function to create a toolbar:

```
#Create UI Design
def createmenu(root):
```

```python
    menubar = tkinter.Menu(root)
    himenu = tkinter.Menu(menubar, tearoff=0)
    himenu.add_command(label="Alpha Demo Data", command=run_sample)
    menubar.add_cascade(label="Database Alpha", menu=himenu)

    dcmenu = tkinter.Menu(menubar, tearoff=0)
    dcmenu.add_command(label="Beta Demo Data", command=run_sample)
    menubar.add_cascade(label="Database Beta", menu=dcmenu)

    etmenu = tkinter.Menu(menubar, tearoff=0)
    etmenu.add_command(label="New", command= file_new)
    etmenu.add_command(label="Open", command=run_sample)
    etmenu.add_command(label="Save", command=run_sample)
    menubar.add_cascade(label="File", menu=etmenu)

    etmenu = tkinter.Menu(menubar, tearoff=0)
    etmenu.add_command(label="Run", command = run_sample)
    etmenu.add_command(label="View", command=run_sample)
    etmenu.add_command(label="Analyze", command=run_sample)
    etmenu.add_command(label="Publish", command=run_sample)
    menubar.add_cascade(label="Audit Reports", menu=etmenu)

    etmenu = tkinter.Menu(menubar, tearoff=0)
    etmenu.add_command(label="Report 1: Bi-weekly Report", command=run_
sample)
    etmenu.add_command(label="Report 2: Failed Tasks", command=run_sample)
    etmenu.add_command(label="Report 3: Monthly")
    etmenu.add_command(label="Report 4: Annual", command=run_sample)

    menubar.add_cascade(label="Custom Reports", menu=etmenu)
    root.config(menu=menubar)
```

Now, let us add an event to the **File -> New** menu:

```python
def file_new():
    clean_ui(root)  #remove the existing widgets
    file_new_design()  # add new set of widgets
```

clean_ui() will look something like this:

```python
#Clean UI Design
def clean_ui(root):
    for widgets in  root.winfo_children():
        if widgets.winfo_class() != 'Menu':
            widgets.destroy()
```

file_new_design() will have new set of widgets added:

```
def file_new_design():
    root_label0 = tkinter.Label(root, text="Enter Database Alpbha Details")
    root_label0.place(x=60, y=10)

    root_label1 = tkinter.Label(root, text="Your Username: ")
    root_label1.place(x=30, y=30)
    root_e1 = tkinter.Entry(root, show=None, font=('Arial', 8), bg='pink',
fg="green")  # Display in text form
    root_e1.place(x=130, y=30)

    root_label2 = tkinter.Label(root, text="Your Password: ")
    root_label2.place(x=30, y=55)
    root_e2 = tkinter.Entry(root, show='*', font=('Arial', 8), bg='pink',
fg="green")  # Display in ciphertext form
    root_e2.place(x=130, y=55)

    root_label3 = tkinter.Label(root, text="8 Digit Access Key: ")
    root_label3.place(x=30, y=80)
    root_e3 = tkinter.Entry(root, width=22, show=None, font=('Arial', 8),
bg='pink', fg="green")  # Display in text form
    root_e3.place(x=200, y=80)

    root.mainloop()
```

The final output looks as shown in *Figure 10.4*. Clicking the **New** menu under **File** will delete the existing set of widgets (by calling **clean_ui()**) and will create a new set of widgets by calling **file_new_design()**.

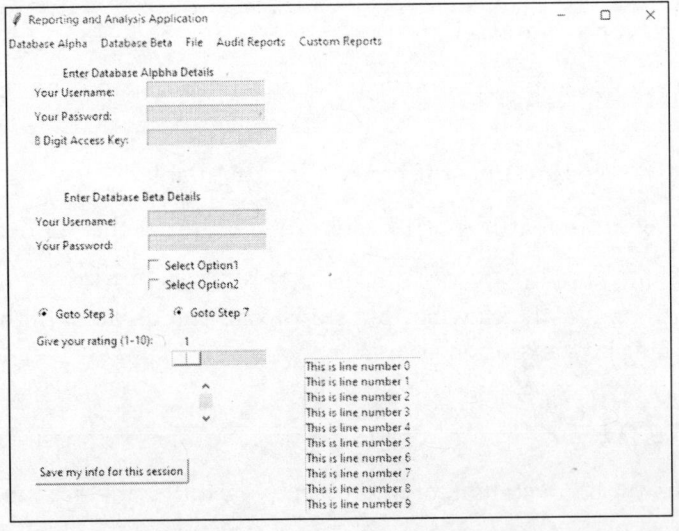

Figure 10.4: Mini project final screen view

Note: This application may look different if you are using macOS.

Developing an application: A quiz game

Learning programming by developing applications is an effective way to gain hands-on experience and develop problem-solving skills. By writing code and creating applications, you can learn to think logically and develop algorithms to solve problems. This process can help you understand the core principles of programming, such as variables, functions, loops, and classes. Let us get started.

Problem statement

This project aims to develop a **Graphical User Interface (GUI)**-based quiz application that allows users to answer multiple-choice questions and receive immediate feedback on their answers. The application should also provide users with a score summary of their performance and allow them to navigate between questions easily. Furthermore, the application should provide some kind of animation to make the application look interesting. So, we will add some concepts from Zango tower-making game to this. For each correct answer, a block will be added to the tower. A player will have maximum three lives to play the game.

Objectives

The objective is to collect as many blocks as possible while avoiding giving wrong answers to the questions asked in the quiz show. Each correct answer will put a block indicating 1 point scored by the player. Along with these, the following features will be added to the game:

- Take the player's name as input.

- Track the points scored. Also, save the highest point scored, along with the player's name.

- Make questions from three difficulty levels available.

- Use the maximum features of Tkinter while building the application.

Creating a quiz game show using Tkinter in Python is a great way to engage users and learn more about them. With a few simple steps, you can create a highly interactive and engaging quiz game show experience.

Requirements

Based on the given problem statement and objectives, following are the requirements:

1. Develop a GUI-based Tkinter quiz game that allows users to answer questions and receive feedback on their performance.

2. Monitor the performance, player is provided with 3 lives, and the number decreases with each wrong answer.

3. Create a user-friendly interface that allows users to answer multiple-choice questions in an interactive way.

4. Create a live scoreboard to show the score. Each correct answer gets one positive point and no negative marks for incorrect answers.

5. Design the game to be intuitive and easy to understand for users of all age groups.

6. Utilize a text file to save the name of the player and score details of the all-time highest scorer.

Solution

The basic steps followed to develop this game are listed here:

1. Define the questions and answers for your quiz.

2. Create a window using the Tkinter library and set the title of the window.

3. Create a Tkinter frame to hold all the elements of the quiz game:

    a. Create a label to hold the questions and answer options.

    b. Create buttons to display the options; the users can click on the button to select their answer.

    c. Create a label to display the player's name, top scorer, number of lives left, and the current scorecard.

    d. On one side, display blocks on top of each other as the score count increases.

    e. Display specific messages using MsgBox to announce the result.

4. Create a function to select the questions from the questions bank randomly and, at the same time, make sure no questions are repeated.

5. Create an **Exit** menu on the menu bar to exit from the quiz.

Design

We will create two screens: the first to accept names and the second with all the components mentioned under the solution. This would look something like *Figure 10.5*:

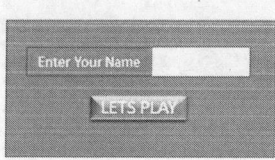

1. Welcome Screen

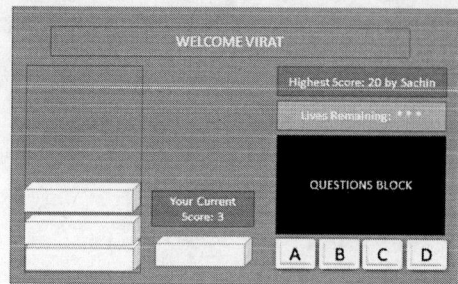

2. Main Screen

Figure 10.5: Screens for the game

For this project, we will create four files:

1. **Databank.py: Databank.py** will contain all the questions and answers. This file will contain three lists, one each for the difficulty-level questions. Each member of the list will be a dictionary that will store the questions and the responses. The list would look something like this:

```
level1_questions = [
    {'question': 'What is 5+3 equal to?',
    'choices': ['5', '8', '3', '4'],
    'answer': 2},

    {'question': 'Sachin Tendulkar played which sports?',
    'choices': ['Hockey', 'Kabaddi', 'Cricket', 'Football'],
    'answer': 3},
    ...
    ]
```

Each member of the list has three keys: question, choices for 4 options, and reference to the correct answer. Similarly, build level2_questions and level3_questions lists.

2. **MyQuizGame.py:** This is the main file where all the actions will take place. We will have different sections within this file, like the following:

Importing modules and libraries:

We will import, of course, **tkinter**, **tkinter.messagebox** along with **pillow (PIL)** for handling images and a random module to select random questions from the questions bank. **Databank** will also be imported to access the questions bank in the list form.

Global variables

Important global variables like current score, highest score, number of lives, and player's name are declared, which will be accessible by all the functions of the file.

Initialization of variables

Read the content of **MyQuizGameScore.txt** and assign this content to the global variables. Also, read the level 1 questions from the **Databank**.

Declare the functions

We will be using the following functions:

- **Fetching_questions()**: This main function will keep the game going. It will keep track of the score and fetch the questions from Level 1 or 2, or 3 list based on the score. It does not take any input or return any value. Question content is updated every time this is run. This function has to run to keep the game moving till the end.

- **a_response()**, **b_response()**, **c_response()**, **d_response()**: These functions handle the responses (button clicks) for options A, B, C, and D. Each button has a different function associated with itself and prints whether the answer is correct or incorrect.

- **check_answer()**: This function checks the number of lives available and if indeed life is more than 1, then continue with the main logic; if the answer is correct, build the tower at the specific position. If life becomes zero, then the game exits, but before that, it checks if the current player has broken the highest score. If yes, then the **MyQuizGameScore.txt** is updated with the player's name and score.

- **gameover()**: The **gameover()** function is called when all the lives are lost to close the game.

- **start()**: It verifies the name entered during the welcome screen.

- **closegame()**: It is used to end the program whenever the user wants.

Driving code

Two windows are created: the main welcome screen that accepts name and the second window for playing the game.

The welcome screen is shown in *Figure 10.6*:

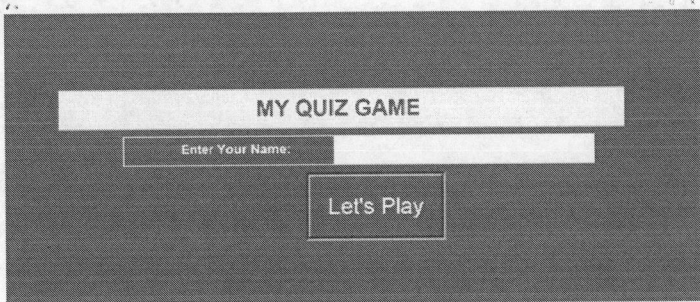

Figure 10.6: Welcome screen of the project

Let us add a menu bar to the main screen. In this case, we will only implement the **Exit** option but will add a label to start a new game and save the existing game for future implementation. The menu would appear as shown in *Figure 10.7*:

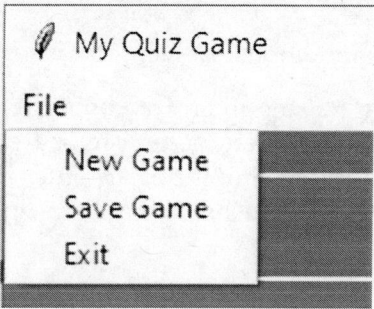

Figure 10.7: Menu bar option

The main screen has all the components and looks like *Figure 10.8*:

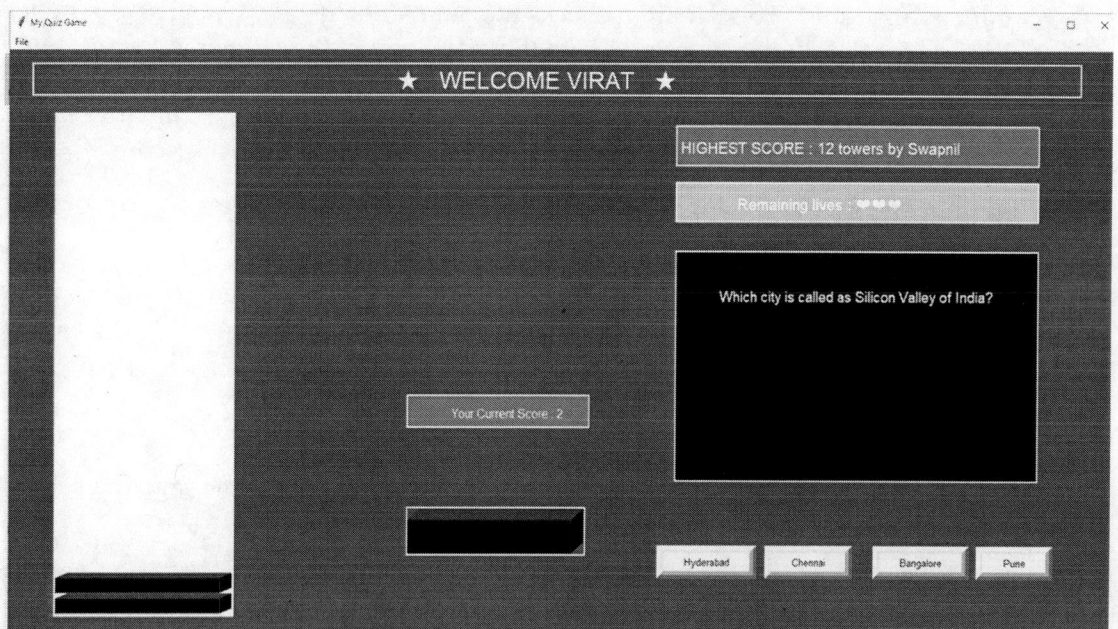

Figure 10.8: Screen 2 when a game is in progress

The complete code has been added under the implementation section for your reference.

- **MyQuizGameScore.txt**: This file will store the highest score information, along with the name. Initially, the file's content would be as shown in *Figure 10.9*. This file will update itself whenever someone scores higher than the previous highest score.

```
MyQuizGameScore - Notepad
File  Edit  Format  View  Help
Name: _
Score: 0
```

Figure 10.9: *Image of the block*

- **Block.png:** This is the image of the block that would appear when the user gets the answer right. The block image would look like *Figure 10.10*:

Figure 10.10: *Image of the block*

Implementation

You have already seen the content of **Databank.py, MyQuizGameScore.txt**, and **Block. png**. In this section, the complete code of the main file, which is **MyQuizGame.py**, is given for your reference. The comment has the details for the code as well.

Here is the entire code for you to practice:

In the next section, we will import the required libraries:

```
from tkinter import *
import tkinter.messagebox as msgbox
from PIL import ImageTk, Image
from Databank import level1_questions,level2_questions,level3_questions
import random
import time
```
Now, let us declare and assign default values to the variables that will be used later, like number of correct answers (answer), score tracking (score), total lives remaining (life), player name, highest score so far, name of the person who holds the highest score, and so on.

```
answer = 0
score = 0
life = 3
player_name = ""
```

```
highest_score = 0
highest_name = ""
level2,level3=1,1
tower_height = 27
timer_text = 30
```

We need to save highest score details so that they can be fetched every time the game is started. We will save it in the **MyQuizGameScore.txt** file. If this file does not exist, then we will create it.

```
try:
    with open("MyQuizGameScore.txt", 'r') as hs:
        if hs.read():
            hs.seek(0)
            data = hs.read().split()
            highest_name = data[1]
            highest_score = int(data[3])

except FileNotFoundError:
    pass

r = random.choice(level1_questions)  #default level 1
```

In the next section, we develop a function called **fetching_questions()** to keep track of the score and fetch the questions from Level 1 or 2 or 3 **List** based on the score. It does not take any input nor does it return any value. Question content is updated every time this is run. This function has to run to keep the game moving till the end. The code for the **fetching_questions()** function is given below:

```
def fetching_questions():

    global r, level1_questions,level2_questions,level3_questions,
level2,level3

    if score<=5:
        level1_questions.remove(r)
        if level1_questions:
            r = random.choice(level1_questions)
        else:
            msgbox.showinfo("Gameover!" , "Sorry, we have run out of
questions.")

            exit()
    elif score <=10:    #level 2
        if level2==1:
            msgbox.showinfo("Moving to the Next Level!","Congratulation!
You now move to Level 2")
```

```
            level2=0

        if level2_questions:
            r = random.choice(level2_questions)
            level2_questions.remove(r)
        else:
            msgbox.showinfo("Gameover", "Sorry, we have run out of
questions!")
            exit()
    else:  #level 3
        if level3==1:
            msgbox.showinfo("Moving to the Next Level!",
                            "Congratulation! You have now moved to the
Level 3")
            level3=0

        if level3_questions:
            r = random.choice(level3_questions)
            level3_questions.remove(r)
        else:
            msgbox.showinfo("AWESOME!", "You have completed the game. Good
Job Genius!")
            exit()
```

Now, we will focus on writing functions to handle the answers. Since we give four options to the user, we will have four functions: one each for options A, B, C and D:

```
def a_response():
    """Handle answer response A if the answer is correct or not"""
    global answer
    answer = 1
    check_answer()

def b_response():
    """Handle answer response B if the answer is correct or not"""
    global answer
    answer = 2
    check_answer()

def c_response():
    """Handle answer response C if the answer is correct or not"""
    global answer
    answer = 3
    check_answer()

def d_response():
    """Handle answer response D if the answer is correct or not"""
```

```
        global answer
        answer = 4
        check_answer()
```

The next function that we will write is **check_answer()**, which will check the number of lives available and find out if at least one life is available for the player. If life becomes zero, then the game ends, but before that it checks whether the current player has broken the highest score. If yes, then **MyQuizGameScore.txt** is updated with the player's name and score. The code for the **check_answer()** function is given below:

```
def check_answer():
    """checks the number of lives available and if indeed life is more than 1
    then continue with the main logic, if answer is correct build the tower at the
    specific position.
    """
    global score, answer, life, r, current_score
    if life > 1:
        if answer == r['answer']:
            score = score + 1
            loc = score * tower_height
            canvas_tower.create_image(2, 660 - loc, anchor=NW, image=new_
image2)
            msgbox.showinfo("Correct!","That's Right! Congratulations!\n "
                                       "Your tower is now higher by one
more block")

        else:
            msgbox.showerror("Incorrect!","Sorry, that's not correct. You
lost a life")
            life = life - 1
        #Play the game
        fetching_questions()
        canvas.itemconfig(ques, text=r['question'])
        canvas1.itemconfig(rem_life, text=f"Remaining lives : {'♥' *
life}")
        b1['text'] = r['choices'][0]
        b2['text'] = r['choices'][1]
        b3['text'] = r['choices'][2]
        b4['text'] = r['choices'][3]
        current_score_canvas.itemconfig(score_current, text=f"Your Current
Score : {score}")

    else:
        if score >= highest_score:
            with open('MyQuizGameScore.txt','w') as f:
```

```
        f.write(f"Name: {player_name}\nScore: {score}")
        msgbox.showinfo("....ohhhh!","The Joys and Struggles of Life: "
                        "You are now the highest rated player and also
the end of your game here")
        exit()
```

Now we will develop two fundamental functions: one for handling the end of the game and another for initiating the game. When **life remaining** reaches zero, we stop the game by calling **exit()**.

For starting the game, we verify the name of the player before launching the game.

```
def gameover():
    """"Game over function when all the lives are lost"""
    canvas_tower.delete("all")
    msgbox.showerror("GAME OVER!", "You lost third life too. The game is
over")
    exit()

def start():
    """"verifies the name entered during the welcome screen"""
    global player_name
    if name.get():
        player_name = name.get()
        first.destroy()
    else:
        msgbox.showerror("Name Error", 'Please Enter Your Name')
```

Let us now define a timer function:

```
# Define a timer.
    def countdown():
        p = 30.00
        t = time.time()
        n = 0
        # Loop while the number of seconds is less than the integer defined
in "p"
        while n - t < p:
            n = time.time()
            if n == t + p:
                timer_text ="Time's up!"
            else:
                timer_text = round(n - t)
```

Next is a function that will chconfirmation before quitting:

```
def closegame():
```

```
    """To end the program whenever the user want to"""
    choice = msgbox.askyesno(root, "Do You Really Want to Quit?")
    if choice:
        quit()
```

In the next section, we will write the driving code that will call the preceding functions:

```
if __name__ == "__main__":
    first = Tk()

    first.geometry("1500x800")
    first.config(bg='#051BFD') #hexadecimal code for blue color
    #Bar to display the Title of the game
    cs = Canvas(first, width=1200, height=80, bg="#F2FD05") #yellow
    cs.create_text(600, 40, text="MY QUIZ GAME ", fill='Blue', font=('',
'35', 'bold'))
    cs.place(relx=0.08, rely=0.25)
    #Second Bar to message and accept the input
    cs1 = Canvas(first, width=450, height=60, bg="#051BFD")
    cs1.create_text(245, 29, text="Enter Your Name: ", fill='white',
font=('', '20','bold'))
    cs1.place(relx=0.17, rely=0.4)
    # accept the name in textbox
    name = Entry(first, width=19, font=('', '40'), relief=RIDGE)
    name.place(relx=0.47, rely=0.4)
    #add the button and the text on it
    sub = Button(text="Let's Play", background='#051BFD', fg='white',
                padx=20,pady=20,bd=10,font=('', '35'), relief=GROOVE,
command=start)
    sub.place(relx=0.43, rely=0.52)
    first.mainloop()

    #Start of second Window
    if player_name:
        root = Tk()
        root.geometry("1920x1080")
        #Create Menu
        menubar = Menu(root, background='blue', fg='white')
        file = Menu(menubar, tearoff=0)
        menubar.add_cascade(label='File', menu=file)

        file.add_command(label='New Game')
        file.add_command(label='Save Game')
        file.add_command(label='Exit', command=closegame)
        root.config(bg='blue', menu=menubar)
        root.title("My Quiz Game")
```

```python
        # metrics and question block
        welcome = Canvas(root, width=1450, height=40, bg="#051BFD")
        welcome.create_text(700, 24, text=f"*    WELCOME {player_name.
upper()}    *", fill="#F2FD05", font=(" ", 24))
        welcome.place(relx=0.02, rely=0.02)

        canvas2 = Canvas(root, width=500, height=50, bg="#DF0A3A")
        curr_score = canvas2.create_text(200, 30, text=f"HIGHEST SCORE : "
                                         f"{highest_score}
towers by {highest_name}", fill="white", font=("", 16))
        canvas2.place(relx=0.6, rely=0.12)

        canvas1 = Canvas(root, width=500, height=50, bg="#F5AC03")
        rem_life = canvas1.create_text(200, 30, text=f"Remaining lives :
{'♥' * life}", fill="white", font=("", 16))
        canvas1.place(relx=0.6, rely=0.21)
        #Questions board
        canvas = Canvas(root, width=500, height=300, bg='black')
        ques = canvas.create_text(250, 60, text=r['question'], fill="white",
font=("", 14), width=490)
        canvas.place(relx=0.6, rely=0.32)

        #placing option buttons
        b1 = Button(root, text=r['choices'][0],font=(" ", 10),
padx=25,bd=10,command=a_response)
        b1.place(relx=0.585, rely=0.79)
        b2 = Button(root, text=r['choices'][1], font=(" ", 10),
padx=25,bd=10,command=b_response)
        b2.place(relx=0.682, rely=0.79)
        b3 = Button(root, text=r['choices'][2], font=(" ", 10),
padx=25,bd=10,command=c_response)
        b3.place(relx=0.780, rely=0.79)
        b4 = Button(root, text=r['choices'][3], font=(" ", 10),
padx=25,bd=10,command=d_response)
        b4.place(relx=0.873, rely=0.79)

        # tower code
        canvas_tower = Canvas(root, width=245,
height=660,background='white')
        img2 = (Image.open("block.png"))
        resized_image2 = img2.resize((245, tower_height), Image.LANCZOS)
        new_image2 = ImageTk.PhotoImage(resized_image2)
        canvas_tower.place(relx=0.04, rely=0.10)

        #Score Label position
        current_score_canvas = Canvas(root, width=250, height=40,
bg="#DF0A3A")
```

```
        score_current = current_score_canvas.create_text(140, 25,
text=f"Your current Score : {score}", fill="white", font=("", 12))
        current_score_canvas.place(relx=0.36, rely=0.55)

        #Display the block  below score card
        canvas_always = Canvas(root, width=245,
height=60,background='#051BFD')
        img1 = (Image.open("block.png"))
        resized_image1 = img1.resize((245, 60), Image.LANCZOS)
        new_image1 = ImageTk.PhotoImage(resized_image1)
        canvas_always.create_image(2, 2, anchor=NW, image=new_image1)
        canvas_always.place(relx=0.36, rely=0.73)

        root.mainloop()
```

Future enhancements

So far, we have developed this application, but if you are interested in taking it forward, you can extend this application and add a few other features, like the ones listed here:

- Provide a mechanism to save the game and load it back when the user wants; only one last game saved would be available.

- Ensure that the quiz game includes a timer to keep track of user progress and provide feedback at the end of the game.

- Provide users with a summary of their performance at the end of the game, including total score, time taken, and number of correct and incorrect answers, through a couple of visualizations.

- Utilize a database to store user data and enable users to track their progress over time.

- Enhance it with additional features such as displaying images and playing audio clips.

In this section, we developed a quiz game. Hopefully, this has given you a chance to practice most Tkinter features. The purpose of adding this example is to help you understand how different program components interact with each other and how to debug and optimize code for better performance.

Conclusion

In this chapter, we saw that the Tkinter library provides an easy way to create and manipulate GUI elements such as buttons, menus, and various kinds of entry fields, and arrange them in a window. It is designed to be used in Python scripts and is available as part of the standard Python distribution. It is written in Python and uses the Tcl/Tk toolkit for the GUI. It is easy to learn and use and is widely available on all platforms. With Tkinter, we created attractive and powerful graphical user interface applications with just a few lines of code.

Python comes with various GUI frameworks, but the Tkinter framework is the only part of the Python standard library. Tkinter offers many advantages, such as its cross-platform compatibility and reliance on native operating system elements to render visuals. This results in applications built with Tkinter appearing as though they are native to the platform they are run on. It is lightweight and relatively easy to use as compared to other frameworks, making it an attractive choice for building GUI applications in Python, particularly when the main focus is to quickly create something that functions well and is compatible with various platforms.

Now, we will focus on developing amazing interactive websites using the Flask framework.

In *Chapter 11, Developing a Flask-Based Web Application*, we will develop a website using Flask. Flask is a lightweight web application framework written in Python. It provides tools, libraries, and technologies that allow developers to build a web application. It is an open-source project maintained by a thriving community of developers.

Join our book's Discord space

Join the book's Discord Workspace for Latest updates, Offers, Tech happenings around the world, New Release and Sessions with the Authors:

https://discord.bpbonline.com

CHAPTER 11
Developing Flask-based Web Applications

The web is the most democratic application platform that has ever existed.
— *Tim Berners-Lee, Computer Scientist*

Introduction

Flask is a powerful web development framework for Python that is designed to make the development of web applications easier. It is a lightweight web application framework that offers an extensive set of features and tools to help developers create highly functional web applications. Flask was created in 2010 by *Armin Ronacher* and was released under the BSD license. Flask is based on the Werkzeug WSGI toolkit and the Jinja2 template engine. The main goal of this framework is to help developers build a solid web application foundation and simplify the development process. Flask is designed to be lightweight, modular, and extensible. It is often called a **microframework** because it does not require particular tools or libraries.

Flask has been used in many projects, including *Pinterest* and *LinkedIn*, and is well suited for creating APIs, simple web applications, and larger web applications. It is often used with other frameworks, such as *Django* and *Pyramid*.

Flask takes advantage of several features that make it an ideal framework for developing web applications. It offers a flexible yet powerful architecture for creating web applications and services. It also uses object-oriented programming, allowing developers to build and maintain complex web applications easily.

Flask provides a great amount of flexibility in terms of the components and features that can be used. It provides several core components that can be used to build a web application quickly. These components include a basic web server and request/response handling, URL routing, and support for templates. Additionally, Flask offers a wide range of extensions and modules that can be used to add new features and capabilities to a web application.

Flask also uses various development tools and platforms that make the development process easier and more efficient. These tools include an **Integrated Development Environment (IDE)**, a debugger, and an integration **Continuous Integration (CI)** server. A CI server is a software tool that automates the process of building, testing, and deploying software changes. It helps teams to continuously integrate code changes from multiple developers into a shared repository and ensure that they are error-free. Additionally, Flask offers several libraries and frameworks that can be used to add functionality to a web application.

Structure

In this chapter, we will discuss the following topics:

- Set up and create a basic application
- Develop a Profile Application
- Templates and static content
- Setting up Database (SQLite3)
- Integrate Flask-Login
- Testing the database

Objectives

The objective of this chapter is to learn Flask, as it is a popular web framework for Python. It provides a lightweight layer of abstraction to allow developers to create web applications quickly and easily, without having to worry about the details of setting up a web server. Flask also provides greater flexibility and customization than many other web frameworks, making it a preferred choice for developers who want to create unique, custom web applications. We will also see how to use existing Python libraries and frameworks to create powerful web applications. We will work to create a personal website using the features of Flask.

Set up and create a basic application

Flask needs to be installed. For this, you do not need to install a server to run a Flask application. Flask is a web framework written in Python. It provides a development server and a debugger that allows you to run your application locally.

We assume that you are already working with Python in VS Code, and we need to install Flask extension now. Create a folder named **FlaskApp**; all our codes will be in this folder. Follow the given steps to get the Flask application running on your local machine:

1. **Create a virtual environment using the virtualenv package:** The first step to creating a virtual environment using the **virtualenv** package is to install the package. To do this, open a command line window and type **pip install virtualenv**, as shown in F*igure 11.1*:

```
PS X:\FlaskApp> pip install virtualenv
Collecting virtualenv
  Downloading virtualenv-20.23.0-py3-none-any.whl (3.3 MB)
                          3.3/3.3 MB 7.2 MB/s eta 0:00:00
Requirement already satisfied: platformdirs<4,>=3.2 in c:\users\hp\appdata\roaming\python\python310\site-packages (from virtualenv) (3.2.
0)
Collecting distlib<1,>=0.3.6
  Downloading distlib-0.3.6-py2.py3-none-any.whl (468 kB)
                          468.5/468.5 KB 9.8 MB/s eta 0:00:00
```

Figure 11.1: Installing virtual environment

This will install the **virtualenv** package. The main purpose of creating virtual environments in Python is to create separate, isolated Python environments for each project. This helps keep project-specific dependencies and libraries organized and separate from other projects. It also helps avoid conflicts between dependencies of different projects.

Once the **virtualenv** package has been installed, you can create a new virtual environment. To do this, open a command line window and type the following:

virtualenv <name of environment>

As shown in *Figure 11.2*, a virtual environment by the name of **env** has been created:

```
PS X:\FlaskApp> virtualenv env
created virtual environment CPython3.10.3.final.0-64 in 9996ms
  creator CPython3Windows(dest=X:\FlaskApp\env, clear=False, no_vcs_ignore=False, global=False)
  seeder FromAppData(download=False, pip=bundle, setuptools=bundle, wheel=bundle, via=copy, app_data_dir=C:\Users\HP\/
    added seed packages: pip==23.1.2, setuptools==67.7.2, wheel==0.40.0
  activators BashActivator,BatchActivator,FishActivator,NushellActivator,PowerShellActivator,PythonActivator
```

Figure 11.2: Creating a virtual environment

This command will create a new virtual environment and place it in the current directory.

2. **Activate the virtual environment**: Once the virtual environment has been created, you need to activate it. To do this, open a command line window and type the following:

Mac OS/Linux: source <name of environment>/bin/activate`

Windows: <name of environment>\Scripts\activate

Make sure to replace `<name of environment>` with the name of the environment you created. This will activate the virtual environment, and you will see the name of the environment in parentheses next to the command prompt. In our case, it would be as follows:

`Mac OS/Linux: source env/bin/activate``

`Windows:   env\Scripts\activate`

Figure 11.3 shows how to run the preceding script:

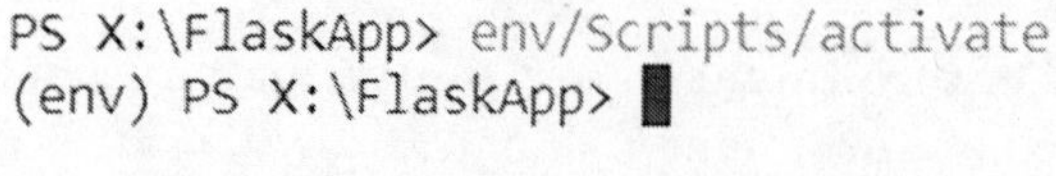

```
PS X:\FlaskApp> env/Scripts/activate
(env) PS X:\FlaskApp>
```

Figure 11.3: *Activate the virtual environment*

Note: You may get the following error on Windows when you try to run the preceding command: activate.ps1 cannot be loaded because running scripts is disabled on this system. For more information, see about_Execution_Policies at https:/go.microsoft.com/fwlink/?LinkID=135170.

The error occurs because the **activate script** command tries to run the **Activate.ps1** PowerShell script (.ps1 is an extension for PowerShell scripts). Windows 10 system has the **Execution Policy** set to **restricted** by default, so PowerShell cannot execute any script. We need to change the PowerShell execution policy to **remotesigned** to fix this error.

Open the **Start Menu** on Windows, search for Powershell, and right-click on it. Click on **run as administrator**. Type the following command in the PowerShell admin window to change the execution policy:

`> set-executionpolicy remotesigned`

You will be prompted to accept the change, type A (Yes to all), and press *Enter* on your keyboard to allow the change. Close the PowerShell admin window, and go back and run the activate command.

3. **Install the Flask extension in Visual Studio Code:** Now that the virtual environment is activated, you can install packages into it. To do this, open a command line window and type the following:

    `pip install <package name>`

    Make sure to replace `<package name>` with the name of the package you wish to install. This will install the package into the virtual environment. The package we will now install is **SQLAlchemy**. **Flask-SQLAlchemy**, a Flask extension, simplifies the integration of **SQLAlchemy** into **Flask** applications, providing useful tools and methods to interact with your database using **SQLAlchemy**. *Figure 11.4* shows how to install **Flask-SQLAlchemy**:

```
(env) PS X:\FlaskApp> pip install Flask Flask-SQLAlchemy
Collecting Flask
  Downloading Flask-2.3.2-py3-none-any.whl (96 kB)
━━━━━━━━━━━━━━━━━━━━━━━━━━━━━━━━━━━ 96.9/96.9 kB 5.4 MB/s eta 0:00:00
```

Figure 11.4: Installing package Flask-SQLAlchemy

You will also need to install **flask_migrate** and **flask_login** for future functionalities.

Flask-Migrate is an extension that handles **SQLAlchemy** database migrations for Flask applications using Alembic. This makes it easy to change your database structure and integrate it with Flask as your application expands. Flask-Login provides user session management for Flask. It handles the common tasks of logging in, logging out, and remembering your users' sessions over extended periods. After installing these libraries, let us import them in our program:

```
pip install flask_migrate

pip install flask_login

pip install flask_wtf

pip install email_validator

pip install pillow
```

We also need to install **flask_wtf**. Flask-WTF is a Flask extension that provides integration with the WTForms library. It helps simplify the process of creating secure forms with minimal code. The extension provides multiple features, such as form generation, validation, and auto-population of fields with data from the database. Flask-WTF makes it easier to create secure, multifunctional web forms on a Flask-based web application.

The **email_validator** module is a Python package that checks the syntax and structure of email addresses. It is an API for validating emails that can be used to prevent users from submitting invalid emails. This library can block invalid email addresses from registering, reducing the amount of spam on a system.

Python Imaging Library (PIL) is a free library for the Python programming language that adds support for opening, manipulating, and saving several different image file formats. It is used by web developers and professional image editing applications. We will import **pillow** to manage the registered user's profile picture.

4. **Create a new project folder and open it in Visual Studio Code:** Now that the virtual environment has been created and activated, you can open the VS Code and start working on it. To do this, open VS Code and select the **File** > **Open Folder...** option. This will open a file browser window. Navigate to the directory where you created the virtual environment and select the folder. The folder structure will look similar to the tree diagram shown in *Figure 11.5*. VS Code will now open the virtual environment, and you can begin working in it.

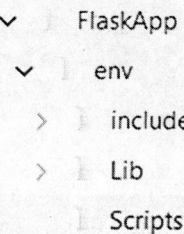

Figure 11.5: Folder structure

5. **Create a file named app.py, which will be the main file for your Flask application:**
Create a new file named **app.py** in the folder we just created (FlaskApp). Now,
let us create a basic Flask application. It will give us a structure for the future
application code. We will write the following code in the **app.py** file:

```
#FlaskApp/app.py
#Import libraries
from flask import Flask


#Set application, referencing this file
app = Flask(__name__)
#Set URL route
@app.route('/')
def hello_world():
    return 'Hello, Flask Application is running'


if __name__ == '__main__':
    app.run(debug=True)
```

App.py is a Python script file in a Flask application that contains the code for the
application. It is the main entry point for the application and contains the code
for setting up the application and its routes. The **app.py** code discussed earlier
typically contains the following:

a. **Import the Flask module**: The first step is to import the Flask module and
other modules that the application may need. This is usually done at the
beginning of the file.

b. **Create the Flask app**: This is done by calling the **Flask()** constructor.

c. **Configure the Flask app:** This includes setting the base URL, the debug flag,
the secret key, the template folder, and other configuration options. We have
not set any of these in this example, but we will do this in the next example.

d. **Create the routes**: This is done using the **app.route()** decorator. This decorator is used to define the URL for each view function that the application will use.

e. **Create the view functions**: This is done by creating functions that will be used to handle requests. The view functions typically take in arguments for the request and return a response.

6. **Open the terminal in Visual Studio Code and run the application:** The final step is to run the application. This is done by calling the **app.run()** method. This will start the application and make it available to handle requests. On the terminal, type the following command:

python app.py

This will launch the server, and the output will look as shown in *Figure 11.6*. Remember, we have launched the development server now. When we complete our work and are ready to deploy, we will switch to the production version instead.

```
(env) PS X:\FlaskApp> python app.py
 * Serving Flask app 'app'
 * Debug mode: on
WARNING: This is a development server. Do not use it in a production deployment. Use a production WSGI server instead.
 * Running on http://127.0.0.1:5000
Press CTRL+C to quit
 * Restarting with stat
 * Debugger is active!
 * Debugger PIN: 104-509-225
127.0.0.1 - - [11/Jun/2023 19:36:08] "GET / HTTP/1.1" 200 -
127.0.0.1 - - [11/Jun/2023 19:36:08] "GET /favicon.ico HTTP/1.1" 404 -
```

Figure 11.6: Python code to execute app.py and the launch of the server

As shown in *Figure 11.6*, the server is running on **http://127.0.0.1:5000**. Open any browser and open **http://127.0.0.1:5000**. You will see that flask is running, as shown in *Figure 11.7*:

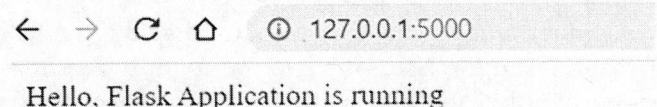

Hello, Flask Application is running

Figure 11.7: Flask application running in the browser

Develop a Profile Application

We will learn the concepts of Flask application by developing an application. Let us call this application My Profile Application and describe the requirements:

- The website will have the following web pages: Home, Education, Expertise, Projects, and Testimonials.

- Home will be a static page, whereas Education, Expertise, Projects, and Testimonials will display the details from the database.

- The website should have a user login page with username/password authentication for access.

- Only the admin users should be able to add content to the database for education, expertise, and projects; any registered user should be able to add testimonials to the page.

- Admin should also be able to control the Testimonial page from the back end.

Flask applications have **Views**. **Views** are functions in a Flask application controller responsible for processing user requests and returning response data to the user. The views are responsible for communicating with the model to retrieve, edit, create, and delete data from a database and for formatting this data as a response to the user. Views are typically written as Python functions that take an HTTP request object and an optional array of parameters as arguments. *Figure 11.8* depicts the **Views** or **Functions** that we will create and add to this website:

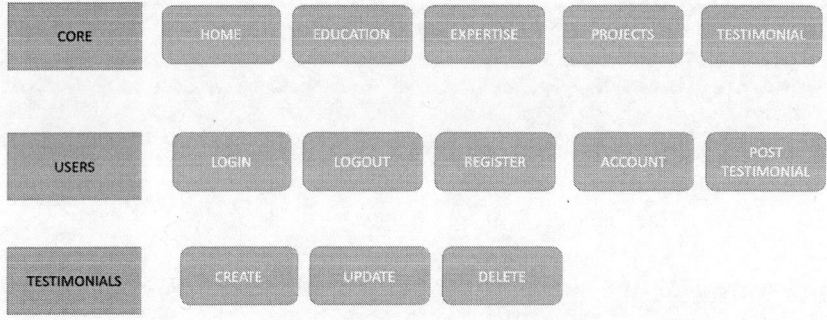

Figure 11.8: Features available in the application

The functionalities shown under the core are to display the content to everyone. Functionalities (or Views) under Users like login, logout, register, account, and post testimonials are to be handled for registered users. Testimonials functionalities are to make edits to Testimonials.

Let us start coding the application in the upcoming sections. But before that, let us create a folder called **myprofile**, where your **app.py** file is placed, as shown in *Figure 11.9*. All the files related to the **My Profile** application will be added to this folder.

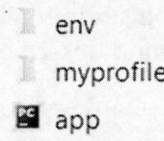

Figure 11.9: Folder structure for the project

We need to add an empty **__init__.py** file in **myprofile** to mark this directory as a package so that Python can recognize it as such. This file can be used to initialize the package or set the **__all__** variable. Under the **myprofile** folder, create three folders named **core**, **users**, and **testimonials** to handle the views related to the functionalities. Now, add an empty **__init__.py** file in all three folders.

Templates and static content

The first set of content that we deal with while developing a Flask application are templates and static. Let us create the **static** and **templates** folders under the **myprofile** folder. Static and **Templates** have special meaning, so Flask knows what to expect in these folders.

Templates in a Flask application are the front-end files used to render HTML. They are written in HTML and use a special syntax to add dynamic content. Flask uses the **Jinja2** template engine to render templates and provide data from the back end.

In Flask, static files refer to files that remain static, for example, image files, CSS, JavaScript, and other files that a web application or website may need in order to render properly. These files are typically stored within a static folder, which is separate from the Python application and template files. Flask provides a useful means to reference these static files through its **static** directory. Flask provides a feature to define these in a folder outside the app's package directory for easy maintenance. This folder can be called **static**, and any files inside it will be loaded whenever the application is run.

The main content for the static folder for this project would be the stylesheet and the images. The **profile.css** file is used as the stylesheet, and the code looks like the following:

```css
*{
    padding: 0;
    margin: 0;
    font-family: 'Poppins', sans-serif;
}

header{
    background-color: rgb(114, 174, 239);
    color: white;
    height: 120px;
    padding: 10px;
}
.resume_title{
    text-align: center;
}
.skills{
    display: flex;
    justify-content: space-around;
}
```

```
.skill_title{
    background-color: rgb(114, 174, 239);
    color: white;
    border-radius: 20px;
    padding: 10px;
    font-size: 30px;
}

.exp_title, .org_name, .org_date, .exp ul{
margin: 15px 0;
}
.exp_title, .org_name, .org_date{
    color: rgb(49, 207, 157);
    font-size:18px;
}
li{
    font-size: 15px;
}
.projects{
    display: flex;
    justify-content: space-around;

}
.project_details{
    margin-right: 13%;
}
.projects ul{
    margin: 15px 0;

}

footer{
    background-color: black;
    color: white;
    padding: 30px;
}

.top_foot{
    display: flex;
    justify-content: space-between;
    align-items: center;
}
.foot-left{
    width: 50%;
    padding: 20px;
    border-right: solid white 1px;
```

```
}
.foot-right{
    display: flex;
    justify-content: space-around;
    width: 60%;
}
.foot-right li{
    list-style: none;
    padding: 5px 0;

}
.foot-right li a{
    text-decoration: none;
    color: white;

}
.foot-right li a:hover{
    color: red;
    transition: 0.7s;
}
.about{
    margin-top: 70px;
    padding: 0 5rem;
}
.testimonial_card{
    margin: 80px 210px;
}
.testimonials{
    margin: 2px;
}
.logo h1{
    font-size: 50px;
}

/* Media Query */
@media screen and (max-width:885px){
    .skills, .exp, .education{
        flex-direction: column;
        padding: 20px;
    }
}
@media screen and (max-width:635px){
    .projects{
        flex-direction: column;
        padding: 0 45px;
    }
    .expert, .project_details{
```

```
        margin: 0 0 10px 0;
    }
}
@media screen and (max-width:770px){
    .about_image{
        margin-top:40px;
        width: 100%;
    }
    .image img{
        width:500px;
    }
    .about_image p{
        width: 100%;
    }
}
@media screen and (max-width:652px){

    .image img{
        width: 250px;
    }
}
@media screen and (max-width:430px){
    .testimonial_card {
        margin: 80px 66px;
}
}
@media screen and (max-width:376px){
    .title{
        font-size: 40px;
    }
    .image img {
        margin-left: -34px;
    }
}
@media screen and (max-width:320px){
    .image img {
        margin-left: -81px;

    }
}
@media screen and (max-width:670px){
    .foot-left{
        border: none;

    }
    .top_foot{
        flex-direction: column;
```

```
        }
        .foot-left{
            width: 80%;
            text-align: center;


        }
}
@media screen and (max-width:570px){
        .foot-right{
            flex-direction: column;
            text-align: center;
        }
}
h1 {text-align: center;}

table, th, td {
    border: 1px solid blue;
    border-radius: 10px;
    border-style: ridge;
} th, td {
    border-color: #96D4D4;
}
```

Put all the required images in the **image** folder. The folder structure within static would look as shown in *Figure 11.10*:

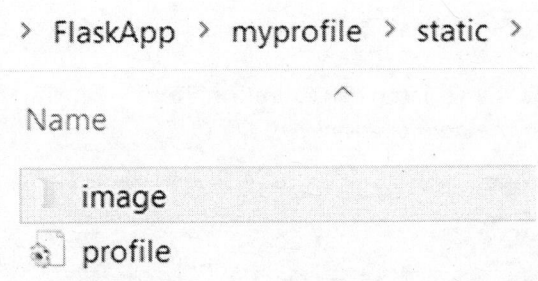

Figure 11.10: Folder structure of static

We will now turn our attention to the **templates** folder. This folder will have all the dynamic HTML content. When a user launches the website and has not yet logged into the website, they should see the following options:

- Home

- Profile

- Extra Curriculars

- Future Goals

- Testimonials

- Login

- Register

The web page view is shown in *Figure 11.11*:

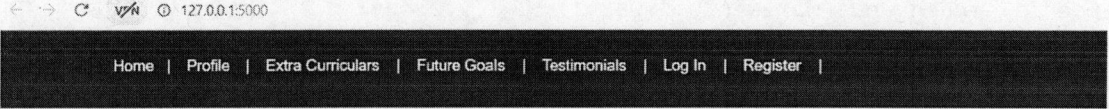

Figure 11.11: *Screenshot of menu from the home page for a visitor*

A logged in user should see the following options on the web page:

- Home

- Profile

- Extra Curricular

- Future Goals

- Testimonials

- Log out

- Account

- Update

The preceding options should have navigation links pointing to the following views, which we will create in the next section:

- **Home: `core.index`**

- **Profile: `core.profile`**

- **Extra Curricular: `core.activities`**

- **Future Goals: `core.goals`**

- **Testimonials: `core.alltestimonials`**

- **Login: `users.login`**

- **Register: `users.register`**

- **Log out: `users.logout`**

- **Account: `users.account`**

- **Update: `testimonials.create_post`**

Now, we have an idea of which folder will have specific views. So far, we have only created views in core and added the home page.

The **index.html** file is the main page of a Flask application. In the **index.html** file, the user will typically find a page with links to the other views or pages of the app. It can also include text, graphics, and other content. The file can be edited to customize the design of the main page of the app. Before we create our **index.html** file, it is recommended to create a **base.html** file that will have header and footer content common to all the main pages. Creating a **base.html** template in Flask helps ensure a consistent look for your web app. This is beneficial for maintaining the visual style of the web app, enabling faster development when making changes to the design. Additionally, by using **base.html**, you can easily add elements such as headers, footers, and navigation menus that appear on every page within your web application.

The **base.html** file (under templates folder) will look like this:

- **Section 1**: First part of any HTML file is, of course, the **<head>** part. We are not adding the head section code here. You can refer to the full code for reference, but feel free to design your own version.

```
<!DOCTYPE html>
<html lang="en">
<head>

</head>
```

- **Section 2**: Now we are looking at the body section. First, the header content is added to the HTML code. Jinja template language is used in the code to make it more dynamic. Jinja is a Python-based templating engine used by Flask that allows you to dynamically generate HTML code. The most common usage of the variable code in an HTML file is to output values from Python code into the rendered template. This can be done using double curly braces **{{ }}**. For example, if you have a variable **name** in your Flask route, you can output its value in the HTML template as **{{ name }}**. When Flask renders this template, it will replace **{{ name }}** with the actual value of the **name** variable passed from the route. Besides outputting variable values, Jinja provides features for control structures like loops and conditionals, allowing you to dynamically change the structure and content of the HTML based on the provided data from Flask.

```
<body>
<header class="p-3 text-bg-dark" style="height:77px;">
  <div class="container" id="navbarForPc">
    <div class="d-flex flex-wrap align-items-center justify-content-
center justify-content-lg-start">
      <a href="/" class="d-flex align-items-center mb-2 mb-lg-0 text-
white text-decoration-none">
```

```
        </a>

    <div id="navigation-bar" class="nav-bar">
    <ul class="nav col-12 col-lg-auto me-lg-auto mb-2 justify-
content-end mb-md-0">
        <li><a href="{{ url_for('core.index') }}" class="nav-link
px-2 text-white">Home    |</a></li>
        <li><a href="{{ url_for('core.profile') }}" class="nav-link
px-2 text-white">Profile     |</a></li>
        <li><a href="{{ url_for('core.activities') }}" class="nav-
link px-2 text-white">Extra Curriculars     |</a></li>
            <li><a href="{{ url_for('core.goals') }}" class="nav-link
px-2 text-white">Future Goals     |</a></li>
        <li><a href="{{ url_for('core.alltestimonials') }}"
class="nav-link px-2 text-white">Testimonials     |</a></
li>
        {% if current_user.is_authenticated %}

        <li ><a  href="{{ url_for('users.logout') }}" class="nav-
link px-2 text-white">Log Out     |</a></li>
        <li><a href="{{ url_for('users.account') }}" class="nav-link
px-2 text-white">Account     |</a></li>
        <li><a href="{{ url_for('testimonials.create_post') }}"
class="nav-link px-2 text-white">Update     |</a></li>

        {% else %}
        <li><a href="{{ url_for('users.login') }}" class="nav-link
px-2 text-white">Log In     |</a></li>
        <li><a href="{{ url_for('users.register') }}" class="nav-
link px-2 text-white">Register    |</a></li>
        {% endif %}

    </ul>
    </div>
    </div>
  </div>
  <div class="container" id="navbarForMob">
    <div class="row ">
    <div class="text-end">
        <button class="btn" data-bs-toggle="offcanvas" data-bs-
target="#offcanvasExample" aria-controls="offcanvasExample"><i
class="bi bi-list text-white fs-2"></i></button>
    </div>

    </div>
  </div>
</header>
```

```
<br><br><br>
<div class="container">
    <div class="top-section">
        <section class="content"><b>
            <h1 class="title">Personal Digital Portfolio </h1></b>
        </section>
    </div>
  {% block content %}

  {% endblock %}
</div>
```

- **Section 3**: Adding the footer part is going to be common for all the pages that we will create.

```
<br><br><br>
<footer>
        <div class="top_foot">
            <div class="foot-left">
                <h1>
                    SACHIN KOHLI
                </h1>
                <p>I'm a software engineer with a passion for
creating cutting-edge applications. I strive to create high-quality
solutions to ensure that users have the best experience possible.</
p>
            </div>
            <div class="foot-right">
                <div class="main_menu">
                    <ul><h4><b>Important Links</b></h4>
                        <li><a href="home">Home</a></li>
                        {% if current_user.is_authenticated %}

        <li ><a  href="{{ url_for('users.logout') }}">Log Out</a></
li>

        <li><a href="{{ url_for('users.account') }}">Account</a></
li>

        {% else %}
        <li><a href="{{ url_for('users.login') }}">Log In</a></li>
        <li><a href="{{ url_for('users.register') }}">Register</a></
li>
        {% endif %}
                    </ul>
                </div>
                <div class="about_menu">
```

```
                        <ul><h4><b>About Me</b></h4>
                        <li><a href="profile">View Profile</a></li>
                        <li><a href="testimonials">Testimonials</a></li>
                        <li><a href="goals">Future Goals</a></li>
                        <li><a href="activities">Extra Curriculars</a></
li>
                </ul>
                </div>
            </div>
        </div>
        <div class="container">

    </div>

        <hr>
        <div class="bottom_foot">
            <h5 class="text-center">
                <marque>Copyright: SACHIN KOHLI      Contact:
sachin@kohli.com</marque>
            </h5>
        </div>
    </footer>
```

- **Section 4**: This involves adding the **Hamburger Menu** code. The hamburger menu is a common design element used in website and mobile app interfaces. It consists of three horizontal lines stacked on top of each other, resembling a hamburger, hence the name. When clicked or tapped, the hamburger menu expands to reveal a hidden navigation menu or additional options, providing a space-saving and intuitive way to access secondary content or features. It is often used in responsive design to optimize the user experience on smaller screens by consolidating menu items into a single icon.

```
<!--hamburger menu-->
    <div class="offcanvas offcanvas-start" tabindex="-1"
id="offcanvasExample" aria-labelledby="offcanvasExampleLabel">
        <div class="offcanvas-header">
            <h5 class="offcanvas-title" id="offcanvasExampleLabel"></h5>
            <button type="button" class="btn-close" data-bs-
dismiss="offcanvas" aria-label="Close"></button>
        </div>
        <div class="offcanvas-body">

            <div class="ms-3 mt-3">
                <ul id="remove">
                    <li class="mb-3"><a href="{{ url_for('core.index') }}"
```

```
class="nav-link px-2 fs-4">Home   </a></li>
               <li class="mb-3"><a href="{{ url_for('core.profile') }}"
class="nav-link px-2 fs-4">Profile    </a></li>
               <li class="mb-3"><a href="{{ url_for('core.activities')
}}" class="nav-link px-2 fs-4">Extra Curriculars    </a></
li>
                 <li class="mb-3"><a href="{{ url_for('core.goals') }}"
class="nav-link px-2 fs-4">Future Goals    </a></li>
               <li class="mb-3"><a href="{{ url_for('core.
alltestimonials') }}" class="nav-link px-2 fs-4">Testimonials
   </a></li>
               {% if current_user.is_authenticated %}

               <li class="mb-3"><a  href="{{ url_for('users.logout')
}}" class="nav-link px-2 fs-4">Log Out    </a></li>
               <li class="mb-3"><a href="{{ url_for('users.account')
}}" class="nav-link px-2 fs-4">Account    </a></li>
               <li class="mb-3"><a href="{{ url_for('testimonials.
create_post') }}" class="nav-link px-2 fs-4">Update    </
a></li>

               {% else %}
               <li class="mb-3"><a href="{{ url_for('users.login') }}"
class="nav-link px-2 fs-4">Log In    </a></li>
               <li class="mb-3"><a href="{{ url_for('users.register')
}}" class="nav-link px-2 fs-4">Register    </a></li>
               {% endif %}

           </ul>
         </div>

       </div>
     </div>
     <!--end hamburger menu-->
     <script src="https://cdn.jsdelivr.net/npm/bootstrap@5.2.3/dist/
js/bootstrap.bundle.min.js"
         integrity="sha384-kenU1KFdBIe4zVF0s0G1M5b4hcpxyD9F7jL+jjXkk+
Q2h455rYXK/7HAuoJl+0I4"
         crossorigin="anonymous"></script>
 </body>
 </html>
```

As you can see, we have combined both **Headers** and **Footers** in this file. This **base.html** file will be imported by all our HTML files. We have used **Block Code** in the **base.html** body where code from other **.html** files will be added:

```
{% block content %}
```

```
{% endblock %}
```

The **{% block %}** tags define blocks that child templates can fill in. All the block tag does is tell the template engine that a child template may override those portions of the template.

Now, we will see the **index.html** file, which will extend the **base.html** file:

```
{% extends "base.html" %}
{% block content %}

    <br>
    <div class="about row">

        <div class="col-lg-6 col-md-12 col-sm-12 image">
            <img src="../static/image/compimage.jpg" alt="Ishana's Profile
Pic" width="550">
        </div>
        <div class="col-lg-6 col-md-12 col-sm-12 about_image">
            <h2><b>About Me</b></h2>
            <p>Hi there, I'm Sachin, and I'm a software engineer with a
passion for creating cutting-edge applications. My journey in programming
began with helping my brother fix his website back in college. That
experience sparked my curiosity and led me to pursue a degree in computer
science. </p>
            <p> In the years since, I've gone on to develop a wide range of
software products, ranging from media players to embedded software. I
have experience in many languages, including C, C++, Java, Python, and
JavaScript, and I'm comfortable working with a variety of platforms, such
as Windows, Mac OS X, and Linux. </p>
            <p>My experience gives me an unusual perspective when it comes to
solving complex software problems. I enjoy working with all aspects of the
development process, from design and coding to debugging and optimization.
I strive to create high-quality solutions to ensure that users have the
best experience possible.</p>
            <p> In my spare time, I like to explore new technologies and ideas,
and I'm a big fan of open source software. I'm also a huge fan of puzzles
and problem solving, and I'm always looking for the next programming
challenge.</p>
        </div>
    </div>
        <div class="row testimonial_card">
            <div class="card testimonials col-lg-4 col-md-12 col-sm-12"
style="width: 18rem;">
                <img src="..\static\image\edu.jpg" class="card-img-top"
alt="...">
                <div class="card-body">
                    <h6 class="card-title text-center"><b>Testimonials</
```

```
b></h6>
                        <a href="testimonials" class="btn btn-primary">View
More</a>
                </div>
            </div>
            <div class="card testimonials col-lg-4 col-md-12 col-sm-12"
style="width: 18rem;">
                <img src="..\static\image\edu.jpg" class="card-img-top"
alt="...">
                <div class="card-body">
                    <h6 class="card-title  text-center"><b>Future Goals</
b></h6>
                        <a href="goals" class="btn btn-primary">View More</a>
                </div>
            </div>
            <div class="card testimonials col-lg-4 col-md-12 col-sm-12"
style="width: 18rem;">
                <img src="..\static\image\edu.jpg" class="card-img-top"
alt="...">
                <div class="card-body">
                    <h6 class="card-title  text-center"><b>Extra
Curriculars</b></h6>
                        <a href="activities" class="btn btn-primary">View
More</a>
                </div>
            </div>
        </div>
```

`{% endblock content %}`

`{% extends %}` is the key here. It tells the template engine that this template **extends** another template. When the template system evaluates this template, it first locates the parent. The **extend** tag must be the first tag in the template to render the contents of the block.

Currently, **app.py** is displaying a custom message. We need to change it to handle the **index.html** file. We need to create **Views** to handle **HTTP** requests. Views in Flask are functions that process incoming requests, perform various operations on the requested resources, and return responses. Views handle the application's logic and are typically used to render templates. They receive requests from the client and decide what to send as responses. We will add **views.py** under the **core** folder of **myprofile**, which will have an **index()** function that would be the default function to call. In this file, we will also have to add code to handle all requests, like goals, activities, etc. We will create a **views.py** file under the **core** folder. Views, often referred to as **controllers**, are modular *handlers* that work with a Flask application's model (back-end database) and template (front-end user interface) layers to provide endpoints to applications. A view function is the code you write to respond to requests to your application. Views handle the logic that manipulates the data (retrieved from the model) and prepares it to be displayed in the template. Views generally return a response object, which the web server then uses to generate the HTTP response. The code in **views.py** will look like the following:

```python
#file location:  myprofile/core/views.py

from flask import render_template, request,Blueprint
from myprofile.models import Testimonials, Details

'''
A blueprint defines a collection of views, templates, static files
and other elements that can be applied to an application. For example,
let's imagine that we have a blueprint for an admin panel. This blueprint
would define the views for routes like /admin/login and /admin/dashboard.
'''
core=Blueprint('core',__name__)

@core.route('/')
def index():
    return render_template("index.html")

@core.route('/goals')
def goals():
    return render_template("goals.html")

@core.route('/activities')
def activities():
    return render_template("activities.html")
@core.route('/testimonials')
def alltestimonials():
    testimonials=Testimonials.query.all()
    return render_template("alltestimonials.html",
testimonials=testimonials)

@core.route('/profile')
def profile():
    details=Details.query.all()
    return render_template("profile.html", details=details)
```

We are using **Blueprint** in the views to enable developers to break larger applications into smaller, more manageable, and better organized components. It gives developers an easy way to design and organize their code into separate files, or *blueprints*, for easy maintenance and organization. Blueprint allows developers to define their application components, such as views, templates, and static resources in separate files, which makes it easier to manage and share them with the team.

The **.route()** decorator binds a function to a URL endpoint. It can be used to handle different requests, such as GET, POST, PUT, and DELETE, as well as bind multiple functions to the same URL endpoint. For example, in the preceding code, the profile endpoint is bound with the **profile.html** page and also returns details that have all the data from the **Details** table. **Details.query_all()** is equivalent to executing query **Select * from Details** in **Structure Query Language** (**SQL**).

The given **app.py** file calls the app file under **myprofile**. The **app.py** file is the main entry point to an application and is typically found where most of the **configuration** and **routing** are done. It is also used to create and initialize the Flask app instance. We can have multiple projects under one application, so it is a smarter idea to handle different project configurations at different places. An application can have only one entry point, so only one **app.py**. It is time to add configurations in **__init__.py** under the **myprofile** folder.

Flask requires views (the functions or methods that handle requests) to be registered with the application instance for the application to know where to look when a request for a particular URL comes in. This way, it can quickly route requests to the appropriate view function, and any additional configuration for that view can be provided as arguments to the decorator. We can see the route in the **views.py** file.

Let us register the views in **__init__.py**:

```
#Filename: myprofile/__init__.py
from flask import Flask

#creating and setting application app
app = Flask(__name__)
# # # # #

#register
from myprofile.core.views import core
app.register_blueprint(core)
```

In a later section, we will come back to register more views, add a path for the database, and activate the login manager. For now, let us move on to creating a database in the next section.

Setting up Database (SQLite3)

For development purposes, SQLite is a usable database due to its lightweight and in-memory capabilities; however, it is not geared toward production use. If an app is planned for deployment, it is recommended to consider a more powerful database such as PostgreSQL. Extra steps will be performed while migrating all database schemas and existing data to PostgreSQL during deployment to the production server. To avoid this issue, it may be best to follow a standard for production-ready databases from the beginning. We will use SQLite database for this exercise. In *Chapter 12, Working With Containers in Azure,* we will move the data to Postgres database. When ready to deploy the application, we will also learn how to migrate an application from one database to another.

We will need three tables to manage the entire thing, so we will create the **DETAILS**, **USERS**, and **TESTIMONIALS** tables. The tables and the columns associated with each table are shown in *Figure 11.12*:

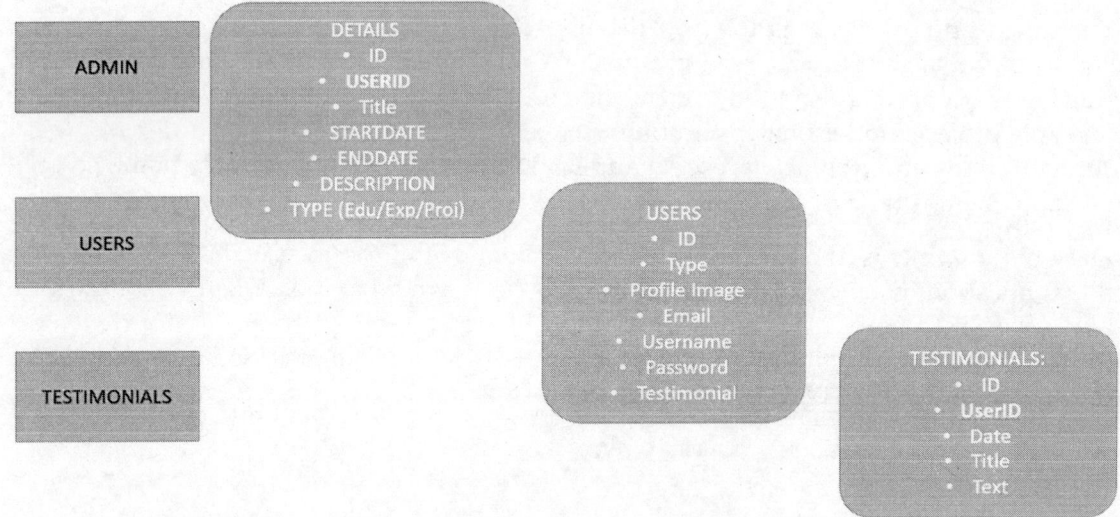

Figure 11.12: Database tables for the project

A model in the context of database in Flask is the structure of the database schema. It is an object-relational mapping that defines models, that is, classes that represent the tables in the database and the relationships between the models. It helps in mapping the objects in Python code to the columns in a relational database. The **models** file contains model classes for the application. These model classes define the data structure and mapping of the application's data and the methods for **Creating, Reading, Updating, and Deleting (CRUD)** information from the database.

The next step is to add a Python file **models.py** to our project. This is where we will add the classes and the database tables will be created after execution. Let us see what the **models.py** file looks like:

```
#FlaskApp/myprofile/models.py
from myprofile import db,login_manager
from werkzeug.security import generate_password_hash,check_password_hash
from flask_login import UserMixin
from datetime import datetime

@login_manager.user_loader
def load_user(user_id):
    return Users.query.get(user_id)
```

```python
class Users(db.Model,UserMixin):

    __tablename__ = 'users'

    id = db.Column(db.Integer,primary_key=True)
    acc_type = db.Column(db.Integer,default=1) # 1 for regular user, 0 for
admin handled within
    profile_image = db.Column(db.String(64),nullable=False,default='default_
profile.png')
    email = db.Column(db.String(64),unique=True,index=True)
    username = db.Column(db.String(64),unique=True,index=True)
    password_hash = db.Column(db.String(128))

    testimonials =
db.relationship('Testimonials',backref='author',lazy=True)

    def __init__(self,email,username,password):
        self.email = email
        self.username = username
        self.password_hash = generate_password_hash(password)

    def check_password(self,password):
        return check_password_hash(self.password_hash,password)

    def __repr__(self):
        return f"Username {self.username}"

class Details(db.Model):
    __tablename__ = 'details'

    id = db.Column(db.Integer,primary_key=True)
    org = db.Column(db.Text, nullable=False)
    startdate = db.Column(db.Date)
    enddate = db.Column(db.Date)
    title = db.Column(db.String(140),nullable=False)
    description = db.Column(db.Text,nullable=False)
    info_type = db.Column(db.Text)  # 1 - for Education, 2 for Expertise 3
for Projects 4 Others

    def __init__(self, org, startdate,enddate,title,description,info_type):
        self.org = org
        self.startdate = startdate
        self.enddate = enddate
        self.title = title
        self.description = description
        self.info_type = info_type
```

```python
class Testimonials(db.Model):
    users = db.relationship(Users)

    id = db.Column(db.Integer,primary_key=True)
    user_id = db.Column(db.Integer,db.ForeignKey('users.
id'),nullable=False)

    date = db.Column(db.DateTime,nullable=False,default=datetime.utcnow)
    title = db.Column(db.String(140),nullable=False)
    text = db.Column(db.Text,nullable=False)

    def __init__(self,title,text,user_id):
        self.title = title
        self.text = text
        self.user_id = user_id

    def __repr__(self):
        return f"Post ID: {self.id} -- Date: {self.date} --- {self.title}"
```

Let us understand the modules we have imported:

- **db and login_manager from myprofile: db** will have the database configuration, and **login_manager** will have **LoginManager** object. These will be added to **__init__.py** next.

- **Werkzeug.security:** It is a Python library that provides a set of secure hashing and salting functions for user authentication purposes. The **generate_password_hash** and **check_password_hash** functions are two of the most commonly used functions from the library. They allow you to securely store and validate user passwords in a database, without needing to store the plaintext version of the user's password. The **generate_password_hash** function takes a plaintext password and creates a secure, salted hash; the **check_password_hash** function takes a plaintext password and a previously created hash and verifies whether the two match.

- **UserMixin:** The **UserMixin** class is in line with the Flask-Login extension and provides generic user account properties that projects may use, such as an id, username, and password.

- **@login_manager.user_loader:** It is a user callback function that is used to reload the user object from the user ID stored in the session. It should take the unicode ID of a user as an argument and return the corresponding user object. This function is used by Flask-Login during the login process to reload a user. Therefore, user implementations should take special care when implementing **get_id**.

The three classes **Users, Details** and **Testimonials** have variables that will get converted into database tables and columns when we migrate them. Each column has a datatype and constraints (like **nullable= False**), just like we write in SQL. We are using the SQLITE database, but you can use any **Relational Database Management System (RDBMS)**.

Now, let us update the **myprofile/__init__.py** file with the following settings:

```
#Filename: myprofile/__init__.py
import os
from flask import Flask
from flask_sqlalchemy import SQLAlchemy
from flask_migrate import Migrate
from flask_login import LoginManager


#creating and setting application app
app = Flask(__name__)


############# CONFIGURATIONS (CAN BE SEPARATE CONFIG.PY FILE)
# Remember you need to set your environment variables at the command line
# when you deploy this to a real website.
# export SECRET_KEY=mysecret
# set SECRET_KEY=mysecret
app.config['SECRET_KEY'] = 'mysecret'


################ DATABASE SETUP  #####
basedir = os.path.abspath(os.path.dirname(__file__))
app.config['SQLALCHEMY_DATABASE_URI'] = 'sqlite:///'+os.path.
join(basedir,'data.sqlite')
app.config['SQLALCHEMY_TRACK_MODIFICATIONS'] = False


db = SQLAlchemy(app)
Migrate(app,db)


#### LOGIN CONFIGS #######

login_manager = LoginManager()

# We can now pass in our app to the login manager
login_manager.init_app(app)

# Tell users what view to go to when they need to login.
login_manager.login_view = "users.login"

#register
from myprofile.core.views import core
app.register_blueprint(core)

#register error pages
from myprofile.error_pages.handlers import error_pages
app.register_blueprint(error_pages)
```

```
from myprofile.users.views import users
app.register_blueprint(users)

from myprofile.testimonials.views import testimonials
app.register_blueprint(testimonials)

from myprofile.details.views import details
app.register_blueprint(details)
```

The **details** folder will have **forms**, using which we will save the data to the database. It will also have **views** that will be used to display all the projects, work experience, and other details from the **details** table. Let us create another folder by the name **error_pages**, which will have the **handlers.py** file to handle 403 and 404 errors.

We have added the final code to the **__init__** file. All the views are registered.

Now, all the folders would be created, and it would look something like *Figure 11.13*:

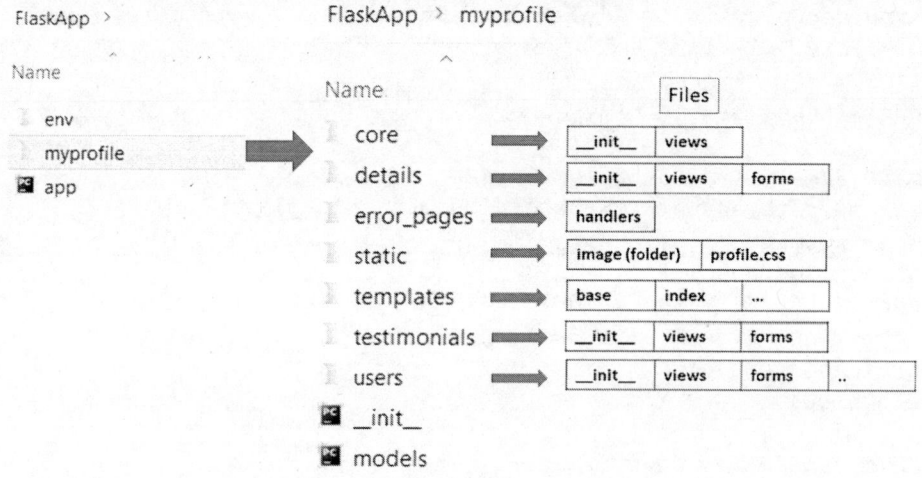

Figure 11.13: *Folders structure*

The code for **handlers.py** file will be as follows:

```
#FlaskApp/myprofile/error_pages\handlers.py
# handlers.py
from flask import Blueprint,render_template

error_pages = Blueprint('error_pages',__name__)

@error_pages.app_errorhandler(404)
def error_404(error):
    return render_template('error_pages/404.html') , 404
@error_pages.app_errorhandler(403)
def error_403(error):
    return render_template('error_pages/403.html') , 403
```

Now, it is time to execute the database code. To create the database, we need to follow these steps:

1. Create a new Python file in the project directory and import **SQLAlchemy** from the **flask_sqlalchemy** package.

2. Create an instance of the **SQLAlchemy** class by providing the Flask application object as a parameter.

3. Define the database model(s) by extending the **SQLAlchemy** base class and adding the required columns, data types, and properties.

4. Create the database by calling the **create_all()** method on the **SQLAlchemy** object.

5. Migrate the changes to the existing database by calling the **migrate** command.

6. Create a shell script to run the application, passing the **Flask** and **SQLAlchemy** objects as parameters.

7. Execute the script to run the application and create the database.

We have already taken care of the mentioned steps while we were working on the __ init__.py file under the **myprofile** project. Now, we need to execute the following commands to create the database:

1. Activate the environment

    a. On Windows, type the following command on the terminal:

    ```
    Env\Scripts\activate
    ```

    b. On Linux/macOS, the following command does the same thing:

    ```
    Source env/bin/activate
    ```

2. Launch Python prompt by typing python on the terminal

    ```
    python
    ```

3. The preceding command will launch Python prompt. First, you will have to set the application context. Import the app from the **myprofile** package and then call **app_context().push()**, as shown here:

    ```
    >>> from myprofile import app
    >>>app.app_context().push()
    ```

4. Now, we need to import **db** and **create_all()** of **db** to create the database:

    ```
    >>> from myprofile import db
    >>> db.create_all()
    ```

5. The final step is to exit from the Python prompt and launch the application in the browser:

```
>>> exit()

python app.py
```

Note: If you encounter the error *"ImportError: cannot import name 'url_quote' from 'werkzeug.urls'"*, it could be because you are using werkzeug version 3.0.0. You might have to downgrade it to werkzeug==2.3.7 to avoid the error.

A database with all tables is created. To verify if the tables have been created or not, look for **data.sqlite** file (file size approx. 24KB) under the **myprofile** folder. If the file is present then it means that the database is successfully created. Now, type **http://127.0.0.1:5000** in the browser. You will see a website similar to *Figure 11.14*:

Figure 11.14: Home page of the website

If you do not get the website but get an error instead, read the error message and fix the error to get the website up and running.

Integrate Flask-Login

The next step would be to create HTML pages that can be referenced from different views to display the information. To add information to the database, like creating a new user, adding education details, adding or editing testimonials, etc., we need to create forms. Forms will take the input from the user, and on submission, they will update the given table with the information. In GitHub, you will have access to all the final versions of the files used while creating this project. In this section, we will specifically focus on login forms and login validation.

Flask-Login can be used to manage user sessions in a Flask application, as it covers common tasks such as logging in, logging out, and remembering user sessions over long periods of time. Even though it is not restricted to a particular database system or permission model, user objects must have methods that can be called upon and a **callback** must be set up to enable the loading of users using their ID.

Flask-Login works via a login manager. To begin using it, we have set up the login manager by instantiating it and telling it about our Flask app in the **main __init__.py** file. Let's check the following code to understand it well:

```
login_manager = LoginManager()

# We can now pass in our app to the login manager
login_manager.init_app(app)

# Tell users what view to go to when they need to login.
login_manager.login_view = "users.login"
```

Users.views has all the options related to login: login, logout, register, check account, and get user type. Admin user is added from the back end, and the account type is set to 0. All other users have type set as 1. This is how you can determine whether or not its admin login or not. Let us see the entire code:

```
# FlaskApp/myprofile/users/views.py

from flask import render_template, url_for, flash, redirect, request,
Blueprint
from flask_login import login_user, current_user, logout_user, login_
required
from myprofile import db
from myprofile.models import Users, Testimonials, Details
from myprofile.users.forms import RegistrationForm, LoginForm,
UpdateUserForm
from myprofile.details.forms import ProfileForm
from myprofile.users.picture_handler import add_profile_pic
```

```python
users = Blueprint('users', __name__)

@users.route('/register', methods=['GET', 'POST'])
def register():
    form = RegistrationForm()

    if form.validate_on_submit():
        user = Users(email=form.email.data,
                    username=form.username.data,
                    password=form.password.data)

        db.session.add(user)
        db.session.commit()
        flash('Thanks for registering! Now you can login!')
        return redirect(url_for('users.login'))
    return render_template('register.html', form=form)

@users.route('/login', methods=['GET', 'POST'])
def login():
    form = LoginForm()
    if form.validate_on_submit():
        # Grab the user from our User Models table
        user = Users.query.filter_by(email=form.email.data).first()

        # Check that the user was supplied and the password is right
        # The verify_password method comes from the User object
        # https://stackoverflow.com/questions/2209755/python-operation-vs-
is-not

        if user.check_password(form.password.data) and user is not None:
            #Log in the user
            login_user(user)
            flash('Logged in successfully.')

            # If a user was trying to visit a page that requires a login
            # flask saves that URL as 'next'.
            next = request.args.get('next')

            # So let's now check if that next exists, otherwise we'll go to
            # the welcome page.
            if next == None or not next[0]=='/':
                next = url_for('core.index')

            return redirect(next)
    return render_template('login.html', form=form)

@users.route("/logout")
```

```python
def logout():
    logout_user()
    return redirect(url_for('core.index'))

@users.route("/account", methods=['GET', 'POST'])
@login_required
def account():
    #user = Users.query.filter_by(email=form.email.data).first()

    if current_user.acc_type==0:
        form = ProfileForm()

        if request.method == 'POST':
            org = form.org.data
            startdate = form.startdate.data
            enddate = form.enddate.data
            title = form.title.data
            description = form.description.data

            info_type = form.info_type.data
            record = Details(org=org, startdate=startdate, enddate=enddate,
title=title, description=description, info_type=info_type)
            db.session.add(record)
            db.session.commit()

        return render_template('addinfo.html', form=form)

    else:   #non admin users
        form = UpdateUserForm()

        if form.validate_on_submit():
            print(form)
            if form.picture.data:
                username = current_user.username
                pic = add_profile_pic(form.picture.data,username)
                current_user.profile_image = pic

            current_user.username = form.username.data
            current_user.email = form.email.data
            db.session.commit()
            flash('User Account Updated')
            return redirect(url_for('users.account'))

        elif request.method == 'GET':
            form.username.data = current_user.username
            form.email.data = current_user.email
```

```
        profile_image = url_for('static', filename='profile_pics/' + current_
user.profile_image)
        return render_template('account.html', profile_image=profile_image,
form=form)


@users.route("/<username>")
def user_posts(username):
    page = request.args.get('page', 1, type=int)
    user = Users.query.filter_by(username=username).first_or_404()
    blog_posts = Testimonials.query.filter_by(author=user).order_
by(Testimonials.date.desc()).paginate(page=page, per_page=5)
    return render_template('user_blog_posts.html', blog_posts=blog_posts,
user=user)
```

Views will handle all the login-related operations. Now we will add forms to get the user input, for example, a form to accept users' details for those wanting to register on the portal. You will see the code to generate forms in **forms.py**. Let us generate the code for **users/forms.py**:

```
# FlaskApp/myprofile/users/views.py
# Form Based Imports
from flask_wtf import FlaskForm
from wtforms import StringField, PasswordField, SubmitField
from wtforms.validators import DataRequired,Email,EqualTo
from wtforms import ValidationError
from flask_wtf.file import FileField, FileAllowed


# User Based Imports
from flask_login import current_user
from myprofile.models import Users

class LoginForm(FlaskForm):
    email = StringField('Email', validators=[DataRequired(), Email()])
    password = PasswordField('Password', validators=[DataRequired()])
    submit = SubmitField('Log In')

class RegistrationForm(FlaskForm):
    email = StringField('Email', validators=[DataRequired(),Email()])
    username = StringField('Username', validators=[DataRequired()])
    password = PasswordField('Password', validators=[DataRequired(),
EqualTo('pass_confirm', message='Passwords Must Match!')])
    pass_confirm = PasswordField('Confirm password',
validators=[DataRequired()])
    submit = SubmitField('Register!')

    def check_email(self, field):
```

```python
        # Check if not None for that user email!
        if Users.query.filter_by(email=field.data).first():
            raise ValidationError('Your email has been registered
already!')

    def check_username(self, field):
        # Check if not None for that username!
        if Users.query.filter_by(username=field.data).first():
            raise ValidationError('Sorry, that username is taken!')

class UpdateUserForm(FlaskForm):
    email = StringField('Email', validators=[DataRequired(),Email()])
    username = StringField('Username', validators=[DataRequired()])
    picture = FileField('Update Profile Picture',
validators=[FileAllowed(['jpg', 'png'])])
    submit = SubmitField('Update')

    def check_email(self, field):
        # Check if not None for that user email!
        if Users.query.filter_by(email=field.data).first():
            raise ValidationError('Your email has been registered
already!')

    def check_username(self, field):
        # Check if not None for that username!
        if Users.query.filter_by(username=field.data).first():
            raise ValidationError('Sorry, that username is taken!')
```

The register form appears over the **register.html** page under the **templates** folder. Let us look at the html code first:

```html
{% extends "base.html" %}
{% block content %}
<form method="POST">
    {# This hidden_tag is a CSRF security feature. #}
    {{ form.hidden_tag() }}
    {{ form.email.label }} {{ form.email() }}<br>
    {{ form.username.label }} {{ form.username() }}<br>
    {{ form.password.label }} {{ form.password() }}<br>
    {{ form.pass_confirm.label }} {{ form.pass_confirm() }}<br>
    {{ form.submit() }}
</form>
{% endblock %}
```

Register.html also extends from **base.html** to pull header and footer information. For every variable in the view, we need to have a textbox and each form will have a label to store the name of the textbox. Let us look at the **register.html** screen in *Figure 11.15*:

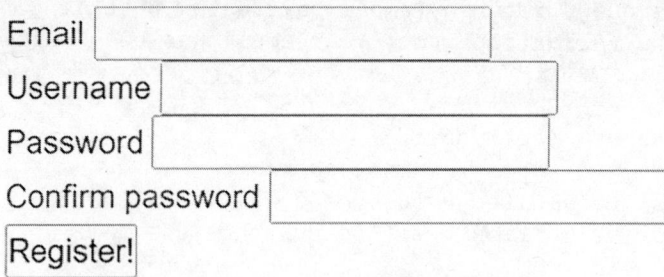

Figure 11.15: Form to register new user

We have covered all the important aspects of Flask programming. In the next couple of sections, we will look at the pending tasks and wrap up the project.

Testing the database

Before we move ahead, let us check whether our database is working fine. We would create a **test.py** Python script to connect to the database and get the data of our choice. This **test.py** file is placed in the **myprofile** project folder.

Flask-Admin is a Python web application development framework that provides administrative tools and interfaces for web applications. It is built on the Flask web framework and designed to provide an administrative interface to applications and databases. It is designed to be simple and fast and provide functionality that is not present in the Flask core framework. It offers features such as authentication, templates, and data management. Flask-Admin also provides a framework for adding additional functionality, such as user management, custom forms, and custom fields.

To use Flask-Admin, you need to install the library using the Python package manager **pip** and then create an **app.py** file in the root of your project. From there, you can create the **admin** page by adding the necessary code. You will also need to create database models to store your data, add the admin interface template, and define custom views for displaying and editing the data. Finally, you will need to add authentication and authorization security. Once everything is set, you can launch the application and access the admin pages. Since we have to customize admin features, let us not use **Flask-Admin** for this application. The way we have designed this application, the admin role is found under the **Users** table with **acc_type =0**. First, create a user from the register option and connect to the database using the **test.py** file to update the **acc_type** of the user. Thus, this user would become our admin user. Since this application is designed to have one admin user only, we are good. The **test.py** file would have code like this:

```
import sqlite3

con =sqlite3.connect("data.sqlite")
```

```
q1  ="Select * from Users"
#query to change the account type to 0 indicating admin role
q2 = "Update Users set acc_type=0 where ID=1"
#execute the command
con.execute(q2)
con.commit()
#query to read the values from Users table
rset = con.execute(q1)
for r in rset:
    print(r)
con.close()
```

Now, let us move on to the next section to complete the other parts of the code.

Completing the Application

Under the **templates** folder, you will see various HTML files; some of these files are designed to pull the data from the SQLITE database and display it on the screen, while others have forms to take input from the registered user and save the data into the database. Refer to *Table 11.1* to understand the purpose of each HTML file:

Filename	Purpose
Error_pages	403: Customized error for 403 error – access forbidden
	404: Customized error for 404 error – page not found
account	When the admin user (acc_type = 0) logs in, they are redirected to addinfo.html
	When other users (acc_type = 1) log in, they can update their profile picture or update their password
activities	Display extra-curricular activities from the database
addinfo	When admin user (acc_type = 0) logs in, they can add their projects, work experience, education, and expertise
alltestimonials	Displays all the testimonials from the database onto the screen
base	Base HTML, and other web pages extend this
create_testimonial	Create and add new testimonials, available for all except the admin
editdetails	Visible to logged-in admin users, they can edit or delete the information present under work experience, education, expertise, and projects
goals	Just like activities, fetches life goals added by the admin user
index	Home page with static content

Filename	Purpose
`login`	Login form with email ID and password
`profile`	Visible to the logged in users only.
`register`	Registration form, take email ID, username, and password
`success`	Validates password
`testimonial`	Logged in users can edit the testimonials posted by them

Table 11.1: List of HTML files

We have already seen the **views.py** for core and users; now, we will look at the contents of the **views.py** file under the **details** folder:

```python
# FlaskApp\myprofile\details\views.py

from flask import render_template, url_for, flash, redirect, request,
Blueprint
from flask_login import login_user, current_user, logout_user, login_
required
from myprofile import db
from myprofile.models import Details, Users
from myprofile.details.forms import ProfileForm, UpdateDetailsForm

details = Blueprint('details', __name__)

@details.route('/submitform', methods=['GET', 'POST'])
def submitform():
    form = ProfileForm()
    if form.validate_on_submit():
        org = form.org.data,
        startdate=form.startdate.data,
        enddate=form.enddate.data,
        title=form.title.data,
        description=form.description.data,
        info_type=form.info_type.data
        record = Details(startdate, enddate, org, title, description, info_
type)
        db.session.add(record)
        db.session.commit()
        flash('Details Saved!')
        return render_template('addinfo.html', form=form)
    return render_template('addinfo.html', form=form)

@details.route('/editdetails', methods=['GET', 'POST'])
def editdetails():
    details = Details.query.all()
    if request.method == 'POST':
```

```
        data_id = request.form['type_radio']
        print('form submit=========>',data_id)
        Details.query.filter_by(id=data_id).delete()
        db.session.commit()
        print('delete done')
        return redirect("/editdetails", code=302)

    return render_template("editdetails.html",details=details)

@details.route('/editform', methods=['GET', 'POST'])
def editform():
    '''
    form = UpdateDetailsForm()
    '''
    flash('Working...')
    return redirect(url_for('details.editdetails'))
```

We have seen the content of views, forms, and **html** files and how they work together to handle data in a Flask application. *Chapter 11* code folder on GitHub has the complete code that you can refer to for developing a web-based personal profile page.

Conclusion

In this chapter, we learned to build web applications using the Flask framework provided by Python. We saw that Flask is a powerful and flexible web development framework. It is designed to make the development of web applications simpler and easier, and it offers a wide range of features and tools to help developers create highly functional and powerful web applications.

Now, we will move to the last chapter of this book. In *Chapter 12, Working With Containers in Azure,* we will learn to use **Containers** from VS Code. The **Containers** extension lets you use a Docker container as a full-featured development environment. The Docker extension makes it easy to build, manage, and deploy containerized applications in Visual Studio Code. In this chapter, we developed a Flask-based website currently hosted on our local server. In *Chapter 12, Working With Containers in Azure,* we will migrate the SQLite database to Postgresql and deploy this website on Azure so that everyone can access it from anywhere.

Let us move on to the next chapter and learn how to deploy a Python Flask application with Docker, Azure Container Registry, and Azure App Services.

Join our book's Discord space

Join the book's Discord Workspace for Latest updates, Offers, Tech happenings around the world, New Release and Sessions with the Authors:

https://discord.bpbonline.com

CHAPTER 12
Working with Containers in Azure

Containers are like having an army of tiny servers, running the exact same code everywhere.
— Joe Beda, Co-founder of Heptio

Introduction

Working with containers on Azure is an efficient way to manage applications and their dependencies. Containers are isolated, compartmentalized software units with their runtime environment, configuration settings, and libraries packaged together. This allows applications to be immediately deployed and moved across different systems and cloud providers easily.

The advantage of containers is that they are lightweight and portable, making them easy to deploy and scale up or down quickly, allowing businesses to optimize resources. With containers, organizations can remain agile and send updates and bug fixes without restarting the system.

By using Azure Container Service, organizations can utilize their existing skills to quickly deploy and manage containers on Azure. Organizations can deploy applications from multiple Docker containers without needing to write and maintain scripts. They can also leverage the scalability of the cloud and have access to world-class networking capabilities. Additionally, providers can increase security using role-based access control, wherein only specific users can access specific containers to address data security risks.

Overall, containers are a great way for organizations to ensure agility and scalability while decreasing costs, accelerating time to market, and increasing security. Azure Container Service is an efficient and cost-effective way to leverage containers on Azure.

In this chapter, we will learn to deploy our already developed Flask application onto Azure using containers. If you want to know how to develop Flask applications, refer to *Chapter 11, Developing Flask-Based Web Applications.*

Structure

This chapter will provide you with a comprehensive guide on how to deploy Flask applications using containers on Azure. It covers the basics of setting up the Azure account and environment, managing the storage and building foundations, and deploying the application. The following topics will be covered:

- Porting FlaskApp database from SQLite to Postgres
- Deploy the Flask application on Azure; this includes following subtopics:

Objectives

This chapter will provide you with an in-depth understanding of deploying a Flask application using containers on Microsoft Azure. Specifically, you will go through step-by-step instructions for setting up a web environment on Azure, deploying a Flask application on a web server, and running a containerized deployment in production. Additionally, you will gain a comprehensive understanding of the best practices for containerizing a Flask application and troubleshooting common deployment issues. Furthermore, you will learn about the various tools and services available on Azure that can be used to facilitate efficient and secure deployments in the cloud. The chapter is aimed at helping you gain the knowledge and skills to quickly deploy, scale, and maintain a Flask application on Azure and also get experience in using Dockers.

Porting FlaskApp database from SQLite to Postgres

Remember the app we developed in *Chapter 11, Developing Flask-Based Web Applications*? It used the SQLite database. While SQLite can be a great tool for standalone, small-scale applications and rapid prototyping, Postgres is more suited for complex, high-volume applications and environments. Let us look at the advantages of using Postgres over SQLite:

- **Scalability**: Postgres is much more scalable than SQLite. It can handle a large amount of data and concurrent users without compromising on performance.

SQLite, on the other hand, is not designed to handle high-volume, high-concurrency database operations.

- **Advanced features**: Postgres supports a wider range of SQL syntax and functionalities, including complex queries, foreign keys, transactional integrity, and multi-version concurrency control. It also supports user-defined data types, operators, and functions.

- **Database connectivity**: Postgres supports network-based connections, allowing multiple users and applications to connect to the database simultaneously from various locations. SQLite is a file-based database, which can lead to issues in multi-user environments.

- **Security**: Due to its network connectivity, there are multiple levels of security in Postgres, including the capacity for host-based access controls; it also supports robust access-control systems. SQLite, due to its simplicity, offers only a basic level of security.

- **Extensions and integrations**: Postgres offers extensive support for third-party extensions and can easily integrate with various front-end and back-end applications.

- **Backups and disaster recovery**: Postgres supports hot backups and point-in-time recovery. SQLite does not provide such types of backups due to its simpler nature.

Migrating to Postgres

Migration from SQLite to PostgreSQL involves exporting the SQLite database into SQL commands, modifying those commands to be compatible with PostgreSQL, and then importing the file into PostgreSQL. It is worth noting that this may be tricky if your database is large or includes formats difficult to convert between SQLite and PostgreSQL. Let us migrate by following these steps:

1. **Export SQLite database to SQL file**

   If you do not have SQLite client, you can download it from **https://www.sqlite. org/.**

   To initiate the sqlite3 program, input **sqlite3** into the command prompt. You can also include the filename of the SQLite database (or ZIP archive). If the specified file is absent, a new database file will be automatically generated using the provided name. If a database file is not defined in the command line, a temporary database will be assembled and subsequently erased when the sqlite3 program closes.

   Use the sqlite3 command-line utility to create a **dump.SQL** file:

   ```
   $ sqlite3 database_name.db .dump > db.sql
   ```

Figure 12.1 shows the command, and *Figure 12.2* shows the screenshot of **db.sql**:

```
X:\FlaskApp\myprofile>sqlite3 data.sqlite .dump >db.sql

X:\FlaskApp\myprofile>_
```

Figure 12.1: *Running the SQLite command to back up the database*

Refer to the following figure:

```
db - Notepad                                    —    □    ×

File  Edit  Format  View  Help
PRAGMA foreign_keys=OFF;
BEGIN TRANSACTION;
CREATE TABLE users (
        id INTEGER NOT NULL,
        acc_type INTEGER,
        profile_image VARCHAR(64) NOT NULL,
        email VARCHAR(64),
        username VARCHAR(64),
        password_hash VARCHAR(128),
        PRIMARY KEY (id)
);
INSERT INTO users VALUES
```

Figure 12.2: *Screenshot of backup file*

2. **Convert SQLite SQL file to PostgreSQL**

   SQLite and PostgreSQL have different syntaxes, so the SQL file needs modification to be compatible. You can do this manually (not recommended unless your DB is tiny) or use a tool like sqlite3-to-pgloader, which automates this process and can be found at **https://wiki.postgresql.org/wiki/Converting_from_other_Databases_ to_PostgreSQL.**

3. **Install PostgreSQL**

   Following are the instructions to install PostgreSQL on Windows, Mac and Linux:

   a. Windows

      i. Go to the PostgreSQL download page:

         https://www.postgresql.org/download/windows/

      ii. Click on the download installer from the web page.

      iii. You will be redirected to the EnterpriseDB site. Then, choose your version and click **download**.

iv. After downloading, double-click on the downloaded file, and you will see the setup window.

v. Follow the steps until you have installed PostgreSQL. Remember the password you give while installing for future use.

b. **macOS**

i. Go to the PostgreSQL download page:

https://www.postgresql.org/download/macosx/

ii. Click on the download installer from the web page.

iii. You will be redirected to the EnterpriseDB website. Then, choose your version and click download.

iv. Double-click on the downloaded file. Now, you will see a PostgreSQL install screen.

v. Follow the steps until you have installed PostgreSQL. Ensure that you remember the password used during the installation process.

c. **Ubuntu Linux**

i. Open a terminal window.

ii. If needed, install the nano editor (**sudo apt-get install nano**).

iii. Now, update apt-get (**sudo apt-get update**).

iv. Install PostgreSQL (**sudo apt-get install postgresql postgresql-contrib**). The postgres user will be created during the installation.

v. Switch to the Postgres account (**sudo -i -u postgres**).

vi. Access PostgreSQL prompt (**psql**).

vii. Exit the PostgreSQL prompt using **\q** and return to the postgres user with exit.

Note: PostgreSQL installation includes the pgAdmin tool. To access it, just go to pgAdmin through your applications menu. You need to give the password you used during installation to connect to the PostgreSQL server using this tool.

4. **Import into PostgreSQL**

Once you have converted the file and have Postgres running on your machine, you can import it into PostgreSQL:

```
$ psql -h localhost -U postgres -d MyProfileDB -f db.sql
```

The username is **postgres**, and the server name is **MyProfileDB**.

You can also copy all the SQL commands from the converted file and run them on the **Query** tool.

5. **Update Flask configuration**

   Update your Flask application configuration to connect to the PostgreSQL server. Open the **__init__.py** file in the **MyProfile** folder and make the following changes:

   a. **Old SQLite database URI:**

   ```python
   SQLALCHEMY_DATABASE_URI = 'sqlite:///app.db'
   ```

   b. **New PostgreSQL database URI:**

   ```python
   SQLALCHEMY_DATABASE_URI         =         'postgresql://myuser:mypass@
   localhost:5432/MyProfileDB
   ```

   You will need to install the **psycopg2** package on the Python terminal. The **psycopg2** package is a PostgreSQL database adapter for Python. It is used to connect to PostgreSQL databases from a Python application, allowing Python applications to execute SQL commands, fetch data from tables, and perform database operations such as **inserts**, **updates**, and **deletes**. It also provides features such as server-side cursors, asynchronous notification, and communication. It is designed for multi-threaded applications and manages its internal buffering. We need to install the **psycopg2** package. This can be installed using a pip command, as follows:

   ```
   pip install psycopg2
   ```

6. **Update Flask models (if needed)**

   If you used SQLite-specific functions or operations in Flask models (for example, operations specific to SQLite's text handling), you would need to update those to use PostgreSQL-compatible functionality.

7. **Perform Flask database migration (if needed)**

   If your database schema has changed, you must use Flask-Migrate or a similar tool to perform database migrations.

Note: It is important to back up your SQLite database before initiating any migration process. Also, test your Flask application thoroughly after the migration to capture any issues that may have arisen due to differences in handling data between SQLite and PostgreSQL.

Deploy the Flask application on Azure

This section will detail the steps for working with containers in Azure from Visual Studio Code using the Python language. **Azure Container Instances (ACI)** allow code to be run in a containerized environment, making it easier to deploy code quickly to the cloud. With the right tools and knowledge, developers can now containerize code written in any language while quickly iterating on cloud-based environments.

We will also cover the steps to follow to deploy Python code to ACI from Visual Studio Code, including setting up a container instance and debugging Python code in Azure.

Step 1: Getting the software ready

Install Docker on your local machine and create a Docker Hub account.

Docker is a platform that allows developers to develop, package, and deploy applications. It allows you to separate your applications from the underlying infrastructure, making it easier to deliver software. Docker provides a consistent framework for managing applications and infrastructure, resulting in faster code deployment. It is compatible with various platforms and can be easily downloaded and installed. The download link is as follows:

https://docs.docker.com/install/

From the mentioned location, download the docket for your operating system and install it like any other software: by double-clicking on the installer.

Now, create an account on the Docker hub. Docker Hub is a cloud-based registry service provided by Docker that allows developers to store, manage, and share their container images. It provides a centralized location for users to access and download container images created by others, and also to publish and distribute their images.

Docker Hub is used for several reasons:

- **Image hosting**: Docker Hub allows us to securely store and host our container images. This provides a centralized and reliable location where our images can be accessed and downloaded by others.

- **Collaboration**: Docker Hub makes it easy to share container images with others. We can grant access to specific users or teams, allowing collaboration on container development and deployment.

- **Automated builds**: Docker Hub allows us to set up automated builds based on source code repositories. This means that every time we push changes to our source code repository, Docker Hub can automatically build and push a new container image.

- **Versioning and tagging**: Docker Hub allows us to apply version numbers and tags to our container images. This makes it easy to keep track of different versions of our images and ensures that users can always access the specific version they need.

- **Integration with other tools**: Docker Hub integrates with other tools and services, such as Docker Compose and Kubernetes. This allows us to seamlessly deploy and manage our containers in various environments.

Overall, Docker Hub provides a convenient and secure platform for hosting, sharing, and managing container images, making it an essential tool in the Docker ecosystem.

Log in to the following link and create an account: **https://hub.docker.com/**

Step 2: Setting up Azure CLI

The next step is to set up the Azure CLI on your local computer. The Azure CLI is a command-line interface for interacting with Azure services, allowing developers to quickly deploy resources to the cloud from their local machine.

Additionally, the Azure CLI provides a way to maintain consistency between environments, helps decrease the probability of errors, and enables easier automation. Refer to the following link on Microsoft to understand how to download and install Azure CLI on various platforms:

https://learn.microsoft.com/en-us/cli/azure/install-azure-cli

The Azure CLI can be easily installed using the following command:

```
$ azure-cli
```

Once the Azure CLI is installed, the Visual Studio Code Azure Tools extension must be downloaded. The Azure tool extension is shown in *Figure 12.3*. This extension contains a set of command-line tools and API wrappers to interact with Azure services, including those related to container instances and debugging capabilities. Refer to the following figure:

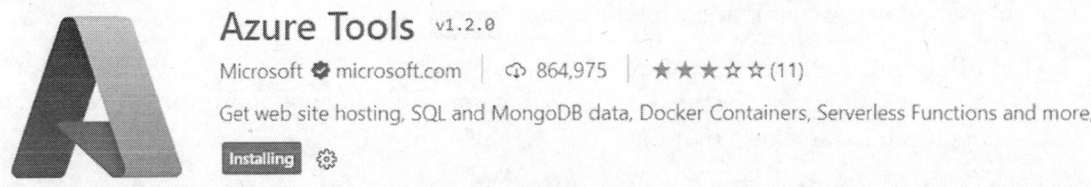

Figure 12.3: Installing Azure tools on Visual Studio Code

Step 3: Creating a container instance

The next step is to set up a container instance in Azure. This can be done using the Azure portal, but it is also possible to provision a container instance with the Azure CLI. The following commands will create a container instance in the same resource group as the CLI environment:

```
```

```
$ azure group create --name <Name_of_ResourceGroup>

--location <Azure_Region_Name>

$ azure container create --resource-group <Name_of_ResourceGroup> --name
<Name_of_Container_Instance> --image <Image_Name>
```

In the preceding example, you can replace **<Name_of_ResourceGroup>** and **<Azure_Region_Name>** with the names of the resource group and Azure region you are working in. You should also replace **<Name_of_Container_Instance>** with the name of your own container instance, and **<Image_Name>** should be replaced with the name of the image you are using to deploy the code to the container instance. We have not created the Docker image yet, and this will be available only after **Step 4** (creating the Docker image).

Working on Azure portal: Docker should not necessarily be running in your local environment to build the image in the cloud. Follow these steps to work on the Azure cloud:

1. Sign in to the Azure portal to complete the steps: **https://portal.azure.com.**

2. In the Azure portal, click on **Create a resource** and search for **Container Registry**. *Figure 12.4* shows the **Create a resource** option, and *Figure 12.5* shows the search result of container registry:

Azure services

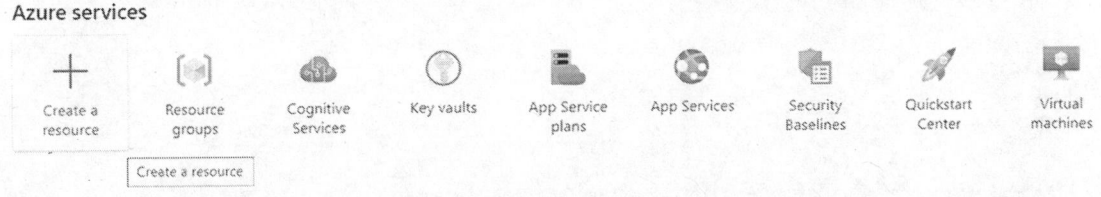

Figure 12.4: Creating a new resource

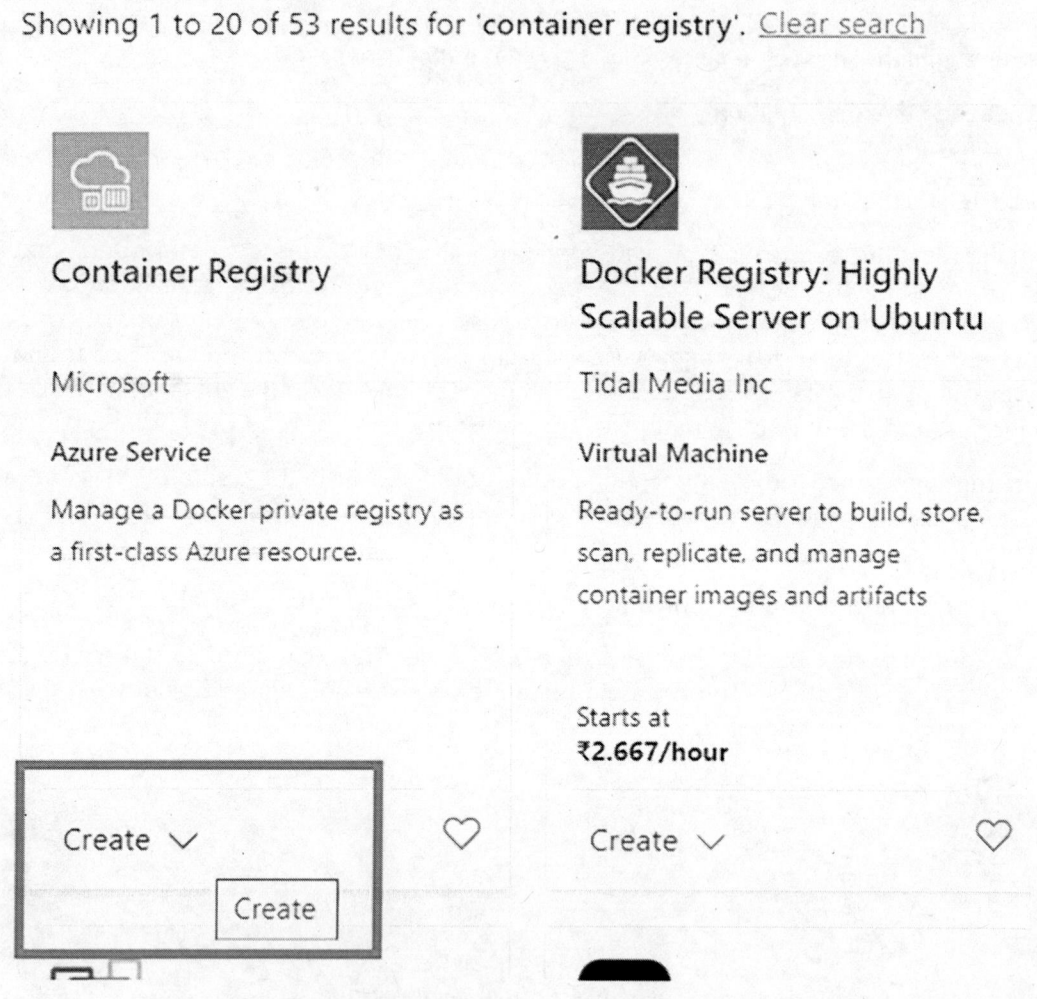

Figure 12.5: Search for container registry

3. Choose a subscription, resource group, and registry name, as shown in *Figure 12.6*.

4. Select the pricing tier and location that suit your needs.

5. Click **Review + Create** and then **Create** to create the ACR.
   Refer to the following figure:

Create container registry ...

Azure Container Registry allows you to build, store, and manage container images and artifacts in a private registry for all types of container deployments. Use Azure container registries with your existing container development and deployment pipelines. Use Azure Container Registry Tasks to build container images in Azure on-demand, or automate builds triggered by source code updates, updates to a container's base image, or timers. Learn more

Project details

Subscription *	Pay-As-You-Go ⌄
Resource group *	(New) ProfileBuilder ⌄
	Create new

Instance details

Registry name *	myprofile ✓
	.azurecr.io
Location *	South India ⌄
Availability zones ⓘ	☐ Enabled

> ⓘ Availability zones are enabled on premium registries and in regions that support availability zones. Learn more

SKU * ⓘ	Basic ⌄

[Review + create]   [< Previous]   [Next: Networking >]

Figure 12.6: Creating container registry

Figure 12.6 shows the values we use for this project for each parameter. It should show validation passed; then, click on **Create** again to create the container registry. The resource should get deployed after a few minutes.

Step 4: Building and pushing your Flask application image to the Azure Container Registry (ACR)

The following steps are to be followed to make the Docker image:

1. In your local development environment, create a Dockerfile in the root directory of your Flask application, which is the **X:\FlaskApp** folder in our case. One way to confirm if you are in the right folder is to look for **app.py** there. Then, make your **requirements.txt** file in the same directory.

2. Create **requirements.txt** using the following:

   X:\FlaskApp> pip freeze > requirements.txt

   This will create a **requirements.txt** file in the root folder.

3. Use a base image that supports running Flask applications (**python:3.9-slim-buster**).

4. Specify the necessary dependencies and configurations in the Dockerfile. The Dockerfile should look something like this:

```
# Use an official Python runtime as a parent image
FROM python:3.9-slim-buster

# Set the working directory to /myprofile
WORKDIR /myprofile

# Copy the current directory contents into the container at /
myprofile
ADD . /myprofile

# Install any needed packages specified in requirements.txt
RUN pip install --trusted-host pypi.python.org -r requirements.txt

# Make port 80 available to the world outside this container
EXPOSE 80

# Define environment variable
ENV NAME env

# Run app.py when the container launches
CMD ["python", "app.py"]
```

5. Build the Docker image locally using the following command, and name it **myprofile**. You can give your name as well. Remember to run the commands on Power Shell running in admin mode.

   docker build -t myprofile .

   To confirm that the image works on the local machine, type the following command and navigate to localhost:4000 in your browser:

   docker run -p 4000:80 myprofile

   Run the following command to create a Docker image:

   `docker build -t <registry-name>.azurecr.io/<image-name>:<tag> .`

   Replace the following values in the preceding command:

   <registry-name> with myprofile

`<image-name>` with **myprofile**

`<tag>` with **tag** (Let us keep it as tag itself for now.)

6. Log in to the ACR using the Azure CLI:

   `az acr login -n <registry-name>`

7. Log in to Docker and push the Docker image to the ACR repository:

   `docker login`

   `docker push <registry-name>.azurecr.io/<image-name>:<tag>`

Step 5: Creating an Azure database for PostgreSQL

Follow these steps to create a database on Azure:

1. In the Azure portal, click on **Create a resource** and search for Azure Database for PostgreSQL. The search result is presented in *Figure 12.7*:

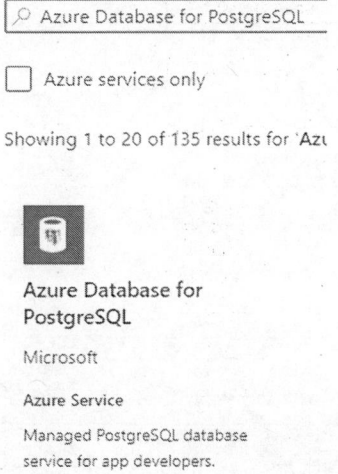

Figure 12.7: Azure Database for PostgreSQL

2. Choose a subscription, resource group, database name, and pricing tier. The information is shown in *Figure 12.8*:

Project details

Select the subscription to manage deployed resources and costs. Use resource groups like folders to organize and manage all your resources.

Subscription * ⓘ   Pay-As-You-Go

Resource group * ⓘ   ProfileBuilder

Create new

Figure 12.8: Adding Azure database

3. Set the server name, admin username, and password. Give the same server name, username, and password as given in the **__init__()** file of FlaskApp, as shown in *Figure 12.9* and *Figure 12.10*:

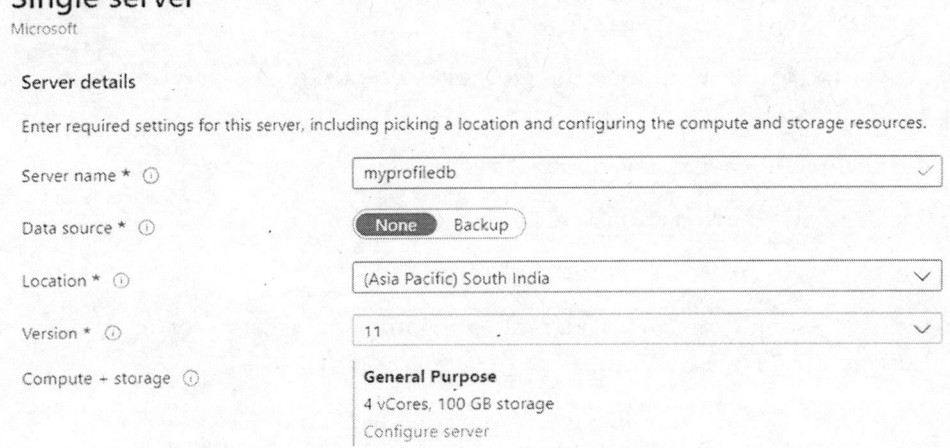

Figure 12.9: Enter server details in Azure database

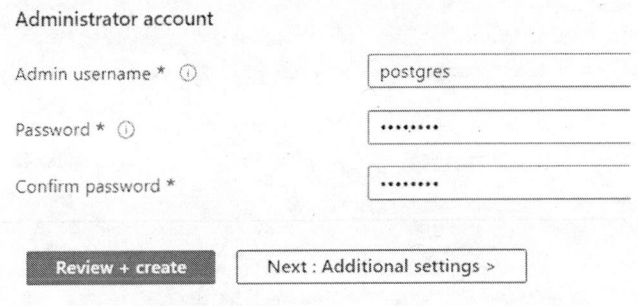

Figure 12.10: Adding username and password

4. Configure other settings (networking, tags) as necessary.

5. Click **Review + Create** and then **Create** to create the database.

Step 6: Configuring environment variables for the Flask application (optional)

In our case, we have used the same server name and login credentials on the Azure database, but if you have used a different one, then it is time to make changes to the FlaskApp settings.

1. In the Azure portal, go to the resource group containing your ACR and database.

2. Open the **ACR** and go to the **Access keys**.

3. Copy the **Login** server and username (both needed for the next step).

4. Go to the database resource and copy the connection string.

5. In your Flask application, configure the necessary environment variables (database URL, credentials) using the values you copied.

Step 7: Deploy the Flask application on Azure

Now, it is time to make the deployment.

1. In the Azure portal, go to the resource group containing your ACR.

2. Open Azure **Container Instances** and click on **Create instance**. The **Container Instances** option is shown in *Figure 12.11*:

Container Instances

Microsoft

Azure Service

The fastest and simplest way to run a
container in Azure

Figure 12.11: *Azure Container Instances*

3. Choose the subscription, resource group, and instance name.

4. Set the instance region and OS type.

5. For **Image Type**, choose **Private** and select your ACR and Docker image.

6. Configure other settings (CPU, memory, ports) as necessary. Set the networking type as public.

7. Click **Review + Create** and then **Create** to deploy the Flask application on Azure.

Step 8: Verifying the deployment

The final step is to verify that our efforts have been successful. Follow these steps to verify the deployment:

1. Once the container instance is created, go to its overview page.

2. Get the public IP address (or DNS name) and the assigned port number.

3. Open a web browser and access the Flask application using the IP address and port.

4. Ensure that the application is running correctly and connected to the database.

You have successfully deployed a Flask application with a database on Azure using Docker and Azure Container Instances.

Step 9: Debugging in Visual Studio Code

Debugging the code in Visual Studio Code is generally the same as debugging locally. However, there are some unique capabilities to debugging code in Azure that make it especially useful when working with container instances. Visual Studio Code offers remote development capabilities, allowing developers to work remotely on the code they have containerized in a remote environment.

To enable remote debugging, you will need to install the Remote Development extension for Visual Studio Code. Press *F1* and select **Extensions: Install Extensions**, and search for remote development. Once the extension is installed, you can select **Start Remote Debugging** from the command pallet.

This will open a connection to the container instance, allowing developers to remotely debug the code in the container instance. The remote development tools also include the **Debug** console, allowing developers to inspect variables, view traces and log messages, and run various commands from the same window.

Conclusion

This chapter detailed the steps necessary for working with containers in Azure from Visual Studio Code using Python. By using the right tools and a bit of knowledge, developers can easily containerize their code in Azure. Additionally, the remote development extension provides unparalleled debugging capabilities, allowing developers to quickly iterate on their code while running it in a container instance.

With that, we have come to the end of the last chapter. We started with the installation of Visual Studio code and moved on to understanding various extensions, learning about Python syntax, and how to deploy a Python application on a public cloud. We hope you enjoyed this journey and have developed a solid foundation for continued learning and growth in Python programming.

Index